HAUNTED STATES

HAUNTED STATES

AN AMERICAN GOTHIC GUIDEBOOK

Miranda Corcoran

Published by Repeater Books

An imprint of Watkins Media Ltd

Unit 11 Shepperton House

89-93 Shepperton Road

London

N1 3DF

United Kingdom

www.repeaterbooks.com

A Repeater Books paperback original 2024

1

Distributed in the United States by Random House, Inc., New York.

Copyright Miranda Corcoran © 2024

Miranda Corcoran asserts the moral right to be identified as the author of this work.

ISBN: 9781914420320

Ebook ISBN: 9781914420337

Printed and bound by CPI Group (UK) Ltd, Croydon, CR0 4YY

CONTENTS

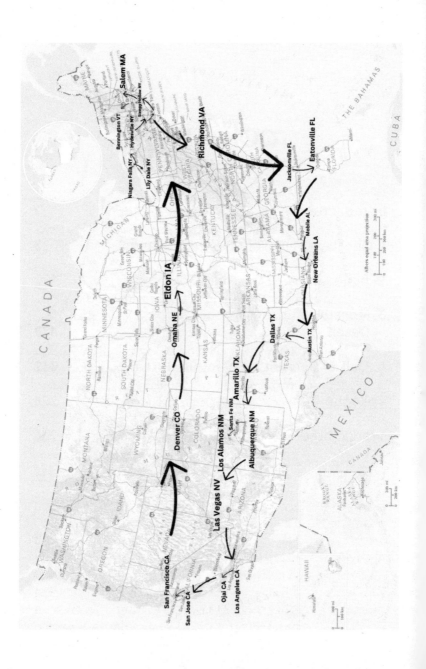

INTRODUCTION

Indeed, as things are for the present, the LAND of SPIRITS is a kinde of AMERICA, and not well discover'd Region
— Joseph Glanvill, *A Blow at Modern Sadducism in Some Philosophical Considerations about Witchcraft*

America is a haunted house
— Leonard Pitts, Jr, "Abominations from America's Past Haunt Us"

I grew up in a haunted house, or at least, I should have. My childhood home was in a council estate built on top of graveyard, and for years I heard about how when builders broke ground in the early 1970s, they discovered a scattered collection of human bones. Some people suggested that perhaps the remains were casualties of a plague or epidemic — maybe cholera, the same disease whose rampage further west, in Sligo, helped to inspire Bram Stoker's *Dracula* (1897). Others wondered whether the skeletal remnants belonged to victims of the Great Famine that ravaged Ireland in the 1840s, when whole communities starved to death even as the crops that did bear fruit were exported to the farthest reaches of the British Empire. There were no answers, and even now I'm unable to find any record of the excavation. Today, I rent an apartment in an imposing nineteenth-century building that was, until recently, a psychiatric hospital. Every taxi driver and delivery person asks if it's haunted. Locals tell stories of elderly parents committed by greedy children hoping to get their hands on an early inheritance, of patients who wandered off the grounds and were drowned in the torrents of a nearby weir. Yet, nothing strange or spectral has ever disturbed my sleep in either of these allegedly haunted homes.

I am interested in ghosts, but ghosts — seemingly — have little interest in me. I have slept under many supposedly haunted roofs and never encountered anything more terrifying than the occasional wayward spider lost in a tangle of sheets or darting beneath the dark crevices of a heavy wooden dresser.

The absence of ghosts in my life has left me a sceptic, albeit an ambivalent one. I don't believe in ghosts, yet my scepticism is soft and pliable. For me, ghosts are oneiric beings, formed out of the ectoplasmic accretions of horror stories, drawn out from beneath the darkest of cinematic shadows and conjured from the deepest crevices of history. The ontological status of the ghost, its reality or lack thereof, means little to me. I am far more interested in what ghosts mean: what they say about the individuals who whisper tales of hauntings, why spirits cleave to certain locations and why they extend their diaphanous forms through the hallways, attics and basements of specific structures — and only those structures. I may not believe in ghosts as real, verifiable phenomena, supernatural or otherwise, but I do think spectres are endlessly helpful, informative beings. They are the tales we tell when we attempt to articulate the disturbing, unsettling powers exerted by sickly places and those lands rendered leaden by the weight of history. Yet, spirits also tell their own tales. They speak of the fears that gave shape to them and the hopes from which they sprung. I am interested in the cultural work performed by ghosts, and indeed by other monsters. Why do we continue to summon such creatures into being? Why do we give them such grotesque shapes and imbue them with fundamentally taboo desires? Moreover, why do we sometimes desire *them*?

In an essay titled "Monster Culture: Seven Theses", the scholar Jeffrey Jerome Cohen constructs a taxonomy of monstrosity that graphs the function of monsters across distinct cultural contexts. For Cohen, "the monster's body is a cultural body". Monsters are imaginative beings cobbled together, Frankenstein-like, from the anxieties, transgressions, taboos and desires of the society that birthed them. Likewise, our ghosts do not simply haunt us. Rather, we summon them to our sides. We need them to express what we cannot articulate, what we do not know how to say. Considering the etymological root of the word "monster", Cohen observes that *monstrum* is that which "reveals, 'that which warns,' a glyph that seeks a hierophant" (4). Monsters are, it seems, puzzles. If we can decode them, read their distinct parts and components, we can interpret them like a language, understanding at last what it is they are trying to tell us about ourselves.

Monsters can be destructive creatures, smashing the categories and hierarchies that we use to structure the world around us. They rip apart our comfortable, quotidian assumptions. Yet, they can also be used to reinforce hierarchies or demonise Others and outgroups. Often, they do both simultaneously, appearing almost paradoxical in their construction. Vampires embody a distinctly parasitic mode of sexual deviance, yet they are also possessed of a desirable and highly eroticised transgressive power. Historically, zombies have represented racial difference in terms of homogeny and multitude, bodies without minds whose numbers pose a threat to "our way of life". At the same time, zombies frequently engender the fantasy of a post-apocalyptic world in which existing social norms are dismantled, even inverted. Ghosts, likewise, regularly speak to the concealed sins of the past. Their return is often violent as they materialise to seek revenge or attest to some historical injustice. Concomitantly, the phantom is often defined by a strange, unexpected nostalgia. Ghosts frequently speak of a lost past, but just as often they gesture forwards to an unrealised future, a dream that failed to come true. Hauntologically speaking, the ghost is a rupture, but also a temporal bridge, drawing together past, present and future. The meaning of the ghost has, likewise, shifted over time, morphing from an objectively real, though invariably diaphanous, being into a potent metaphor for guilt, trauma and psychological disorder: we haunt, and we are haunted.

This book materialised out of my own curiosity, my desire to know why it is that people persist in making monsters. Why do we repeatedly retreat into our cursed laboratories and fuse together disparate parts to create beings that are nothing if not mirrors of ourselves? While I have no faith in spirits or the supernatural, I am fascinated by the social, political and imaginative functions of such beings, their diverse reasons for being. I have often wondered whether the supernatural is consistent across cultures, or if every spirit, every monster, is simply an echo of its own time and place. Do we all make monsters in the same way, or is it possible that the unique historical patterns or environmental contours of a given place could breed radically different monsters?

Such questions are at the heart of this book, and they provided the impetus for me to write it as a travelogue as opposed to, say, an academic study or a linear historical narrative. I wanted to move around, physically, between different places, shifting between histories, cultures and peoples in order to experience the environments that birthed the ghosts, monsters and vampires I am studying.

I am not the first person to conceive of the otherworldly in terms of travel and exploration. Writing about the world of the undead, seventeenth-century philosopher Joseph Glanvill claimed that "the LAND of SPIRITS is a kinde of *AMERICA*, and not well discover'd *Region*". Glanvill was trying to develop a rational system through which to study and understand the spirit world, one that married Christian faith with newly emerging scientific principles. When he describes the spirit world as "a kinde of AMERICA", he is framing the supernatural in terms of colonial enterprise. As things stood at the end the 1600s, we humans knew as much about the spirit world as Europeans did about America, upon whose shores the first English settlers were just beginning to carve out their New World. Despite its entanglement with colonialist power structures, Glanvill's spatial metaphor is an intriguing one. His words suggest a kind of materiality, an emplacement of the supernatural that would allow us to map its contours as though charting the perilous coastline of a strange land.

At the same time, however, travel seems oddly inimical to ghosts, as if movement is somehow opposed to the traditionally stagnant Gothic mode. Ghosts, after all, are defined by their connection to the properties they haunt. They are eternally bound to a single space, and in that constrictive space, they are often caught in a repetitive loop, performing the same actions again and again for years, decades, centuries. If travel is dynamic, emblematic of perpetual change and renewal, then surely this runs counter to the Gothic's preoccupation with the oppressive weight of history. When the Gothic does travel, its voyages are defined by unremitting loneliness (*Melmoth the Wanderer*, *Frankenstein*) or figured as part of some monstrous invasion (*Dracula*). The Gothic rarely travels simply to explore, and within the confines of horror fiction, travel, where it does appear, facilitates a descent into depths of horror unimaginable in the home place (*The Narrative of Arthur Gordon Pym of Nantucket*, *The Texas Chain Saw Massacre*).

This is a book about the American Gothic, the unique modes of horror that cleave to distinct regions of the vast, unfathomable landscapes of the United States. This book could have been set anywhere. My own home country — Ireland — has enough horrors buried in rural fields and beneath crumbling convents to fill any number of hefty tomes. However, I am interested in the tension between the mythos of the great American road trip, with its attendant promises of freedom and unfettered possibility, and the dark, sepulchral power of the Gothic. Though American road trips often end in tragedy or horror (think *Easy Rider*, *Bonnie and Clyde* or the crushing, existential dread of Jack Kerouac's *Big Sur*), we still consider transcontinental crossings to be essentially liberatory movements. Such journeys invariably unfold, as mine did, East to West, and in popular culture this trajectory is imagined in terms of freedom, the opening up of the land below and the sky above to new possibilities, new discoveries. When we visualise such a movement, we see the thickly forested East Coast, with its dense, smoke-filled cities, flattening out into prairies and plains, vanishing into the great red deserts of the West. Such a fantasy is, of course, a product of earlier permutations of the American dream, with its emphasis on boundless liberty and endless possibility, at least for some. From the first Puritan settlers, who conceived of the North American continent as a tabula rasa upon which they could inscribe their own godly vision, to the mythic space of the frontier, such narratives have been the engine that propelled the US forward. How, then, might such visions of freedom coexist with the oppressive terrors of the Gothic mode?

In the early 1960s, a US academic named Leslie A. Fiedler wrote a massive tome called *Love and Death in the American Novel*. However, the book — which constituted a broad survey of nineteenth- and twentieth-century

American fiction — was not simply an overview of the nation's literary output. Instead, Fiedler was preoccupied with a single question, which he obsessively pursued over some five hundred pages: Why is it that a nation ostensibly committed to ideals of freedom, justice and equality produced a body of literature that is so overwhelmingly bleak?

Early in the book, Fiedler maintains that American literature is an essentially Gothic literature, writing that US authors have time and again produced a "literature of darkness and the grotesque in a land of light and affirmation" (xxiv). When he comes to answer the question of why American literature might be so deeply haunted, Fiedler returns, inevitably to the tense relationship between American history and the stories America tells about that history. The terrors that benight American literature — Melville's monstrous whale, Poe's live burials, Hawthorne's witch-haunted woods — are manifestations of historical horrors that cannot be otherwise articulated. Dark imagery of excessive violence, sadism and the supernatural becomes the only means Americans have to express the contradictions that plague both their history and their identity. Similarly, in her 1992 book *Playing in the Dark*, Toni Morrison queries the violence and terror embedded in much early American literature, positioning this darkness in contrast to the nation's foundational myth of New World innocence. For Morrison, American literature's deployment of the "thematics of innocence coupled with an obsession with figurations of death and hell" are responses to what she calls "a dark, abiding, signing Africanist presence" (6). Essentially, Morrison charges that the fundamentally Gothic nature of American literature is a product of the nation's history of slavery and racist violence, a history which it perennially seeks to disavow. Yet, if the Gothic is anything like the ghosts it portrays, it will not let such histories lie undisturbed. The Gothic — as it manifests in art, literature and film — is a resurrectionist mode, reviving everything we seek to bury and forcing to confront its terrifying visage.

As a literary mode, the Gothic shares its birthday with the United States. Both were products of the Enlightenment, that age when new philosophies and emerging scientific paradigms promised a new and better world founded upon natural justice and innate human rights. However, as scholar Fred Botting explains, "A negative aesthetics informs Gothic texts", and so it is a mode that seeks to challenge the values of the Enlightenment (1). Born at a time when human endeavour was, supposedly, guided by ideals of rationality, empirical reasoning and vague conceptions of equality, Gothic works, Botting maintains "are, overtly but ambiguously, not rational, depicting disturbances of sanity and security, from superstitious belief in ghosts and demons, displays of uncontrolled passion, violent emotion or flights of fancy to portrayals of perversion and obsession" (2). The Gothic is, in essence, the tenebrous underside of the Enlightenment, its dark reflection.

Over the centuries, the Gothic, and its close cousin horror, has continued to trouble our fantasies, our sense of who we are. It has always given form to those unspoken, and unspeakable, facets of ourselves that we would rather not confront. In the US, the role of the Gothic has been to challenge the nation's idealised sense of self. Leonard Pitts, Jr, writing in 1998, provided another helpful spatial metaphor for thinking about history: "America," he writes, "is a haunted house". Like Glanvill, Pitts constructs the supernatural as a physical space, one that can be discovered, explored and perhaps known. However, in this particular scenario, America is a structure whose dusty attics and icy hallways teem with the restless spirits of the past, wispy forms who speak to historical transgressions and abuses whose memories we might prefer to bury deep beneath its foundations.

Part of what I hope to explore in this book is the perpetual haunting of America by its own past. I want to wander the rooms and corridors of that haunted house, commune with its ghosts and dwell in its dark spaces. At the same time, I want to discover whether the Gothic might have other uses. Beyond giving voice to the horrors of the past or the injustices of today, can ghosts and monsters have other functions? Can they be benevolent, gentle or loving? Is it possible for such beings, or the stories we tell about them, to be joyful, subversive or liberatory? Can we tell ghost stories to celebrate, to resist or to laugh? Moreover, is the American Gothic a monolithic imaginative form, or do conceptions of horror shift as they incarnate across different regions? If a monster — be it a ghost or something more tangible — comes into being in the verdant mountains of New England, does it differ substantially from a creature birthed in the oppressive, sucking swamps of Louisiana? When these beings take form in the arid desert, their bodies shaped by hot blasts of sand-heavy winds, surely their skins harden and their limbs grow large and strong. When some undead terror crawls, slow and turgid, from the sticky soup of the swamp, their body must bear traces of the thick, primordial mud that revitalised it.

In my travels around the US, I wanted to investigate both the tactile physical environments that produced distinct manifestations of the American Gothic and the less tangible but nevertheless very real histories that engendered its most iconic monsters. Without wanting to silo off different expressions of the Gothic or discount the dynamic potential of hybrid modes, I divided my trip into four key sections: New York/New England, the South, the Desert and California, with a brief excursion to the Midwest towards the end. What I'd hoped to investigate was how different topographies and diverse histories lend themselves to different forms of monstrosity and regionally distinct hauntings. As such, I chose to focus on ghosts and spiritualists during my time in New York and New England; vampires, the undead and Voodoo in the South; atomic monsters in the desert; and cults in California. In the course of my journey, I visited regions associated with distinct manifestations of monstrosity in hopes of better understanding how unique permutations of horror might arise out of particular histories or distinct physical environments. In this way, while this book is very much a cultural history and a work of literary criticism, it also plays in the tenebrous realm of psychogeography. A mode of exploration that eschews what philosopher Guy Debord terms "the determinant action of general natural forces"— soil composition, climate conditions — psychogeography maps the effects of geographical environment, both built and natural, not only on the emotions and behaviour of individuals, but also on the cultural artefacts they produce and consume.

Monsters are not exhibits in a museum, and they do not inhabit the kinds of carefully delineated habitats constructed for zoo animals. They overlap and intermingle. They refuse purity and trouble the taxonomies of species and origin. Stories of vampires can be found among the ghosts of New England, as they could during the nineteenth century, when cadaverous blood-drinkers proliferated, alongside tuberculosis, in the rural towns of Vermont, Massachusetts, Rhode Island and Connecticut. Likewise, ghosts themselves are often difficult to distinguish from their undead brethren, vampires and zombies. In medieval Europe, people told stories of "revenants" — from the French *revenir*, meaning "to return" — who climbed out of their tombs at night to torment the living (Owens 17). Returning to their own towns or villages, these revenants haunted their former abodes with the stubbornness of spirits, yet they possessed physical bodies. They could touch and be touched; they battered down doors and tore the flesh from the bones of the living. Horror is filled with hybrids, with beings that traverse categories of time, place and being.

As such, this book is not intended as a fixed cartography of terror, but rather as a dynamic, ever-shifting phantasmagoria, a light show in which figures flicker, dance and then disappear into the gloom. In these pages, ghosts and monsters of various sorts come into view, delicate wisps congealing into an image that is almost solid, almost tangible, but they do not remain. There are absences in this book — I do not discuss Stephen King's Bangor or Lovecraft's Providence — which arose primarily out of the exigencies of sustained travel. I simply couldn't find time to cover everything. However, I hope this book will serve as a starting point, a source of inspiration for anyone seeking to explore America's haunted history, whether by travelling across its immense, sometimes terrifying, landscape or by immersing themselves in its equally terrifying literary and cinematic output.

1. GHOSTS OF NEW YORK & NEW ENGLAND

The whole neighborhood abounds with local tales, haunted spots, and twilight superstitions; stars shoot and meteors glare oftener across the valley than in any other part of the country, and the nightmare, with her whole ninefold, seems to make it the favorite scene of her gambols.

— Washington Irving, "The Legend of Sleepy Hollow"

Niagara Falls, New York

On an oddly still evening in mid-June, with the sun low in the sky and a cold, sticky vapour creeping along the streets, I found myself sitting at a plastic table between the Misty Dog Grill and the Twist O' the Mist ice-cream stand, not far from Niagara Falls State Park. The Misty Dog is a shiny metallic hut beneath a green awning that advertises hamburgers, wings, sweet potato fries and hotdogs. Each evening, as the sunlight fades, its windows and service hatches hum with the glow of red and green neon signs. I sat eating deep-fried onions nestled in slick, chequered paper as enthusiastic little sparrows hopped back and forth under the table. A few feet away, the Twist O' the Mist rose above neatly trimmed hedge rows. Like the Dog, Twist O' the Mist is a small food stand, but its commitment to simulacrum is what makes it truly impressive. In the grand tradition of

American roadside architecture — office buildings shaped like wicker baskets and refreshment stands made to look like over-sized coffee pots — Twist O' the Mist has been constructed in the shape of a huge ice-cream cone. The base is criss-crossed with latticework, which suggests the texture of a wafer, while the fibre-glass roof rises into a perfect white swirl, a gentle heaping of faux soft-serve ice-cream. The effect is completed by a little red cherry that sits enticingly atop the roof. The streetlights that surround the Twist O' the Mist are topped with smaller ice-cream cones that glow like minute torches at night.

Earlier that day I arrived at the City of Niagara Falls Transit Terminal on the other side of the Niagara River, an immense body of water where Southern Ontario meets upstate New York. Catching a bus across the road from the abandoned Hotel Europa, an early twentieth-century commercial building whose unoccupied rooms remain screened by firmly closed white curtains, I was shuttled from the empty, cracked streets and boarded-up windows of downtown to the bustling Falls Avenue, with its high-rise hotels and casinos, its tourists strolling along in shorts and flip-flops.

I'm not sure at what point I made the decision to cross the US-Canada border on foot. The notion of merely stepping across the border between two nations appears to undermine the very notion of border-crossing, making it seem prosaic, everyday. However, to walk across the US-Canada border is also to re-enact a journey that was once common, ordinary, before the division of these lands by European settlers. Although the landscape seems to create a natural divide between the two countries, with the Niagara River neatly bisecting the narrow strip of land that runs between Lake Ontario and Lake Erie, the border is an infinitely more complex entity. Prior to the arrival of European colonisers, the region had been occupied by the six nations that would eventually comprise the Haudenosaunee Confederacy: the Mohawk, Oneida, Onondaga, Cayuga, Seneca and Tuscarora. These peoples had maintained traditional territories for thousands of years, but when the new nations of Canada and the United States were established, their borders were laid down on top of already existing Indigenous nations, supplanting and ultimately erasing original territorial markers.

The US-Canada border makes me think of a palimpsest, a document whose original text has been erased to make room for new writing, yet upon whose surface traces of that initial wording remain decipherable. We find palimpsests among medieval manuscripts, used parchments scraped clean in preparation for hosting a new text, but we also make our own palimpsests, half-heartedly erasing pencilled notes to scribble new words on top of their faint spectres. Likewise, the US-Canada border has simply been etched over the territories of colonised peoples, effacing older communities and nations, whose histories nevertheless remain legible in both the landscape and the names that still cling to the region's towns, rivers and mountains.

I walked alone across the Rainbow Bridge, carrying a huge, bulky backpack. Although there is a pedestrian path, most people drive, leaving me a lone figure, hair whipped about by the high winds, trudging across the bridge. Midway, there was a marker telling me that I was now in the United States. The actual, bureaucratic process of entering the US took place in a small room where TSA staff peered at travellers over the rim of a high countertop. The agent who checked my documentation asked me for advice on visiting Ireland — he likes fishing — and sent me on my way. As I passed through the turnstile into the United States, paying my entry toll with a one-dollar coin procured from a machine on the wall, I felt a deep gratitude for both my Irish passport and the American tendency to romanticise a vision of Ireland that has not existed in my lifetime and perhaps never did.

That evening, I cycled downtown from my room in a guesthouse where overstuffed throw pillows and sleeping cats sprouted from every soft surface. When I arrived, the owner was throwing a birthday party for her grandson, but she let me borrow a bicycle from the garage. I pedalled through the streets of Niagara Falls, passing shop windows concealed behind sheets of brown paper, car parks consumed by grass and weeds, dilapidated bars and a hotel whose outside sign was missing letters and read "Cosed for eason" even though it was already June.

Later, sitting between the Misty Dog and Twist O' the Mist, as the last shards of evening light were drawn from the sky, I was struck by the silence of Niagara Falls. The city seemed so empty, and its wide streets only accentuated its loneliness. Unlike many of the other locations on my itinerary, I hadn't bothered to research Niagara Falls. For me, it was a crossing point, a place where I could take in some natural scenery before heading south to chase the ghosts of New York and the Hudson Valley. I hadn't expected to find Niagara haunted in the same strange way. I knew that Niagara Falls had once been a hugely popular tourist destination, and I expected to find it a bit like the seaside resorts that dot the Irish and British coastlines: in decline, certainly, what with the growing accessibility of international travel, but still there; still holding on with souvenir shops, arcades, fast food restaurants, maybe a Ferris wheel and some bumper cars. Niagara Falls, however, feels as though it was abandoned, hastily at first, with shop windows carefully boarded up and signs dismantled, then all at once, as displays of plastic furniture, nautical paintings and artificial flowers were left to yellow in decades' worth of sunlight.

If you watch a lot of movies from the early part of the twentieth century, you'll recognise Niagara Falls as America's premier honeymoon destination. In Frank Capra's 1944 black comedy *Arsenic and Old Lace*, Cary Grant plays Mortimer Brewster, a reformed playboy whose attempts to bring his new bride to the falls are repeatedly thwarted by the antics of his murderous spinster aunts. "But, darling, Niagara Falls," his wife pleads as Mortimer is dragged into another chaotic scheme. "It does?" he responds. "Well, let it." A decade and half later, in Billy Wilder's boundary-pushing comedy *Some Like It Hot*, Jack Lemmon's character, who has gotten himself engaged to a millionaire while posing as a female musician, deliberates as to whether he would prefer to honeymoon on the French Riviera or in Niagara Falls.

Old photographs and film strips show a teeming, vibrant city, cluttered with brilliant signs advertising bars, restaurants and shows. Pedestrians crowd the pavements, streaming in and out of small souvenir shops. In silent Super 8 mm films, girls in headscarves smile as they lean against the railings of the Rainbow Bridge, the falls mutely roaring in the distance. Brightly tinted postcards from the 1950s show sleek aquamarine tour buses gliding through the streets alongside huge convertibles with hoods like the bows of ships. Others advertise clean white motel cabins with names like "Star Motel" or "Memory Lane". The Niagara Falls of the 1950s is so bright, so full. It seems like one never-ending party.

It did end, of course. Niagara Falls slipped into decline sometime around the early 1960s. As automobiles supplanted rail travel, the once steady stream of tourists riding the rails up from New York City began to dwindle. Almost simultaneously, other industries began to fail. In the early decades of the twentieth century, the US side of Niagara Falls thrived as a hub for industry, particularly manufacturing and petrochemical plants, which were powered by the falls. However, by the 1960s, this economic sector had started on the path to decline, with the wide availability of electricity across the nation making Niagara's hydroelectricity increasingly redundant. Slowly, companies moved south, where labour was cheaper. Worse still, not only were petrochemical companies abandoning Niagara Falls, but the damage they wrought during their time in the region was becoming increasingly apparent. In the 1970s, a number of public surveys and newspaper reports began to emerge detailing abnormally high levels of illness — asthma, epilepsy, leukaemia, chronic migraines — as well as birth defects and miscarriages in the working-class neighbourhood of Love Canal, a one-time dumping ground for the Hooker Chemical Company.

Today, Niagara Falls is a ghost, empty and mute. Though there are shops lining Old Falls Street, a casino, and an aquarium, the further you go from the falls, the more the city seems drained of life. The population of Niagara Falls peaked in 1960, with the city calling itself home to more than 102,394 residents. At last count, in 2021, the population had decreased to 48,360. When those tens of thousands of residents abandoned the city, they left behind them vestiges of the past — silent living rooms frozen in time behind shuttered windows, Christmas decorations boxed in attics, vacant motel rooms grown thick with dust and the wispy corpses of spiders — but they also relinquished a promised future. In the first half of the twentieth century, Niagara Falls pointed towards the future, a vision of tomorrow defined by comfort, financial security, family togetherness and ample leisure time. Yet, somewhere along the way that dream had been punctured.

Niagara Falls, as it stands now, might be best understood in terms of hauntology. This term, which was coined by the French philosopher Jacques Derrida in his 1993 book

Spectres de Marx, replaces the solidity of ontology — being and existing in the here and now — with the ambiguity of the ghost. Caught between life and death, past and present, spectres destabilise certainties and disrupt linear time (Davis 373). Taking this idea even further, another philosopher, Mark Fisher, understands hauntology as the state of being haunted not only by the past, but also by the future, by all the longed-for futures that never materialised. If Niagara Falls is haunted, then this is precisely the nature of its haunting. In the eternally vacant motels and the blank, boarded-up windows that stared blindly from empty buildings along Main Street, there was a sense that past and future had collapsed in upon themselves. Time was out of joint in Niagara Falls. The structures that had been built to accommodate bright futures — honeymooning couples; growing families; a bigger, brighter, happier America — had fallen to ruin, become sickly monuments to a vanished yesterday and a stalled tomorrow. Fisher writes that haunting "happens when a place is stained by time, or when a particular place becomes the site for an encounter with broken time" (19). Niagara Falls is certainly stained by time. In fact, it is saturated by it. Marked by the ruins of twentieth-century consumer culture, the city is a testament to failed futures. Later, as I moved south, down through New York State, and then headed east, with the Erie Canal running alongside me, I thought a lot about haunting as a confluence of past, present and future. In other towns and cities, whether famous for table-rapping spirits or spectral horsemen, it seemed that the ghosts of the past also carried with them hopes and fears about the future.

Night fell, and the Twist O' the Mist glowed red and green from its small square windows. The white swirl of faux ice-cream was bathed in an ectoplasmic light. I cycled back to the guesthouse through dark streets. Niagara Falls was a strange little temporal juncture. Marking the site where new national borders had attempted to efface their ancient precursors, whatever haunted the streets now was not merely the scattered traces of the past, but the promise of a future that had sparked, sputtered and ultimately faded out. Unlocking the guesthouse door, I saw that the party had dissipated, leaving behind a few deflated balloons and tattered streamers. I petted the cats and curled up in a bed overflowing with pillows.

Lily Dale, New York

The central and western regions of New York State brim with ghosts. You find them flinging exhibitions from shelves in dusty local museums, overturning furniture in suburban homes and clattering along hotel corridors in the off-season. Yet, despite their seeming ubiquity, not all of these ghosts are frightening and not all are unwelcome. Indeed, many of New York's ghosts are invited guests, long-lost relatives returning after decades of absence, or famous poets and orators, once again thrilling audiences with their words. In dimly lit parlours, these spirits find old friends, bringing comfort to mourners and joyfully describing the peaceful existence that awaits souls after death.

The influx of ghosts to New York State began in the middle decades of the nineteenth century. The region, which then constituted the western edges of the American frontier, was aflame with religious fervour, with at least thirty new spiritual movements and utopian communities establishing themselves in upstate New York. For a hundred years, from the advent of US independence in 1776 until the close of the nineteenth century, the region pulsed with spiritual energy. As migrants moved west, following the new economic opportunities that had opened with the completion of the Erie Canal in 1825, they sloughed off the dogma of established churches, mostly New England

Protestantism, and began to explore new faiths. Historian Whitney R. Cross described the spiritual transformations that attended this period of migration and upheaval as a "psychic highway" stretching west across the Finger Lakes region, through booming industrial centres like Rochester, all the way to the US-Canada border. Free from the conservatism and hierarchical structure of East-Coast Christianity, new religions sprang up like mushrooms in the rapidly developing West. The United Society of Believers in Christ's Second Appearing, better known as the Shakers, founded their first community based on the egalitarian teachings of Mother Ann Lee in 1776 near Albany. By 1826, they had expanded further west, founding another community in Groveland, Central New York, where they continued to practise celibacy and gender equality. Two years later, in 1828, Joseph Smith discovered the golden plates that would form the basis for the Book of Mormon, and the new religion of Mormonism, buried in the earth not far from the canal town of Palmyra. The Millerites, a sect that expected Christ's return to take place in 1844 and out of whose "Great Disappointment" emerged the still thriving Seventh-day Adventist Church, were also active in the region. New York State also played host to more unconventional movements, such as John Humphrey Noyes's utopian Oneida Community, which was distinguished by the communal ownership of goods and property and, most controversially, by the practice of "complex", or group, marriage. So fervent was the spirit of religious and mystical awakening that swept across Central and Western New York that critics christened the region the "Burned-over District", adopting, in Cross's words, "the prevailing western analogy between fires of the forest and those of the spirit" (3).

Perhaps the most unusual movement to emerge from the flames of the Burned-over District, Spiritualism has become an icon of modern popular culture, a Gothic staple that endures on page and screen. The vestiges of Spiritualism can be found in strange places, often far removed from its origins as an idealistic religious system that sought to marry faith and science in a rapidly modernising world. In horror movies, Ouija boards, tools developed out of Spiritualist séances, become portals to demonic realms, while mediums are brought in to cleanse suburban houses of ghostly energy. In mystery novels, fraudulent seers are unmasked as unscrupulous killers or caricatured as vainglorious old women. In actuality, though, Spiritualism is one of the most important religious and social movements to emerge out of the ideological ferment of the nineteenth century. Founded in 1848, Spiritualism was grounded in the belief that life persists after death and that the dead can communicate with the living. Andrew Jackson Davis, a prominent Spiritualist who was nicknamed the "Poughkeepsie Seer", described a cosmology in which, after death, the soul ascends through various planetary spheres. The closest of these, "Summer-Land", remains accessible to the living and was often understood in terms of beauty, peace and rationality:

> The spiritual is real ... so the entranced and clairvoyant of this age behold delightful fields, landscapes, gardens, flowers, fruits, rivers, lakes, fountains, vast assemblages of spirits, musical bands, lyceum gatherings, sportive children, scholars of design, art galleries, magnificent mansion, and architectural abodes of beauty where loving hearts beat and throb as one (quoted in Troy 8).

Spiritualism was diffuse, with no central church or governing body. Indeed, the movement was inimical to hierarchy and rank. Because Spiritualists believed that divine truth was accessible to all individuals, regardless of race or gender, the movement incorporated a wide range of belief systems and produced little in the way of orthodox dogma. The earliest mediums employed relatively simple techniques for communicating with the other world: tapping sounds or the gentle movement of the table around which the sitters had gathered spelled out words and phrases. Later, more elaborate equipment was added. The spirit cabinet — developed in the 1850s — served as what one paranormal researcher called a "spiritual storage battery". Mediums would be bound, placed in the cabinet, and while still immobile, spectacular manifestations would appear to emanate from the structure. Another device utilised in séances from the 1860s onwards was the planchette, a small board placed on wheels with a pencil attached near the front (Natale 132). Planchettes were typically used in automatic writing, a practice whereby mediums would channel the words of the spirits through their bodies to produce messages on a page. Like the more well-known "talking board", or Ouija board, the planchette was later successfully marketed as a toy or parlour game (Natale 132).

Although Spiritualist practices thrived in parlours and private homes, adherents nevertheless arranged public spectacles, intended to demonstrate the very real possibility of spirit communication to the masses. Mediums often performed in hotels, theatres and music halls. Sometimes, spirits would speak through the mediums, essentially puppeteering the body of another in order to give a public address. On other occasions, mediums would cause sprits to materialise, ephemeral yet seemingly very real, before an enraptured audience. North American Spiritualist groups even went so far as to organise summer "camp meetings" at scenic locales such as beaches and lakesides (Braude 174). Typically taking place over a period of two weeks, camp meetings featured lectures, séances and various forms of light entertainment. In stark contrast to the serious tone of more conservative Protestant denominations, Spiritualist camp meetings encouraged guests to take part in frivolous activities like boating, dancing and even roller-skating (Moore 238). A visitor to one such camp meeting described a programme of events that included a "phantom party", where guests came clad as spirits, and an "Old Folks Concert", where all the performers donned costumes from the 1700s and imitated the style of the previous century (Natale 26). While many camp meetings packed up at the end of their two weeks, dismantling wooden furniture and folding up tents until next year, some developed into permanent resorts, with hotels, restaurants, assembly halls and cottages (Braude 174). One such resort, a summer camp that solidified into a vibrant community filled with brightly painted homes and clean white woodland temples, is the small hamlet of Lily Dale. Created by the mediums and Spiritualists who would meet each summer on the shores of the Cassadaga Lakes, Lily Dale still stands today, almost 150 years later, as the largest modern-day Spiritualist community.

***

I made my way to Lily Dale by bus, travelling from Niagara Falls to Buffalo and then heading west along Route 5, hugging Lake Erie through towns like Athol Springs, Mt Vernon and Fredonia, all the way to Cassadaga. A small village whose name in Seneca means "water beneath the rocks", Cassadaga is little more than a single street flanked on one side by a Tim Horton's doughnut shop and on the other by a red-brick restaurant that seemed to have served its last customers decades ago. When the bus shuddered to a halt outside a lonely petrol station, I tossed my backpack onto the pavement and climbed down behind it. Before turning right onto County Road 48, I passed an ice-cream shop whose sign read "King Kone". Above the service window, a massive plastic King Kong swung from the wood-panelled wall. His eyes blazed brilliant orange, and he brandished an over-sized ice-cream cone.

I walked a mile and a half from Cassadaga to reach Lily Dale. The narrow rural road unspooled along the lower and middle portions of the Cassadaga Lakes. I was arriving early — Lily Dale's summer season would not begin for another two weeks — so the road was quiet and free of traffic. US flags fluttered on telephone poles and porches. Stars and Stripes bunting adorned every window. The next day would be Flag Day, a national holiday celebrating the adoption of the US flag on 14 June 1777. Beneath a sign welcoming visitors to "the beautiful Cassadaga Lakes", a small noticeboard advertised a yard sale and an upcoming "strawberry social" on the beach. Gentle sunlight streamed through the trees, dandelion seeds floated on the breeze, and waves lapped gently against the lakeshore. At regular intervals, I spotted tiny fishing huts and small cabins adjacent to private marinas. One wooden house, painted a striking red, floated on its own diminutive island, which was connected to the shore by a little curved bridge. In a garden on the other side of the road, a gaggle of geese convened in the shade of a hedgerow.

I knew I had reached Lily Dale when I passed a wooden building with vibrant purple awnings and an octagonal turret that looked out onto the lake. Foxgloves and bluebells danced in the garden, and the sign by the entrance read: "Fellowships of the Spirit: Lakeside Learning Center". A few metres further along the road I found the entrance to Lily Dale. A wrought iron sign, bearing the words "Lily Dale Assembly" in white letters, arched over a red brick pillar on the roadside. At one point, this archway seems to have been the main gate. Sepia photographs from the turn of the twentieth century show ladies in long white summer dresses, hair coiffed in Gibson Girl swirls beneath the shade of parasols, strolling under the arching letters, arm in arm with gentlemen in bowler hats. Now this original entry sign sits off to the side of the road. Underneath it, more-recent signage, deep royal blue and decorated with a lily pad, welcomes visitors to "Lily Dale Assembly: World's Largest Center for the Religion of Spiritualism".

Lily Dale seemed caught in the sticky, molasses grip of the past. Time had slowed to a crawl; it lurched forwards in tiny increments, moving reluctantly, haltingly. The streets were narrow and unusually quiet. Numbered streets went no higher than 4th Street; others bore names like Library St and Cottage Row. I felt like I had opened a toy box. On each street, wooden Victorian houses, painted in pastel shades of yellow, green and purple, were lined up like the

Post office in Lily Dale, New York

habitations of delicate porcelain dolls. Wind chimes jangled on porches and crystals gleamed enticingly on window ledges. Stone fairies and ceramic angels guarded pathways. The houses appeared friendly, inviting. That evening, one of Lily Dale's resident mediums told me that many of the windows and porches are over-sized in comparison to the houses themselves, making them appear even more welcoming. Outside a small white building with a wide porch, a sign read "United States Post Office, Lily Dale, NY" and an American flag fluttered in the breeze. Small pathways and trails snaked out from the centre of the hamlet, leading visitors through Leolyn Woods — a mossy old-growth forest — or down to small lakeside beaches. Other paths wound past Inspiration Stump, a locus of spiritual revelation, or through the Lily Dale pet cemetery,

Lily Dale's Forest Temple

Marker in Lily Dale's pet cemetery

where lovingly tended markers honoured Sampson, "Best of the Bassetts", and Smokey, "Dedicated Beagle".

My main point of contact in Lily Dale was Joanne Mansfield. A lively and intelligent woman in her seventies, when I first encountered Joanne, in June 2022, she was vice president of the Lily Dale Assembly. We met at the community's administrative office, where staff were busy preparing for the start of the summer season. Though the walls were adorned with images of famous mediums — Kate and Margaret Fox, Thomas Lake Harris, Andrew Jackson Davis — the office atmosphere was like any other. Email notifications pinged; photocopiers lurched as they spewed out streams of paper. The anticipation was palpable. Every year, Lily Dale comes to life for the summer when the year-round population of around 300 permanent residents swells to over 22,000. Visitors come from all over the world. Some are committed Spiritualists, while others are curious tourists, eager to see this unusual community or to learn what the future holds for them.

"Lily Dale Assembly," Joanne explained, "went through a series of names." In the 1840s, a man named Jeremiah Carter, who at the time had been suffering various health problems, began to practise mesmeric trances in hopes of healing his afflictions. In his trance state, Carter communicated with the dead and was encouraged by the spirits to hold meetings on the land of a local farmer, Willard Alden. Carter's group, which called itself the First Spiritual Society of Laona, subsequently purchased eighteen acres of land adjoining Alden's property, where they established the Cassadaga Lake Free Association in 1879. The community was renamed the City of Lights in 1903, before being rechristened Lily Dale, in honour of the abundant local flora, in 1906. Today, Joanne continued, "Lily Dale is most known for healing, more than the mediumship, really." In fact, one of the community's most important spiritual centres is its healing temple, a sparse white building flanked by thick neoclassical columns. "Mae West dedicated that," Joanne noted. "She was not a Spiritualist, but she did come for readings." Later, I would learn that West, an icon of classic Hollywood best remembered for her quick wit and salacious double-entendres, had possessed a profound connection with the spirit world: attending séances, communing with the other world and even dictating screenplays in a trance state.

Joanne walked me to the Lily Dale auditorium, unlocking the main door and ushering me inside. The building's immense wrap-around windows — which provided ventilation for crowded events in an age before air conditioning — were still shuttered. The freshly polished wooden floors gleamed even in the sparse light. Rows and rows of vacant seats stretched to the back wall. On the stage, three wooden chairs sat empty behind a wooden podium. Nearby, a small organ and a piano waited patiently for the start of summer meetings. Although it was currently empty, the auditorium reverberated with the joyous echoes of history, of past summer lectures and spectacular displays of mediumship. I asked Joanne what made Spiritualism such a unique religious movement. "They were the first women that went on stage," she explained. "They gave women a voice. They were the first ones to be allowed to go on stage and say something." I nodded enthusiastically. For me, this was one of the most intriguing facets of Spiritualism. Early mediums, most of whom were female, were among the first women to speak publicly on a variety of social and political issues. In an age when the division between the public sphere of commerce and politics and the private sphere of home and domesticity had hardened into an intransigent ideological divide, Spiritualism encouraged women to assume an active role in public life. While few other nineteenth-century religious organisations even countenanced women speaking in church, Spiritualism afforded them equal opportunities for leadership and spiritual development (Braude 3). Spiritualists, both men and women, were active in the suffragist movement, fighting for women's right to vote, and many early feminists were drawn to the radical equality espoused by Spiritualist groups. Susan B. Anthony, one of America's foremost women's right activists, spoke at Lily Dale's Women's Day celebrations on at least five occasions, giving lectures in the very auditorium in which I now stood.

In the nineteenth century, many Spiritualists believed that while all humans possessed some degree of mediumistic potential, women were best suited to the practice due to their natural passivity and openness. Even now, the majority of mediums in Lily Dale are women. Today, the notion that women are natural mediums because of an inherent feminine passivity might strike us as somewhat misogynistic. However, Spiritualism as a movement was deeply committed to equality and actively manipulated popular stereotypes of feminine fragility and incompetence. As the historian Ann Braude explains, mediumship was a subversively empowering practice because it "allowed women to discard limitations on women's role without questioning accepted ideas about woman's nature" (83). In darkened theatres across America, women — often young, in their late teens and early twenties — took to stages to address rapt audiences. As conduits for the spirit world, these women discoursed on some of the most important issues of their day: women's suffrage, the abolition of slavery and the treatment of Indigenous populations. They balanced right on the edge appropriate female behaviour but, clasped in the ectoplasmic embrace of the spectral, never toppled over the line.

After locking the auditorium behind us, Joanne accompanied me the short distance to the Maplewood Hotel, built first as a stable and later transformed into a residence for vacationing Spiritualists. We climbed the steps of the wrap-around porch and entered the lobby, unchanged since the latter part of the nineteenth century. Behind a high reception desk, the walls were lined with tiny nooks, each housing unclaimed keys. A little wooden telephone booth, a relic of the pre-mobile phone era, stood in the corner of the lobby. A sign on the wall read, "No Séances, Readings or Healings Allowed in the Hotel." Joanne brought me upstairs to show me the empty rooms. The floors were carpeted with deep, rich patterns, and the curtains that hung on the high windows were thick and heavy. The hotel was not yet open for the season, so stray pieces of furniture, piled high with fresh, crisp bedsheets and soft, downy towels, crowded the hallways.

Back downstairs, we wandered around the Azur Room, named for the life-sized oil painting of "Azur the Helper" that dominates the space despite being currently propped against a chair. "He's just returned from the Minneapolis Institute of Art," Joanne told me. "He was in their exhibition. That's why he's not on the wall." Azur, an old man with kind eyes and a grey beard, was the spirit guide of English businessman and Spiritualist Allen Campbell. Campbell worked alongside another man, Charles Shourds, and while the pair operated as "The Campbell Brothers", they were most likely a gay couple (Schill 38). Together, they produced "precipitated paintings", images that materialised, seemingly at the behest of invisible spiritual hands, on blank canvases. Azur manifested this way in June 1898. Campbell channelled him while sitting inside a spirit cabinet. To ensure the veracity of the work, a number of different witnesses occupied the cabinet alongside Campbell. Each time the cabinet was opened to allow a change of sitter, the rest of the assembled witnesses saw that more of the image had materialised. At the end of the session, Campbell emerged with a richly textured painting of Azur clad in the flowing white robes of an ancient mystic. The witnesses claimed that following Campbell's emergence, a six-pointed star, which had not originally been part of the painting, slowly became discernible behind Azur's head (Buckland 60). On other spots, on other walls, hung additional precipitated paintings channelled by the Campbell Brothers. Among them, visitors can find the sage visage of Abraham Lincoln and doe-eyed Nora, a little girl whose grieving mother requested the painting following her child's death but then balked at the possibility of accepting an image she thought of as "the devil's work".

***

Later that afternoon, I visited a few of Lily Dale's thirty-three registered mediums. In a boardroom at the administrative offices, I spoke to Alison, who told me that her first psychic visions came in the form of events unfolding on a television screen. The spirits would show her a TV set, and she would watch events unfolding, as if she were watching a movie, on the screen. Afterwards, I called to one of the community's many art galleries to meet Sally, who practises physical mediumship in the form of spirit-inspired art. At the door of the gallery, Sally's little dog greeted me happily and led me inside. Much like the Azur Room, back at the Maplewood Hotel, the walls were adorned with colourful paintings. These, however, were newer works, and most were not precipitated paintings. Instead, Sally's walls teemed with portraits of benignly smiling spirit guides, auragraphs and trance paintings. My favourite pieces were the abstract images — swirling lines and jostling blocks of colour — revealed during séances, and Sally kindly gave me a small one to take with me when I left. As I stood admiring the images, Sally told me that she was picking up some energy around me. I started. I had never had a psychic reading, though in the small seaside town where I grew up, fortune-tellers would crowd the pier front each summer, reading tarot cards and deciphering shapes in crystal balls from the backs of vans. "There is a woman near you," Sally announced. She was unable to tell me more, and we never determined who it might have been.

Towards the end of the day, I sat in the shade of a screened porch and drank lemonade with a friendly middle-aged woman named Michelle. "So, yeah," she said, pouring another glass, "I was accidentally electrocuted in a kitchen." I paused and put down my drink. "When?" Michelle thought for a moment: "I was five... maybe just five. Anyway, I touched appliances, and one wasn't properly grounded. And I ended up in the hospital. And I think that seems to have opened up some things." She went on to relay a series of strange events, flashes of knowledge that she couldn't

The Victorian houses and temples of Lily Dale

possibly possess and strange forebodings that followed her throughout her life. In middle school, Michelle excelled in French exams without ever really studying the language, and she now believes she was absorbing some kind of psychic residue, perhaps a past life or the wisdom of a spirit guide. Throughout her life, working in diverse careers — first as a journalist, and later as a communications manager — Michelle would catch glimpses of future events or hear voices from the past. In the 1980s, she started working at psychic fairs, gaining clients because she dressed like an executive: "I didn't have any flowy clothes. I had a big blouse with a bow on the blouse and the pearls, you know, pencil skirt, high-heeled pumps. I looked ridiculous." I laughed: "Very *Working Girl*." Michelle had recently joined the Lily Dale community as an officially registered medium, so I asked about the process. "You do a half-hour reading for three people who then score you," she explained, "and then you do a public demonstration, and you give messages to three people that you choose from the audience. And they also do the scoring." Securing membership in the Lily Dale Assembly is a rigorous process, and only registered mediums can give readings in the community. Applicants are carefully tested, and are asked to prove their capabilities before the Assembly Board and in public demonstrations. The procedures sound almost scientific with their emphasis on securing empirical evidence of psychic capabilities and the replicability of tests.

Considering the history of Spiritualism, this scientific rigour makes sense. Emerging in the middle decades of the nineteenth century, amid a profusion of new technologies and scientific innovations, Spiritualism has always defined itself as both a religion *and* a science. In an age when newly laid railroads crossed the American continent, condensing time and space in a flurry of steam and steel, and telegraphs sent messages almost instantaneously across vast distances, Spiritualism sought to bridge the divide between the scientific and the spiritual. The movement's agenda was rational in nature, as it aimed to prove the endurance of life after death by opening up a line of communication with the spirits of the deceased. Séances were thought of by some as replicable experiments: if the same conditions were reproduced in each sitting, contact with the spirits would certainly be made. Witnesses carefully observed mediums, whether seated at a table or concealed in the darkness of a spirit cabinet, to ensure the legitimacy of their practices. Spiritualists articulated their endeavours through the language of cutting-edge technologies and new scientific discoveries. Connecting the capacity of mediums to commune with the dead to new communications technologies, many Spiritualists referred to mediumship as the "spiritual telegraph".

Spiritualism, then, is a movement that exorcises many of our preconceptions about ghosts and hauntings. While so many ghosts appear as ephemeral, translucent accretions of trauma, the spirits summoned into the parlours and materialised on the stages of nineteenth-century mediums were hopeful beings. From their homes in the peaceful environs of Summer-Land, they returned with joyful messages, hoping to better the world they had departed. Speaking through mediums or manifesting as gauzy ectoplasmic configurations, these spirits were not simply echoes of a remote past. Rather, they inhabited a liminal space between past, present and future. While they returned from the far reaches of the past, old friends or departed historical figures, the very act of receiving a message from the beyond suggested a dawning future in which science and rationalism might illuminate even the tenebrous realm of the dead.

Hydesville and Palmyra, New York

In March 1848, a small cottage in the Finger Lakes region of New York State trembled and shook as mysterious knocking sounds vibrated through its timber frame. Something powerful but unseen knocked on walls, banged on ceilings and floors and caused furniture to shake throughout the building. The house, located in the tiny hamlet of Hydesville, not far from the Erie Canal, belonged to John and Margaret Fox. The couple had moved to the area only a few months prior with their young daughters, Margaret (Maggie), aged fourteen, and Catherine (Kate), aged eleven. In a signed testimony, later published as a pamphlet, the elder Margaret described how the strange, jarring sounds would always commence just after the family had retired to bed. "It sounded like someone knocking in the east bedroom, on the floor," Margaret claimed. "Sometimes it sounded as if the chair moved on the floor; we could hardly tell where it was." That first night, the Fox family lit a candle and attempted to root out the source of the discomfiting thuds. However, as Margaret later testified, "The noise continued while we were hunting, and was heard near the same place all the time."

The banging continued for a number of weeks until finally, on the night of 31 March, something shifted. There was a change, the chaos ebbed and the inchoate "tremulous motion" transformed into conversational raps. By now, the family were exhausted. The continuous nocturnal sounds had disturbed their rest so much that Margaret was on the verge of sickness. A late snowfall lay thick on the ground and darkness had not yet fallen when the two girls, Kate and Maggie, began to communicate with whatever was making the sounds. Lying in their beds, the adolescent sisters started to imitate the sounds by snapping their fingers. Each time Kate, the youngest girl, snapped her fingers, the family would hear a knock. The more she snapped, the more knocks would follow, imitating precisely the number and pattern of Kate's snaps. Maggie then addressed the source of the knocks, banging her hands together, and commanding the force, "Now do this just as I do. Count one, two, three, four." The invisible force responded by imitating Maggie's claps, "repeating every blow that she made". Maggie was startled, but her mother, Margaret, proceeded to further test the force. She asked it to count to ten, and then quizzed it by asking the ages of her children. The entity answered correctly, counting out their ages in raps. By now, Margaret understood what was happening in her home. She enquired of the force whether it was a spirit, and if so, asked it to respond in the affirmative by knocking twice. Through this system of rudimentary communication, Margaret ascertained that the source of the unsettling thuds was a spirit, a man who had been murdered in the house and whose remains were buried beneath the dwelling.

Margaret sent for the neighbours. People began pouring into the cottage: Mrs Redfield and her husband, Mr and Mrs Duesler, the Hydes, the Jewells; a group of men night-fishing on the Ganargua Creek stopped by to see what all the fuss was. The excitement must have been palpable. By the following evening, several hundred people — roughly half the population of Arcadia, the larger town of which the hamlet of Hydesville forms a part — had begun to crowd the house. Visitors wanted to see the house and the family; they wanted to hear the strange rapping spirits for themselves. By now, diligent neighbours had determined through a series of yes/no questions that their interlocutor was the spirit of a peddler, his throat cut with a butcher knife for the five hundred dollars he had been carrying.

As wagons filled with curious visitors daily pulled up in front of the Fox home, termed by some the "spook house", the spectral raps continued, seeming to follow young Kate and Maggie wherever they went. Margaret decided to separate the girls, sending Kate to stay with their older sister, thirty-five-year-old Leah, in the nearby city of Rochester. Yet, even then, the disturbances continued, so Leah moved Kate and her own daughter, Lizzie, to a new house, fearing the first had been haunted. Margaret and Maggie joined them, and after a single night of peace, the spirits resumed their boisterous antics.

It was at this time, while living in Rochester, that the Fox sisters became reacquainted with Amy and Isaac

Post, a Quaker couple they had known as children. The Posts, who were already committed abolitionists, became ardent supporters of the Fox girls and their spiritual gifts. Indeed, it was Isaac who introduced the practice of reciting the alphabet so that the spirits, banging at the appropriate letter, could spell out words and create more complex communications. Leah also discovered her own mediumistic powers while living with Kate and Maggie in Rochester. Entering magnetic trances in hopes of curing her recurrent headaches, Leah found that in this state she could easily communicate with the spirits.

After about a year, the spirits decided to go public, instructing Isaac Post to rent the city's largest venue, Corinthian Hall, for three nights and charge an admission fee of seventy-five cents (Braude 15). Four hundred people gathered in the hall on 14 November 1849 to witness the Fox Sisters commune with the spirits. The demonstration was widely discussed in the popular press, with both supporters and sceptics dissecting the girls' performance. A short while later, in 1850, the sisters began conducting séances in New York City, where they garnered even more attention. Occupying a room in the Barnum Hotel, on the corner of Broadway and Maiden Lane, the girls became bona fide celebrities. Leah later recalled that journalists from major newspapers would call to their rooms on a daily basis and that advertisements and shop window displays used the "Rochester Knockings" to sell a variety of goods (Natale 72).

The heady swirl of celebrity was, unsurprisingly, transitory. Their careers lasted almost half a century, but the girls were perpetually hounded by sceptics who hoped to expose them as frauds, and preyed upon by opportunistic reporters, eager to dissect the private lives of the young mediums. For Kate and Maggie, who were only teenagers when they were unveiled as the public faces of the burgeoning Spiritualist movement, fame was a difficult course to navigate. Leah settled into a comfortable life of middle-class respectability, but the younger girls were plagued by tragedy, with both eventually succumbing to alcoholism and poverty. Kate and Maggie's later years were marked by struggle and heartbreak, as well as by a series of spectacular confessions, retractions and recantations that never fully succeeded in extinguishing the spark of Spiritualistic fervour that had been ignited on a cold March night in Western New York.

***

It was still dark when I arrived in Newark, New York, the nearest settlement in what remains of Hydesville. There are only two buses per day between Rochester, where I was currently residing in a leafy suburb, and Newark. The morning bus departs the Rochester Transit Centre at 5:00am and returns at 5:30pm. If you miss either, then tough: you're stuck. I walked through the centre of the village, a collection of brick commercial buildings that branched out into highways lined with auto repair shops and fast-food franchises. A pale pink morning light was barely visible beneath the heavy curtain of pre-dawn blackness, and a diaphanous mist rose out of the Erie Canal.

On a patch of neatly trimmed grass, nestled between farmland and clapboard houses with SUVs parked in their driveways, I found what remains of the little cottage where modern Spiritualism was born. A single-storey wooden cabin stood alone amid a cluster of tall elm trees. It was a comparatively modern building, with thick double-glazed windows. A green sign read, "Hydesville Memorial Park", while a few feet away, just by the roadside, a royal-blue historical marker identified the site as the origin point of a major religious movement.

The site of the Fox sisters' house in Hydesville, New York

Tracy arrived with the first rays of sunshine. Hopping out of her black SUV, she greeted me with a sunny smile and introduced herself as the property's caretaker. "Hydesville is just a road now," she told me as she unlocked the cabin door. The little hamlet had simply vanished over time, gradually disappearing into the surrounding towns until the only evidence of its existence was the nearby Hydesville Road and the small memorial park in which I now stood. Inside, the cabin was bright and airy. Light streamed in through large, clean windows, and white-washed ceilings vaulted to a point high above my head. The cabin, however, was not the main attraction. In fact, it wasn't the attraction at all. People come to Hydesville to see the low stone walls that occupy most of the structure, preserved like Pompeian ruins beneath the cabin's protective roof. I walked about between the walls; the highest ones barely reached my waist. Crumbling stone and concrete, these are the foundations of the Fox cottage, all that remains of the haunted house that birthed a new religion.

The house itself was long gone. In 1916, it was purchased by a member of the Lily Dale Assembly and moved to the community's grounds. "They just took everything apart," Tracy said. "They put it on a barge, it went up the Erie Canal to Buffalo and then they put it on a truck." The Fox house spent almost forty years in Lily Dale, where the medium who took up residence in the cottage claimed to be in regular contact with the spirits of the Fox sisters. Sadly, the house burned to the ground in 1955. During my time in Lily Dale, I was able to see the plaque — which survived the fire — memorialising the cottage as the birthplace of Spiritualism, and the tranquil little garden that now commemorates the Fox family. A trunk, ostensibly belonging to the murdered peddler, was salvaged from the blaze and currently resides in the Lily Dale Museum. In 1967, a man named John Drummond attempted to reconstruct the Fox cottage using old colour postcards as his primary reference. That house, too, burned down, and while Drummond hoped to rebuild the cottage, he died before he could realise his dream. Today, the stone foundations, enclosed within an unassuming wooden cabin, are the last vestiges of the Fox home.

Tracy led me around the foundations, showing me the original parts and the sections that were added later by Drummond when he tried to build his replica. The house had clearly been very small, with two rooms on the ground floor and a small loft upstairs. No wonder the ghostly knocks had reverberated so powerfully throughout the structure. "It wasn't anything fancy," Tracy told me. "Nothing really was back then." Dotted around the structure, I saw small displays featuring letters, photographs and some early Spiritualist memorabilia. On one wall hung a (recent) child's drawing of the Fox sisters, coloured in bright Crayola hues. A wooden dolls' house, inhabited by plastic figures in period dress, recreated the layout of the original Fox home.

I wondered what it had been like for Kate and Maggie, two adolescent girls, to live in this little cottage in rural New York during the middle years of the nineteenth century. When the Fox family moved to Hydesville in the late 1840s, the community was only around thirty years old. It had been founded by and named for Henry Hyde, a doctor from Vermont, who moved to the area to practise medicine in 1814. Realising that he had settled on a popular route for travellers heading west, Hyde opened a tavern. Later, he started purchasing land in the area, building houses and renting them out to migrants who decided to stay in the region. Hydesville was a young settlement when the Foxes arrived, but it never grew to maturity. Unlike other communities in the region, the hamlet failed to flourish. Tracy explained that this was because a group of local farmers objected to the construction of the Erie Canal so close to their land. They feared disease and contamination from dirty, stagnant water. One night, after surveyors had laid out the stakes marking the site of the canal's trajectory, the farmers snuck out and moved the stakes south, away from their land. Without the commerce associated with the canal, Hydesville flagged, never becoming more than a small, loosely connected assemblage of houses.

Katie and Maggie's home lives were likely just as staid. John Fox, the girls' father, had once been a hard-drinking gambler, but by the time his two youngest daughters were born, he had repented, becoming a sober, observant Methodist. The girls were lively and intelligent in school, but like many young women of the day, they would have been expected to work in the home, helping their mother with household chores. Contemporary witnesses described the girls' terror when the rappings began, but I wonder if it had also been somewhat thrilling for them, a fantastic intrusion upon an endless, grey winter. Perhaps they had felt a little shiver of excitement as their home pulsed with unsettling noises.

Unsurprisingly, Kate and Maggie were accused of fakery, of producing the sounds through nefarious means in order to dupe the credulous and gain attention for themselves. Years later, Maggie — worn down by poverty and alcoholism, and still reeling from the death of her great love, the arctic explorer Elisha Kane — would stand before a packed auditorium to announce that the sisters had produced the rappings themselves by loudly cracking the joints in their toes. Although she later retracted her confession, many still hold to the theory that the Fox sisters were nothing more than talented tricksters. If this was the case, did two little girls conjure a haunting that made headlines throughout the region — and eventually around the world — simply to alleviate the tedium of an adolescence spent on the western fringes of the New York frontier?

I asked Tracy about the source of the knockings and whether there was any truth in the story that the house had been host to strange occurrences even prior to the arrival of the Foxes. She seemed convinced that there was something otherworldly residing in the Fox cottage. "In 1904," she told me, "there were actually kids playing in here. And that's when they discovered the bones of the peddler, okay, because the kids were in the basement messing around in the spook house." As it turns out, the travelling peddler whose spirit was believed responsible for the first knockings was not buried in the floor of the cellar, where many interested parties had already searched, but behind a wall. According to one contemporary article, a local physician who examined the bones estimated that they were about fifty years old, though, like everything else in this case, doubts remain.

Tracy, who has worked at the Hydesville site for twenty-three years, has heard some strange noises and observed a number of unusual occurrences: "Sometimes I come in, it's quiet, and I'll hear, you know, little giggling." On other occasions, locals will call Tracy to tell her that someone is moving around inside the locked enclosure. However, when she asks them to describe what they've seen, they will usually describe Mr Drummond, the man who, before his death, was attempting to reconstruct the Fox home. "He's still here," Tracy added.

***

The remains of the Fox cottage are not the only haunted house in the region. In towns and villages all along the Erie Canal, ghosts are busily slamming doors, overturning furniture and disturbing sleeping families. Tracy drove me to nearby Palmyra, a small canal-side town named for an ancient city in the Syrian Desert. Today, it is famous as the site where the first edition of the Book of Mormon was published in 1830. In addition to caring for Hydesville Memorial Park, Tracy also oversees five museums in the centre of Palmyra: the Alling Coverlet Museum, the Palmyra Historical Museum, the Wm. Phelps General Store and Restoration Property, the Palmyra Print Shop and the Erie Canal Depot. Because it was summer break, Tracy worked alongside two teenage interns, Casey and Maria, who showed me around the museums. As they explained the history of the town, the girls also spoke to me about their plans for college and filled me in on the local social scene (not great for teenagers, was the verdict). We wandered around the Historical Museum, which was built as a tavern and boarding house in 1826 and now plays host to twenty-three themed exhibition rooms, each showcasing a unique facet of the town's history. In the religion room, a daguerreotype of Kate and Maggie Fox sits in front of a menorah, while in the toy room, a bookcase overflows with dozens of grinning ragdolls. My guides walked me through each of the buildings, telling me in solemn tones about a fire that claimed the lives of a mother and her six children back in the 1960s, when the building was still a private residence. The children, I'm told, still play in the museum's hallways.

The girls were most excited to show me the Wm. Phelps General Store and Restoration Property because, it seemed, we might run into an old friend. Casey unlocked the heavy wooden door, pushing it open with a soft grunt. A gentle slant of early afternoon light shone through the display windows, illuminating shelves packed with brightly coloured boxes, most bearing the names of cleaning products I'd never heard of: Rinso, Dreft, Fab. Across the room, coffee tins gleamed red and orange. Ancient boxes of Corn Flakes sat undisturbed where they had been stocked almost a century ago. A pair of brass weighing scales stood on the countertop alongside a huge, ornate cash register. Casey punched in a few numbers so I could hear the little bell ring up a sale. Apparently, Julius Phelps, who had inherited the store from his father, William, simply decided to shut up shop one day in 1940. He locked the front door behind him and never returned, leaving the store to sit, frozen in time, until it was reopened as a museum decades later.

Above the store, the family residence also remains unchanged since the last member of the Phelps clan, Julius's daughter Sybil, passed away in 1976, at the age of eighty-one. Tracy told me all about Sybil earlier in the day. She had been something of a local character. As a young woman, in the 1920s, Sibyl had moved to New York City with dreams of becoming an actress. When she returned a few years later, out of luck and money, she shocked her staunch Episcopalian family by announcing that she had become a Spiritualist. Sybil lived in the apartments above the general store for the rest of her life. After her parents passed away, she refused to change the layout of the rooms or buy any new furniture because she wanted to ensure that their spirits would feel comfortable when they inevitably returned. In later years, Sibyl — who always wore black and kept at least a dozen cats — gained a reputation as a witch. To me, she sounded like a stylish animal lover. Tracy also told me that Sibyl is still very much an active presence in the house. Her footsteps can be heard on the stairs, and the odd spectral meow has been known to echo along the landing.

Sibyl is a well-known ghost, and the Palmyra museums are considered among the most haunted locations in the already ghost-ridden Finger Lakes region. For this reason, paranormal investigators have come from all over the country in hopes of capturing proof of Sibyl's presence. The museums have featured on shows such as the Travel Channel's *Kindred Spirits*, A&E's *My Ghost Story* and NEPA Paranormal's *Ghost Detectives*. Regardless of who the investigators are, Tracy always checks with Sibyl to make sure she is happy to have visitors: "Usually, before we have these investigators come in, I will go to the house and say, 'Okay, Sybil, you know, we're going to have visitors tonight and I hope it's okay. But this is how we make money [...] We want to keep the doors open.'" Sibyl is, apparently, quite amenable to guests, although her father, Julius, can be, in Tracy's words, "a little grouchy". Casey and Maria also spoke warmly of Sibyl, joking about her antics as if she were an eccentric yet beloved aunt. If visitors criticise Spiritualism or mock Sibyl's belief in the afterlife, she has been known to slam doors with unusual force. Yet, as I joked with the girls about Sibyl's occasional tantrums, I didn't sense any fear. They seemed genuinely fond of the old lady. In fact, the entire community seems to adore her. Each year, the museum celebrates Sibyl's birthday with cake, refreshments and psychic readings.

As I left the museum, waving goodbye to Tracy and the girls, I felt the air grow heavy. The day had been oppressively hot, and the air crackled with a barely restrained electrical energy. I sat beneath a gazebo in the town park and watched as grey clouds rolled in, slowing and then stopping as though they had been speared by the steeples of the four great churches that sit across from each other at the main intersection. Thunder rumbled and sharp winds whipped debris through the streets. As the sky split apart and rain poured down, I thought about the unique ghosts of the region. From the welcoming spirits of Lily Dale, nestled snug in the curve of the Cassadaga Lakes, to the friendly ghosts of Palmyra and Hydesville on the banks of the Erie Canal, the supernatural appeared truly wondrous. Here, ghosts were not startling, grotesque apparitions but lifelong companions, looked upon with warmth and love. I wondered if this supremely joyful conception of the afterlife and its inhabitants arose out of Western New York's former status as a frontier region. Was that the source of such optimism? Were the spectres that haunted this land so beloved because they brought with them not just memories of the past, but a promise for the future of the nation?

Sleepy Hollow, New York

I moved east, following the course of the Erie Canal as far as Albany, before turning south to trace the curves of the Hudson River downstream to Sleepy Hollow. Reversing the trajectory of America's colonial endeavour, I was working backwards, moving ineluctably towards some of the oldest European settlements on the continent. As the train wound its way along the banks of the Hudson, I sat close to the window and watched as we sped through the many towns and villages that had embedded themselves in the coves and curves of the river. We flew past huge expanses of reeds, soggy marshland thick with water lilies, old bridges turned to rust and the opulent upstate mansions of nineteenth-century robber barons. The valley is a lush green; trees reflected in the river imbue it with a striking verdancy. In other places, great bulky machines line the precipices of quarries. The metal frames of old factories dot the landscape like the skeletons of ancient monsters, while mountains roll and arch towards the sky.

After stopping briefly in Croton-Harmon to change trains, I arrived in the village of Sleepy Hollow. In my imagination, Sleepy Hollow had always appeared as a small cluster of wooden houses, perennially shrouded in mist and blanketed year-round in a crisp, golden layer of fallen leaves. However, as I would soon learn, nothing is ever small in America. Even the tiniest villages seep outwards, extending beyond densely packed centres, to form vast webs of box stores, car dealerships and petrol stations. In Sleepy Hollow, one of the many convenience stores I passed on my way from the riverside train station was decorated with a colourful image of the village's most famous resident, the Headless Horseman. Sitting atop his steed, his arm raised, wielding a pumpkin, the Horseman welcomes visitors to Sleepy Hollow. A little while later, as I trudged through a picturesque suburb where each house was surrounded by carefully maintained flowerbeds, I noticed that the

The Headless Horseman as school mascot in Sleepy Hollow, New York

immaculate symmetry of the green lawns was occasionally broken by signs congratulating the Sleepy Hollow High School seniors, the class of 2022. These too featured images of the galloping Horseman, who I would later learn is the school mascot. Further south, where Sleepy Hollow meets the neighbouring village of Tarrytown, a massive complex of new condominiums is bisected by streets bearing names like Legend Drive and Horseman Boulevard.

Everyone knows the Horseman, and not just here in Sleepy Hollow. He has become a bona fide piece of American folklore. Though he had antecedents in European tales of spectral riders and local tales stemming from the Revolutionary War, it was Washington Irving's short story "The Legend of Sleepy Hollow" (1820) that transformed the Headless Horseman into the most powerful and well-known of American ghosts. Irving's story follows a schoolmaster named Ichabod Crane, a gaunt and gawky man with a snipe nose that makes his head appear "like a weathercock perched upon his spindle neck to tell which way the wind blew". Despite his lanky frame, Crane is distinguished by his immense appetites, for food, women and wealth. One night, after a quilting party at the house of a rich landowner whose daughter Crane has set his sights upon, the hapless schoolmaster is pursued through the woods by a ghostly rider who carries his head on the pommel of his saddle. The next day, the townspeople discover that Crane has vanished, leaving behind only a hat and a shattered pumpkin. It is left to the reader and the town gossips to determine if Crane really was spirited away by the Horseman or if he was chased out of the village by a love rival. Over the past two centuries, the story has circulated widely in various forms. "The Legend of Sleepy Hollow" has been the subject of paintings, television shows, music and theatrical productions. It has been adapted to film numerous times, beginning in the silent era and continuing into the twenty-first century. I remember how, as a child, I watched the Disney version, *The Adventures of Ichabod and Mr Toad* (1949), and was vaguely discomfited by the shift in tone as the scene changed from the bumbling antics of the erudite yet awkward Ichabod to his wild nighttime pursuit by the ghastly rider.

I had come to Sleepy Hollow to see the Old Dutch Church on the outskirts of town. Built by Dutch settlers in 1685, the church is one of the oldest buildings in New York State. It sits atop a gentle slope encircled first by a peaceful green churchyard, and then by the wider expanse of Sleep Hollow Cemetery. In the oldest parts of the burial grounds, the headstones are engraved with winged death's heads, grinning mementos mori and restful cherubs, recalling the souls of the deceased. At one of the highest points in the cemetery, in the shade of a great elm tree, one can find the Irving family burial plot and the grave of Washington Irving. Towards the base of cemetery, as the green hill sweeps downwards to a gently babbling brook, there is a little wooden caretaker's shed, decorated on its north-facing wall with brightly painted clogs that hang beside the window.

In Irving's story, it is here, in the Sleepy Hollow churchyard, that the Headless Horseman tethers his horse by night, and it is to these hallowed grounds that he must return before daybreak. The Horseman is not the only spectre to roam the green pastures of the churchyard. As Irving writes, "The sequestered situation of this church seems always to have made it a favorite haunt of troubled spirits." However, the spectral rider is the most famous resident, being "commander-in-chief of all the powers of the air". Walking further down the slope towards the centre of the village, I arrived at a wide concrete bridge crossed by multiple lanes of traffic. Heavy trucks rattled past and traffic lights swayed gently overhead. A blue historical

Old Dutch Church, Sleepy Hollow, New York

marker informs would-be ghost hunters that "The Headless Horseman Bridge described by Irving in 'The Legend of Sleepy Hollow' formerly spanned this stream at this spot." The original wooden bridge, across which Ichabod flees from the Horseman, has long since rotted away and been replaced by a succession of new structures.

With his bridge long collapsed, his hunting grounds long since paved over, I wondered where the Horseman might now spend his nights. Perhaps he still rides forth each night in search of his head. It's difficult to know because, like many of the ghosts that haunt the Hudson Valley, the Horseman is conspicuously silent. In contrast to the notoriously chatty ghosts summoned by the Spiritualist mediums of Western New York, here, in this secluded valley the spirits are silent, wispy and ephemeral.

In her study of Hudson Valley hauntings, Judith Richardson observes that ghosts in this area are frequently understood "in terms of vagueness, colorlessness, wispiness, incompleteness; they are most often recognized and defined precisely by their lack of definition or identifiers" (26). Moreover, these ghosts rarely attempt to communicate: "Hudson Valley ghosts are often either dead silent or, when they do try to communicate, are heard as muffled or otherwise incomprehensible" (27). In another of Irving's tales, "Rip van Winkle", the titular layabout encounters the famed explorer for whom the region is named, Henry Hudson, playing ninepins deep in the mountains with a group of men dressed in the doublets and jerkins of the previous century. The spectral group unsettle Rip precisely because of their silence: "Though these folks were evidently amusing themselves, yet they maintained the gravest faces, the most mysterious silence."

The steadfast silence of the Hudson Valley's ghosts may be attributable to the region's unique history and topography. Ghosts, after all, are invariably produced by the very communities they haunt. For sociologist Avery Gordon, "haunting is one way in which abusive systems of power make themselves known and their impacts felt in everyday life" (xvi). Ghosts are, in this context, echoes of painful, unresolved histories. Where we, as individuals and societies, fail to address the horrors of the past, spirits materialise to remind us that the injustices and abuses of earlier centuries will always reverberate through time. Haunting disrupts expected chronologies, stalling the forwards movement of history and dragging us inextricably into an uncomfortable confrontation with the past. The Hudson ghosts do not talk, because unlike the vocal spectres who commanded so much attention at Spiritualist séances, they have no messages to deliver. Instead, they are silent materialisations of historical wars, mute phantasmagorias replaying the brutal conflicts of centuries past.

The village of Sleepy Hollow was located right on the front lines of the Revolutionary War. Positioned between the British command centre in New York City and Benedict Arnold's stronghold, further north, in West Point, the small community played host not only to battles and raiding parties, but to bitter divisions between friends and family members who had taken opposing sides in the conflict. In "The Legend of Sleepy Hollow", the Headless Horseman is characterised as the spirit of a Hessian — a German soldier in service of the British cause — who rises from his grave in search of his head, lost in battle. As an incarnation of a war whose canons and muskets have long since fallen silent, the Horseman and his night rides give form to the region's painful history and testify to its enduring trauma.

Moreover, while the Horseman emerges as a vibrant and terrifying echo of the past, his ambiguous nature also suggests a crisis of the future. In true hauntological fashion, the ghostly rider of Sleepy Hollow is an obscure, incorporeal site where past, present and future all overlap.

Irving's story is infused with humour, which sometimes mingles uneasily with the sinister atmosphere that pervades the tale, and he draws his narration to a close with the somewhat bathetic possibility that Ichabod's encounter with the Horseman was merely a prank. Indeed, if the story's narrator is to be believed, the ghostly rider may have simply been Ichabod's rival, Brom Bones, who — playing on the pedagogue's superstitious nature — chased him down, a pumpkin in place of a severed head, and ran the unfortunate teacher out of town. These two competing possibilities — a supernatural visitation, on the one hand, and a rational explanation, on the other — place the story at a fraught historical juncture where America is torn between an adherence to the superstitions of the past and the rationalism of the future.

A number of other factors may also have contributed to the region's susceptibility to haunting. The Hudson Valley has a history of diverse settlement, with significant Dutch, English, Indigenous, German, Irish and African American populations inhabiting the area. Not only did this produce conflicts, on occasion it led to a curious intermingling of disparate folkloric traditions. At the same time, the region's distinctive geographical features also helped to produce a ghostly atmosphere. In "The Legend of Sleepy Hollow", the landscape is possessed of a peculiarly enchanting quality:

> The place still continues under the sway of some witching power, that holds a spell over the minds of the good people, causing them to walk in a continual reverie. They are given to all kinds of marvellous beliefs, are subject to trances and visions, and frequently see strange sights, and hear music and voices in the air.

Some attribute this ghostliness to atmospheric effects produced high in the Catskill Mountains, while others blame the frequent thunderstorms that roll in over the peaks. Still others are convinced that it is the mists that rise up from the Hudson or the vivid reflections cast upon the river's surface that conjure armies of restless spectres (Richardson 16).

***

As the warm summer afternoon cooled to a violet dusk, I caught the ferry from the nearby village of Ossining to Haverstraw, on the opposite bank of the river, where I planned to spend the night. Crossing the river, it is possible to see the hazy outline of the New York City skyline materialising like an apparition in the distance. Haverstraw is a little village that clings, mollusc-like, to a bay of the same name. The streets are lined with clapboard houses, tiny constructions dwarfed by the rolling green foothills of High Tor Mountain rising up behind them. Stories told by local Indigenous populations relate how High Tor was present at the creation of the world and later became a prison for evil spirits. Stories also circulate that it was from the summit of High Tor that members of the Lenape tribe first witnessed a Dutch ship sailing up the Hudson.

As in Sleepy Hollow and Tarrytown across the river, many of the spirits that haunt Haverstraw are linked to the region's history of colonisation and brutal suppression of tribal resistance. In 1609, when the first European settlers began to explore the valley, there were somewhere between six and twelve thousand Native Americans living along the banks of the Hudson. These included the Lenape (Delaware) and Mohicans. By the latter half of the nineteenth century, these populations had been devastated — first through disease and conflict, and later as a result of "Indian removal" policies that forcibly relocated tribes to less-valuable land west of the Mississippi River.

Legends culled from Native tribes imbued numerous natural features — mountains, rivers, trees — with spiritual attributes that contributed to lingering tales of their haunting. Spectral "Indians" have also been thought to exert a powerful influence over the mountains and woodlands of the Hudson Valley. In "The Legend of Sleepy Hollow", for instance, the narrator speculates that one reason for the "drowsy, dreamy" ambiance that pervades the village is that "an old Indian chief, the prophet or wizard of his tribe, held his powwows there before the country was discovered by Master Hendrick Hudson". Other ghostly Natives wander fields and streams, visibly but incorporeally attesting to the violence that made the European conquest of the New World possible. These phantoms challenge one of America's most generative foundational myths: that Europeans settled a vast, empty wilderness. Indigenous ghosts bear witness to the lived reality of the diverse peoples who inhabited the American continent before the arrival of Europeans and to the decimation of their communities by voracious colonial forces.

For Renée Bergland, the enduring presence of spectral Indians serves two distinct functions. On the one hand, this "ghosting of Indians" may act as "a technique of removal" (373). Writing about Indians as ghosts has the effect of removing them "from American lands, and [places] them, instead, within the American Imagination" (374). Like in the stories of "ghosts, witches, *and Indians*" (italics added) that Rip van Winkle delighted in telling the local children, the conflation of Indigenous peoples and spectrality works to confine these groups to the past or to a land of make-believe and fantasy. It enables us to forget those who survived, dispossessed of their ancestral lands, into the modern age. At the same time, however, Bergland argues that the ghosting of Indians empowers writers and storytellers of all kinds to challenge the hegemonic narratives of American imperialism. When Indigenous peoples return as ghosts, they are refusing the burial given them by dominant histories, and returning to rupture the clean, heroic narrative of American history.

That night, I slept among the silent hills of Haverstraw. Nothing stirred except for the occasional low thud of a large, white moth battering its body against my window as it traced confused circles in the dark. In Lily Dale and Palmyra, my ghosts had been joyful, mischievous creatures, but here in the dark mountains, as the immense body of the Hudson surged southwards to New York Harbour, where it would empty itself into the cold water of the Atlantic Ocean, the spirits remained silent.

Salem and Danvers, Massachusetts

I made my way to Salem on a series of trains. After taking the Hudson line from Croton-Harmon down to New York City, switching to a noisy subway car whose vibrations shuddered through me as we lurched past packed underground stations, dashing across 8th Avenue, and boarding a late afternoon train, I finally arrived in Boston. In the city's North Station, I sat beside a middle-aged man who told me that he was a professional gambler. He'd made a fortune in casinos up and down the East Coast, but his ex-wife had taken everything in the divorce. "Bitch," he snorted, inhaling dramatically before spitting on the floor. On the short ride to Salem, I was blissfully alone. Moving through Chelsea and Revere, the Boston skyline gradually receded as the train cut through flat salt marshes. Dense thickets of grass swept by on both sides of the track and then disappeared, replaced by the creeping expanses of concrete car parks and suburban shopping centres.

In Salem, I walked from the train station to the town centre, my unwieldy backpack balanced precariously on tired shoulders. The narrow streets were a swirl of life and colour. Artisanal ice-cream parlours, Japanese restaurants and vintage clothes shops hummed with customers. In the historic centre, where many of the most popular tourist sites can be found, the shop windows were crowded with T-shirts and hooded sweatshirts, all featuring witches or witch-themed slogans: broomstick-riding witches silhouetted against full moons, black cats, faux college logos embroidered with the words "Witch City, est. 1626". Fridge magnets displayed outside shop doors bore slogans like "Don't be a salty witch", while quirkier vendors sold stuffed toys shaped like the demonic entity Baphomet. Colourful signs encouraged visitors to have their picture taken in historical dress or in the black robes and pointed hat of a storybook witch. I passed a tour guide telling a group of assembled tourists that in one house in the town, "things would move around on their own". I wondered if that had anything to do with the Salem witch trials, or if it was another story entirely. Performers dressed in flamboyant breeches and tricorn hats distributed flyers advertising guided tours that promised thrilling tales of witches and pirates.

In Lappin Park, I stopped to take in Salem's infamous *Bewitched* statue. Erected in 2005, the monument depicts Samantha Stevens, heroine of the classic 1960s sitcom *Bewitched*, sitting astride a broomstick, grinning mischievously. In the television series, best known to my generation from endless Saturday morning reruns, Samantha is a glamorous modern-day witch who, for some baffling reason, marries a dreary advertising executive, moves to the suburbs and promises never to use her powers again. Of course, she does use magic — often at the behest of her meddling mother, Endora — and each episode sees Samantha's chaotic spells go awry and threaten to destroy her husband's placid, middle-class existence. *Bewitched*, as I would later discover, really made Salem what is today. In 1970, a fire at the Californian studio where *Bewitched* was usually filmed forced the cast and crew to find a new, temporary setting for the show. Relocating to Salem, presumably because of its connection to historical witchcraft persecutions, the makers of *Bewitched* filmed eight episodes of the show in the city. While Salem had previously featured in films and literature, most notably in Arthur Miller's 1953 play *The Crucible*, it was *Bewitched* that brought the city of Salem to national attention and solidified its connection to a campier, more fantastical type of witch.

Although *Bewitched* was responsible for a massive upswell in the number of tourists visiting Salem, the nine-foot bronze Samantha remains a controversial addition to the city, with many residents feeling that a frivolous monument to a television character makes light of the very real tragedy that occurred in the area three centuries ago. When the monument was unveiled in 2005, a local resident hung a banner with the word "SHAME" printed on it from the window of a building that faced the park. The statue has also been defaced, usually with red paint, on a number of occasions, with the most recent act of vandalism taking place in 2022, just prior to my visit.

On nearby streets, between bustling burger joints and crowded gift shops, I found a variety of eclectic museums jostling for attention. There was Count Orlok's Nightmare Gallery, featuring wax figures modelled after various horror movie monsters; the Witch History Museum, comprised of "15 life-size scenes" that recreate the witch trials in wax; and the Witch Board Museum, the "world's ONLY Ouija museum". Closer to the waterfront, where the oldest settlements in Salem encircle a wide natural harbour, I passed more-sober museums, recreating colonial-era houses and expounding on the city's storied maritime history. Out beyond the marinas, the brilliant white sails of nearby yachts bobbed like sea foam on the waves.

It was a warm afternoon and the city teemed with visitors. In small green parks, boisterous packs of college-aged kids formed circles on the grass, laughing and shouting as the sea breeze rustled the branches of full, verdant trees. Couples drank coffee outside brightly painted cafés, and parents wrangled small children in witches' hats. Because it was Pride Month, businesses across the city erupted in brilliant colours. Rainbow flags fluttered gently on awnings; bursts of red, orange, yellow, green, blue and purple radiated from windows and doorways. Gentle pastel hues quivered on pole tops. Packs of tourists in baseball caps and sunglasses crowded footpaths or traipsed through busy squares, trailing guides who held umbrellas aloft to indicate their positions.

The swirl of noise and colour that surrounded me could not have been more remote from the fledgling colonial settlements where the Salem witch trials occurred. When the accusations that led to the trials commenced, in the early months of 1692, Salem Town was less than seventy years old. Salem Village, a nearby community where the first reports of witchcraft emerged and which has since been renamed Danvers, had only existed as an independent parish for twenty years. Inhabited primarily by Puritan settlers, Salem Village and its larger namesake — as well as other towns in what was then the Massachusetts Bay Colony — were little more than outposts on the edge of a vast, impenetrable wilderness. Although Salem Town flourished, becoming rich from the trade of fish, livestock, coffee, sugar and enslaved humans, many of the communities that had grown up further west, close to the frontier, were isolated, vulnerable to both the caprices of nature and escalating tensions with Indigenous populations.

One of the most famous chroniclers of the witch trials, the Reverend Cotton Mather, wrote in his 1693 treatise *The Wonders of the Invisible World* that the wilderness surrounding the New England colonies was the domain of the Devil and that it was his influence — and his ire at seeing a godly people settle in his realm — that caused the outbreak of witchcraft in the area. Mather goes on to describe New Englanders as "a People of God settled in those, which were once the Devil's Territories". Like many Puritan intellectuals of the time, Mather worried that the New England colonists had settled not in a bucolic new Eden, but in a dreadful, frightful wilderness. He posited that "Indian Powawes, used all their Sorceries to molest the first Planters here", and avers that the Devil, or the "Black Man" (as witches supposedly call him), might easily be mistaken for an Indian. For Mather and his cohort, there was something innately terrifying about the New World. Its deep forests, alien landscapes and mysterious inhabitants challenged the colonists' belief that they had crossed the Atlantic Ocean to establish God's kingdom on earth. Given the uncanny qualities of the landscape and the isolated positions of many colonial settlements, it is hardly surprising that when two little girls in Salem Village began to complain of spectral assaults — attacks by invisible foes who bit and pinched them — neighbours and friends, jurists and ministers were quick to believe their claims.

Not only were the Puritan settlers surrounded by an immense, unknown landscape, but, like most Christians at the time, they believed that the Devil was a real and tangible force, an enemy abroad in the world of men. Witches, too, were very real threats, capable of withering crops, souring milk and causing both children and animals to sicken. Witches could fly, commanded familiar spirits and regularly sent their own spectres to harass victims. It was these spectres — disembodied forms in their own shape that a witch could send to do their bidding — that proved most troublesome. After the first accusations, spectres began to appear throughout Salem Village and in neighbouring towns. They pinched and bit, scratched and choked, all with the aim of torturing the innocent into joining the Devil's legions. The spectre of an elderly woman who was previously much respected in the town leapt on the bed of a young girl and threatened to tear the child's soul from her body if she did not give herself over to Satan. At the same time, a five-year-old girl, the daughter of a woman already imprisoned for witchcraft, flew in spirit form about the village, biting and pinching her victims. Other strange creatures were also seen roaming Salem Village on those dark nights in early 1692: a hog, an immense black dog, cats and various other diabolical apparitions. Crowds of witches were also reported to have held a nocturnal meeting in a field where they "partook of a Diabolical Sacrament in Bread and Wine then administrated".

Following the first claims of spectral assault, accusations spread across the entire region such that in a short time not just Salem Village, but the whole of Essex County appeared thronged with witches and their roving, malign spectres. Witches were identified in the neighbouring towns of Lynn, Beverly, Topsfield and Andover. Satan's emissaries were found as far away as Boston, and, in one case, a former Salem minister was tracked down in Maine and returned to the town to stand trial. Over the course of the next few months, accusations and condemnations proliferated. Legal proceedings began in late February of 1692 with the arrests of the first "witches", quickly escalating into public examinations in the meetinghouse of Salem Village before culminating in full-fledged trials in Salem Town's Court of Oyer and Terminer (meaning "to hear" and "to determine"). The trials and subsequent executions of those found guilty of witchcraft, which began in June, continued until the autumn of that year, with the Court of Oyer and Terminer being dissolved in late October. In those few brief months, fifty-four people had confessed to witchcraft (including the little girl who had allegedly sent her spirit to bite victims), nineteen people had been hanged, one had been crushed to death by stones, and five people, including an infant, had died in prison (Norton 7).

The Salem trials were neither the first nor the only witch trials in colonial New England. The region's first execution for witchcraft, the hanging of Alse Young, had taken place in 1647 and initiated a witch-hunt that would result in a total of eleven executions in the state of Connecticut over the next sixteen years. A few years later, an Irish housekeeper named Anne Glover was hanged for bewitching her employer's wife and children. Yet there is something about the events in Salem that haunts both the town itself and the American imagination more broadly. Beyond the spectres that accosted townspeople in their beds and tormented the godly with pinches and bites, Salem has been possessed by the ghosts of history, the restless echoes of past atrocities that refuse to lie still.

***

Hoping to learn a bit more about why US culture has been so gripped by the Salem trials, why its principal figures continue to haunt American folklore and fantasies, I went to visit the Salem Witch Museum. The building in which the museum is housed was, once upon a time, a Unitarian church. Built in the middle decades of the nineteenth century, the brownstone building is dominated by the foreboding arched windows characteristic of the Gothic Revival style that was fashionable at the time. Sitting between brightly painted wooden houses, the museum appears rather sinister. Centuries before, the building had been the site of a house occupied by a minister, John Higginson, who examined some of the accused during the trials and whose own daughter was later arrested on charges of witchcraft. In the middle of the intersection in front of the building, a huge statue of Salem's founder, Roger Conant, stands proudly atop a rock. His flowing cape and tall hat have, apparently, tricked many tourists into believing that the statue represents a witch.

In the offices that occupy the back rooms of the grand Gothic building, I met Rachel Christ-Doane, the museum's director of education. Warm and friendly, Rachel appeared to be about my age, and we bonded over a shared millennial love of the Disney film *Hocus Pocus* and the memory of dressing as witches every Halloween. I asked Rachel what she thought made the Salem witch trials so unique, why did this series of persecutions enter American popular culture and become a part of the national mythos when so many comparable atrocities have been forgotten. For Rachel, as for many historians, the Salem trials endure in American memory because they constituted "a perfect storm". "It's the fact that they were so intense. And they're also happening quite late," she explained. "Witchcraft is decriminalised about twenty or thirty years later in England." Not only did the Salem trials involve an unprecedented number of accusations, confessions, arrests and executions in the space of a few short months, the trials themselves occurred late in the seventeenth century. In Europe, witchcraft persecutions peaked between 1580 and 1630, entering a steady decline as new philosophies, theological perspectives and scientific paradigms began to erode the terrifying power of Satan (Behringer 8). Salem, a comparatively remote colonial outpost, had its trials long after the European witch-hunts had begun to taper off. Rachel went on to describe how the anxieties about witchcraft emerged just as Salem, and the entire Massachusetts Bay

Colony, was wracked by new doubts about the settlement's future. The accusations coincided with increasingly violent confrontations with Indigenous tribes in neighbouring Maine and New Hampshire, and many of the key accusers were refugees displaced from these nearby territories by the conflicts. At the same time, when the first spectres began to materialise in Salem Village, Massachusetts was without a legally established government, since the charter that governed the administration of the colony had been revoked (Nissenbaum and Boyer 6). When the first examinations of suspected witches took place, in early 1692, they could not be brought to trial since legal proceedings were unable to advance without the charter, which did not arrive until May.

In Salem, as in Hydesville and Sleepy Hollow, it seems that spectral activity was born out of anxiety. Ghosts embodied the horrors of the past — and indeed many of Salem's spectres spoke of past crimes and concealed murders — but they also warned about the future. Nervously awaiting their new charter, the people of Salem Village and the surrounding towns must have wondered what the future held for them: Would Massachusetts always remain an English colony? How would they govern? Would the Puritans succeed in building a new Jerusalem in this strange, wild continent? Was some diabolical conspiracy threatening to destroy their godly community?

After I left Rachel behind at the museum, I wandered down to Salem's Charter Street Cemetery. It is here, where small dusty paths weave between headstones that stand like proud sentinels, that the town's haunted quality feels most pronounced. The names engraved on these headstones constitute a litany of Salem's most influential residents, but the most intriguing grave is a small, crumbling marker topped by a half-eroded death's head and encased within a modern concrete frame, presumably to prevent further deterioration. This grave is the resting place of John Hathorne, one of the most important judges to preside over the Salem trials. Though well respected in his lifetime, Hathorne's actions were a source of deep shame for his descendants, most notably the nineteenth-century author Nathaniel Hawthorne, who allegedly added the "w" to his surname hoping to distinguish himself from his notorious forebearer. Hawthorne was born in Salem and was a prolific writer, producing dozens of short stories early in his career before later switching to novels. Hawthorne's most famous work, especially in the US, where it is taught to thousands of high school students each year, is his 1850 novel *The Scarlet Letter*. The tale of a young woman shunned by her narrow-minded Puritan community after she gives birth to a child out of wedlock, it's hard not see the parallels with the persecutory spirit of the Salem witch trials. In the opening chapter of the book, Hawthorne writes of his own ancestors, describing John Hathorne as a man distinguished by a cruelty so severe that it brought a curse upon the subsequent generations of his family. According to his descendent, Hathorne "made himself so conspicuous in the martyrdom of the witches, that their blood may fairly be said to have left a stain upon him. So deep a stain, indeed, that his old dry bones, in the Charter Street burial-ground, must still retain it, if they have not crumbled utterly to dust!"

I thought of this image as I walked among the tombstones of the Charter Street Cemetery: the blood of unjustly executed "witches" seeping into the very flesh of this zealous Puritan judge, its scarlet hue imprinting the ivory white bones that lie uneasily in the deep New England soil. Hawthorne seemed deeply preoccupied with the tainted blood of his ancestors, imagining it as a pollutant tarnishing the souls of every member of the dynasty. Like Lady Macbeth, he might scrub and scrub, but he would never be free of that hideous stain.

Blood, stains and mysterious birthmarks appear in countless works by Hawthorne, a testament to his profound sense of historical guilt. In his second novel, *The House of the Seven Gables* (1851), another stern Puritan is marked with the blood of his unfortunate victims. In the 1600s, Colonel Pyncheon, a cruel and vindictive figure, accuses an innocent man of witchcraft so that he may seize his lands and build a grand house upon them. Not long after Pyncheon moves into his new home, his relatives find him dead, and upon approaching his corpse they see "that there was blood on his ruff, and that his hoary beard was saturated with it". The gruesome discovery is presumed by Pyncheon's descendants to be the fulfilment of the curse pronounced by the dying "wizard" that "God will give him blood to drink!"

This, too, has its roots in the sad history of the Salem witch trials. Sarah Good, a beggar who regularly implored her neighbours for charity, was one of the first people to be accused of witchcraft in 1692. According to legend, just as she was about to be hanged, the Reverend Nicholas Noyes pressed her to repent and confess her crime. She responded by shouting at Noyes, "I'm no more a witch than you are a wizard, and if you take away my life God will give you blood to drink." Years later, the historian Thomas Hutchinson learned from Salem residents that Noyes had indeed died from a haemorrhage, choking on his own blood and thereby fulfilling Sarah's curse (though, like many Salem stories, there is no evidence or documentation to support this). In Hawthorne's novel, this curse haunts the Puritan's descendants for generations. The family is plagued by violence and death. Their beautiful house — the titular House of the Seven Gables — becomes an oppressive, mouldering tomb, stifling and suffocating its inhabitants. Today, the house still exists, standing proudly on Salem's waterfront. Visitors can take guided tours, wandering through ornate living rooms or climbing narrow, winding staircases to low-ceilinged attics.

Although he thought of his novels as Romances — in the sense of their not adhering to the rigorous realism demanded by serious novels of the day — Nathaniel Hawthorne was very much a pioneer of the American Gothic form. In a contemporary review, Herman Melville drew attention to what he saw as the duality inherent in Hawthorne's writing: "For spite of all the Indian-summer sunlight on the hither side of Hawthorne's soul, the other side — like the dark half of the physical sphere — is shrouded in blackness, ten times black." This contrast, the tension between light and dark, is at the heart of the American Gothic as it would develop from Hawthorne to Poe, from Stephen King to David Lynch. America's foundational mythology is deeply preoccupied with the perceived newness of the nation, what scholar Teresa A. Goddu calls "new-world innocence" (11), and so the prevailing story of the US is one of purity and possibility. A new world built on the philosophies of the Enlightenment — liberty and justice for all — America, it was understood, could never be haunted in the deep, enduring way that Europe is. Yet, despite such luminous promises, the nation's earliest sins — slavery, genocide, witchcraft persecutions — endure in the cracks and crevices which that light does not reach. The American story is one of light and shadow, and of the dark things that grow in those shadows.

In Hawthorne's fiction, it is possible to trace a map of New England's historical trauma. His stories often feature real Salem locations, reconceived as explicitly haunted sites. The implicit curses and figurative ghosts of Salem become very real phantoms, the faint memory of historical horrors congealing into dense, sticky pools of blood. Almost a century later, another New England writer, Howard Phillips Lovecraft, would create his own dark mirror of Salem. In his alternate version of the town, past horrors re-emerge in the form of grotesque cosmic abominations, perverse cults and isolated, inbred populations. Stories such as "Herbert West–Reanimator" (1922), "The Colour Out of Space" (1927), "The Dreams in the Witch House" (1932) and "The Thing on the Doorstep" (1933), among others, all take place in the Massachusetts town of Arkham. A fictionalised version of Salem (with a bit of Danvers thrown in for good measure), Arkham is "witch-cursed and legend-haunted" (quoted in Bridle 3). Lovecraft also transposed the mythology of the Salem witch trials onto his imagined town. "Dreams in the Witch House" features a grotesque witch's familiar named Brown Jenkin, described as a rat with a "sharp-toothed, bearded face" that appears "evilly human". This monstrous hybrid sounds eerily similar to the chimerical familiar spirits described by one of the first accused witches to testify in 1692. According to her, a fellow witch possessed two diabolical companions: "a thing with a head like a woman with 2 leggs and wings" and "a thing all over hairy" that "goeth upright like a man" and was "around two or three feet tall". Similarly, one of the beings found within the titular witch house is described as "a tall, lean man of dead black colouration" whose feet click, perhaps like hooves, when he walks. Although this entity is a part of Lovecraft's own cosmic pantheon, it also recalls the descriptions of the Black Man that appeared throughout the Salem trials. Generally assumed to have been either Satan or one of his servants, the "Black Man" was known to tempt villagers, asking them to sign their names in his infernal book and to whisper in the ears of those standing trial.

In Lovecraft's Arkham, the streets and landmarks recall precisely the layout of its real-world counterpart, as though the author simply traced over a map of the town. Beyond the dense cluster of streets and buildings, Arkham — like

Salem — vanishes into wild hills, dense forests and the silver threads of woodland brooks. To wander among the colonial houses, to step along the cobbles of its oldest streets, is to wander Lovecraft's Arkham. At the same time, there is a strange sense of doubling inherent in navigating the twists and turns of this literary town. In many of his stories, Lovecraft describes Arkham as existing alongside Salem and Boston, a fictional town ensconced between the real cities that inspired it. Arkham is Salem, but Salem itself also exists somewhere in Lovecraft's complex geographical imaginary. His stories mingle past and present, fantasy and reality to create an uncanny in-between space, neither wholly real nor entirely conjured from the misty ream of imagination.

Lovecraft's vision of Salem, rendered on the page as Arkham, is that of city permeated, perhaps even poisoned, by its history. In one story, "The Festival" (1923), he evokes the unsettling omnipresence of the past, portraying the white spires of austere New England churches perched atop mouldering crypts, their depths thronged with ghouls. Like Salem, Arkham is a failed utopian project, a godly community that has slid irrevocably into decadence and decay. The lofty ambitions of the town's Puritan settlers have degenerated into a set of archaic rituals practised with cultic fervour by lost communities of inbred monsters. In another early story, "The Unnameable" (1923), Lovecraft expands an unfinished tale by Hawthorne, *Dr Grimshawe's Secret* (1882), into a short, shocking account of a monstrous child secreted away in the top rooms of a house overlooking the Charter Street Cemetery (Ringel 269). The story, as told by both Hawthorne and Lovecraft, has its origins in the history of Mary Dyer, a heretic hanged in 1660 after converting to Quakerism and defying an order banishing members of that faith from the Massachusetts Bay Colony. In 1637, Mary apparently gave birth to a stillborn infant.

71

Community leaders who later saw the child's remains described it as

> so monstrous and misshapen, as the like has scarce been heard of [...] The arms and legges [...] were as other childrens [sic], but in stead of toes it had upon [...] each foot three claws, with talons like a young fowle [...] It had no forehead, but in the place thereof, above the eyes, foure hornes, whereof two were above an inch long, hard, and sharpe, the other two were somewhat shorter (quoted in Winsser 24).

The story was circulated widely by Puritan authorities, who viewed the deformed child as evidence of God's wrath come down upon a heretic, an apt punishment visited upon a woman who threatened the ideological purity of their community.

Lovecraft's version of the story sees the grotesque infant surviving and growing to adulthood hidden in the attic of a Salem house. Here, Lovecraft's tale differs from the many iterations relayed by the Puritans. Rather than a sign of divine displeasure, Lovecraft envisions the twisted flesh of the monster as a testament to what he calls the "ghastly festering" of seventeenth-century New England society, which "bubbles up putrescently in occasional ghoulish glimpses". The Puritans, he suggests, created a world devoid of beauty and freedom, a "rusted iron strait-jacket" inside which "lurked gibbering hideousness, perversion, and diabolism". The monster born of that oppressive society is an embodiment of Puritan repression, its body twisted in reflection of the sickly ideologies and rigid minds that proliferated among Salem's original founders. The story ends with the narrator and his friend hospitalised after an encounter with the "unnameable" monstrosity that haunts the old Salem house to this day, gazing from its attic room to the cemetery below, where the bones of witch trial judges and Puritan leaders lie crumbling in the ancient earth.

***

In Salem, I felt the past as though it were a real, tangible presence. Gravestones, historical markers and houses that have stood overlooking the same streets for centuries all attest to an almost tactile history, as though one could simply reach out and touch the past. Yet, Salem is also defined by absence, as many of the sites central to the town's most notorious historical event are long gone, razed and replaced with modern buildings and roads. The jail where many of the accused witches were imprisoned is long gone, replaced with an office building on the corner of St Peter's and Federal Streets. Likewise, the meetinghouse where accused witches were examined is also gone, as is the courthouse where nineteen innocent people were condemned to death. A road — Washington Street — now runs through the empty space where the courthouse stood.

Foremost on this litany of absences, there are no graves where the victims of the trials might finally rest or where visitors might pay their respects. Though one can locate the tombs of judges, political leaders and ministers, those whose lives were unjustly taken during the witchcraft panic seem to have simply been lost to history. Burial sites have been suggested, and there is much speculation, but gaps in the historical record and the disdain with which the remains of the executed "witches" were treated have made it impossible to locate anything resembling a grave. Recent scholarship has identified an area now known as Proctor's Ledge as the most likely location for the hangings. Some of the deceased may also have been interred here. According to one seventeenth-century source, their bodies were simply dumped in holes or makeshift graves near the site of the executions, though some remains may have been recovered by family members and buried with more reverence in unmarked graves on their own properties (Hill 98).

In the heart of Salem Town, the names of the victims are memorialised in the absence of any material remains. Leaving the Charter Street Cemetery, I walked down to the small stone enclosure located next to the burial ground. In the centre, in the midst of a green lawn, tall black locust trees stand as forlorn symbols of unjust execution. At regular intervals rectangular slabs of stone jut out from the wall. These are each engraved with the names of those whose lives were lost to intolerance and fear: Bridget Bishop, Georges Burroughs, Martha Carrier, Mary Eastey, Giles Corey and his wife Martha, Sarah Good, Elizabeth Howe, George Jacobs Sr., Susannah Martin, Rebecca Nurse, Alice Parker, Mary Parker, John Proctor, Ann Pudeator, Wilmot Redd, Margaret Scott, Samuel Wardwell Sr., Sarah Wildes and John Willard. Perhaps this is apt. In *The Crucible*, the play's nominal hero, John Proctor (loosely based on one of the historical "witches"), refuses to sign a false confession because to put his name to such a document would be to surrender the last of his integrity. "How may I live without my name?" he asks. "I have given you my soul; leave me my name!" If nothing else, this monument gives the accused back their names, their identities. On each of the slabs, residents and visitors leave flowers, while inscriptions at the entrance record words spoken by the victims. Some of the sentences are cut short, interrupted to suggest lives snuffed out too soon (Hill 96).

In a juxtaposition that succinctly encapsulates Salem's many fascinating contradictions, the sombre memorial to the victims of the witch trials is located almost directly opposite the Salem Witch Village, an attraction that

Part of the Witch Trials Memorial, with a dedication to Bridget Bishop, the first person hanged in for witchcraft in 1692, Salem Massachusetts

professes to separate the myths from the reality of actual witchcraft. In addition to resident spellcasters and guided tours, the attraction also hosts a gift shop filled with Wiccan and Neo-Pagan supplies. Visitors can purchase the "Hysteria Pass", which provides discounted admission to the Witch Village and the nearby wax museum. It's often difficult to reconcile the two distinct faces that Salem presents to tourists. On the one side, solemn monuments recall the history of intolerance and cruelty that culminated in the deaths of at least twenty-five individuals. On the other, brightly coloured cartoon witches stand guard outside of gift shops selling T-shirts and bumper stickers. There seems to be a constant and uneasy tension in Salem between carnivalesque play and serious commemoration which — even after decades of witch-themed tourism — remains unresolved. Sometimes, this tension manifests itself in malicious or tasteless ways. During my visit to the

Salem Witch Museum, Rachel told me that one of the most repulsive pieces of merchandise she encountered in the town was a T-shirt bearing the slogan "I got stoned in Salem". Although stoning wasn't a method of execution employed in colonial New England, it has been and continues to be used in many parts of the world. Moreover, one of the victims of the witchcraft panic — Giles Corey — was pressed to death with stones during an interrogation. Yet Rachel, like many Salem residents, remains optimistic about the town's tourist industry. Locals are acutely aware of the economic benefits of even the most garish witch-themed attractions, ultimately accepting their hometown's unusual reputation as a fruitful source of revenue. Rachel explained that, as a historian, she embraces Salem's haunted-house atmosphere because "it's an amazing learning opportunity". The average tourist, she noted, might come to Salem because they love witches or are drawn in by the spectacle of the town's annual Halloween festivities. However, most visitors end up learning something, uncovering a profound and meaningful story not only about the history of colonial New England but about the very real people who, three hundred years ago, found themselves caught up in a fatal admixture of religious fervour, political instability and human cruelty.

***

It's hard not to feel like an outsider in Danvers. Located just under five miles from Salem, the small town has received barely a fraction of the attention that its larger, more infamous neighbour has. Yet it was here, in what was once a loose collection of farmhouses, that the Salem witch trials began. Today, the town clusters around an innocuous main street. Small cafés and delis are grouped alongside wide pavements, and a steady stream of cars trickles through the main intersection. On one corner, a shop called Glitterati sells prom dresses to excited teenage girls passing their last, lazy summer at home before dispersing to colleges and careers across the country.

Early in the morning, I took the only available bus as far as the Liberty Tree Mall, disembarking outside a Best Buy and resolving to go the rest of the way on foot. After a short walk, clinging to embankments alongside busy roads, past box stores and car parks, the industrial finally melted into the suburban. I stopped in a small diner crammed with middle-aged couples. In one corner, a group of movers in matching overalls chatted animatedly in Spanish. My coffee came in a big brown mug and was refilled at regular twenty-minute intervals. The news hummed at a low volume on a TV set above the counter. An older man in a baseball cap asked, in a broad Boston accent, "Whad, you givin' food away for free today? Lotta people?" I couldn't have been further from the plastic witches and costumed tour guides of Salem.

Following Hobart Street west through quiet communities where neat, green lawns encircled clapboard houses and American flags swayed gently on porches, I reached the oldest part of Danvers. At one point, this was the heart of Salem Village. The streets were very much the same then as they are now, with Hobart Street opening out onto Center Street. In a clearing between the lawns and driveways of this still, peaceful neighbourhood, I found the Danvers Witchcraft Victims Memorial. Sheltered by the full branches of sycamore trees, the monument is comprised of a granite block engraved with the words "In memory of those innocents who died during the Salem witchcraft hysteria of 1692." Atop the block rests a replica of a Bible box and a sculpture of an open book, which reads "The Book of Life". On each side, broken shackles represent the "chains of falsehood smashed asunder by truth" (Hill

121). A figure engraved on the opposite wall stands in for either a minister or a judge. Below and beside this imposing silhouette are the names and execution dates of the Salem "witches". The far walls are emblazoned with testimonies from the accused: "I am an innocent person. I never had to do with witchcraft since I was born. I am a gospel woman"; "The Lord above knows my Innocence"; "I can say before my Eternal Father I am innocent and God will clear my innocency".

Walking further along Hobart Street, past an elementary school, and turning onto Center Street, I eventually came to the epicentre of the witch trials. At the end of a grassy pathway between two unassuming houses lie the ruins of the Salem Village parsonage, tucked away behind suburban backyards where empty swings hang from tree branches and boisterous chickens flap in their coops. I felt strangely incongruous standing there, behind family homes, with my backpack and camera. Yet, there was also something oddly peaceful about the secluded little grove. Everything was so green, and a soft, silvery light fell upon the exposed stone foundations that are now the only remnants of the old parsonage. It was here, in the cold depths of January 1692, that the spectres of Salem first made themselves known.

At that time, the parsonage was home to the village's minister, Samuel Parris — a contrary and controversial figure — as well as his wife, three children, an adolescent niece who had fled the Indian wars on the Maine frontier, and two Indian slaves, Tituba and John. The horrors that would ultimately consume the entire region began when Parris's niece, Abigail, aged eleven, began to exhibit strange behaviours, followed not long after by the minister's nine-year-old daughter, Betty. The girls reported that they were being tormented by invisible forces, that unseen spirits bit, pricked and pinched them. On occasion, they would fall insensible, losing the power of speech; other times, they

The Parris Parsonage, where the events of the Salem witch trials began

would transform into wild, feral creatures, barking, yelling and crawling beneath furniture. Sometimes they would be seized with inexplicable fits, stiffening with rigid spasms or simply going limp. One of the girls was noted to have crawled down a well, while Abigail apparently attempted flight. The local physician, William Griggs, examined the girls, and discounting afflictions such as epilepsy, diagnosed them as being "under an Evil Hand". The Devil had come to Salem.

The girls worsened, their odd behaviour escalating as their suffering intensified. John Hale, a minister in the nearby town of Beverly who provided one of the few first-person accounts of the girl's afflictions, wrote that they

> were bitten and pinched by invisible agents; their arms, necks, and backs turned this way and that way, and returned back again, so as was impossible for them to do of themselves, and beyond the power of any Eplieptick [sic] Fits, or natural Disease to effect [...] sometimes they were taken dumb, their mouths stopped, their throats choked, their limbs wracked and tormented so as might move an heart of stone, to sympathize with them, with bowels of compassion for them (quoted in Norton 20).

Fans of horror cinema will undoubtedly recognise the girls' bizarre contortions and animalistic noises as symptomatic of possession. Undoubtedly, the people of Salem, equally familiar with the Devil's machinations, easily identified signs of diabolical interference. News spread quickly in the small, rural village, and gossip swiftly circulated about the girls' odd behaviour. Their guardian, Rev. Parris, fasted and prayed, seeking the Lord's guidance in such trying times. Other members of the community, however, sought different, more unorthodox remedies to aid Abigail and Betty.

A neighbour named Mary Sibley settled on a cure derived from traditional counter-magic, instructing the Parris's slaves in the art of baking a witch cake. Combining the girls' urine with rye meal, Tituba and John baked the mixture in the ashes of the hearth and fed the resulting concoction to the family's dog. While it is not entirely clear how this process worked, work it did, and the two little girls identified the enslaved woman, Tituba, as the witch who had afflicted them. Although the "witch" had been identified, Rev. Parris was furious when he discovered the method by which she had been revealed. He denounced Mary Sibley from the pulpit before his entire congregation, charging that Mary had gone "to the Devil for help against the Devil", and that by doing so, she had succeed in raising demonic forces within the community. Tituba was also swiftly dealt with; she was arrested alongside two other village women, Sarah Good and Sarah Osborne. But it was too late: the affliction had spread. seventeen-year-old Elizabeth Hubbard and twelve-year-old Ann Putnam, Jr were also claiming harassment by spectral forces.

Following their arrests, Good and Osborne were examined along with Tituba at the Salem Village meetinghouse. Although both women protested their innocence, Tituba confessed in spectacular fashion, weaving an elaborate tale filled with witches, devils and colourful familiar spirits. Sadly, little is known of Tituba, one of the most important and enigmatic figures to take part in the trials. In the accounts of the trial, her name was variously recorded as "Tituba", "Titibe", "Tattaoa" and a host of other appellations. In some records, she was described as "black", leading subsequent historians, writers and filmmakers to assume she was of African descent. However, early European settlers in North America often referred to Indigenous peoples as "black". It was also a descriptor they frequently applied to the Devil. Scholars have posited a number of possible origin stories for Tituba, with the most likely hypothesis being Elaine G. Breslaw's claim that she came from one of the Arawak-related tribes that inhabited the northeastern parts of

South America and was sold into slavery in Barbados before being brought to the English colonies (12). As mysteriously as she entered the historical record, Tituba vanished again after the witchcraft hysteria of 1692, having been sold to a new owner to cover the cost of her jail fee. Stories and legends about Tituba endure in the absence of real facts. For centuries, historians and writers of popular fiction imagined that Tituba initiated the Parris girls' affliction by teaching them the art of fortune telling. In his play *The Crucible*, Arthur Miller even has Abigail perform blood rituals with the slave woman deep in the forests surrounding Salem Village. This, however, is simply a myth, and like much of Tituba's sad history, there is no written documentation to substantiate such claims.

As scant as her biography may be, Tituba was for a brief moment the most notorious of the Salem witches. During her examination, judge John Hathorne demanded to know why she tormented the Parris children. Tituba responded that it was not she who harmed the children, but the Devil himself. She explained that one day, while tending to her duties at the parsonage, a tall, white-haired man in a black coat appeared to her and ordered her to hurt the children, threatening to torture her and cut off her head if she did not comply. Satan, when he appeared to Tituba, was accompanied by four companions: Sarah Good, Sarah Osborne and two unknown individuals from Boston. The Devil, she said, had a yellow bird with him, and he himself could shapeshift into a stunning array of colourful animals. He assumed the guise of two red cats, one huge black cat, a hog and a black dog. He promised that if she became his servant, Tituba could have a yellow bird of her own. Tituba described being harassed by the spectres of Good and Osborne, who tormented her until she agreed to join them in afflicting the children. She flew about houses, pinching the innocent girls, and even journeyed as far as Boston. When asked how she accomplished such a feat, Tituba explained that she flew "upon a stick or pole, and Good or Osborne behind me".

Tituba's tales were elaborate, featuring impossible acts and a range of fantastic characters. The assembled villagers were enraptured, and according to Elaine G. Breslaw, it was Tituba's brilliance as a storyteller that saved her life while at the same time enflaming the burgeoning witchcraft hysteria with her descriptions of a cabal of unknown, mysterious witches operating both in Salem Village and further afield.

***

A chicken squawked in the neighbouring yard, the sound tearing through the silence of the still afternoon. It flapped its wings loudly. The gentle roar of car engines rose up from the road that was, I had forgotten, only a few feet away. It was strange to think that the witchcraft panic for which this region has become known started here, in what was then a quiet village covered in silent winter snow. Salem had, I thought, much in common with Hydesville, another story of young girls isolated in dense wilderness. Once again, the spirits had invaded, coming clattering down chimneys and barrelling over windowsills. I imagined how, all the way out here, in the dark of moonless nights, every sound must have taken on a sinister aspect. As in Hydesville, Abigail and Betty's accounts of spectral contact sparked intense speculation. A lighting strike to the heart of a dull frontier town, their claims stoked the passions of all who heard them. Yet, where Hydesville engendered a new religion and transformed America's understanding of the spectral, Salem became a byword for intolerance and cruelty. At the start, though, there was little to distinguish them: two little girls on the edge of a vast, howling wilderness, listening to spectres prowling in the night.

Bennington, Vermont

When I was young, I often wondered, as I do now, what makes a house haunted. What uncanny accretions of events, of histories, need to pile up in order to entice a ghost back to a dwelling place long deserted? In his study of haunted houses on screen, Barry Curtis writes that "'ghosts' and the dark places where they dwell have served as powerful metaphors for persistent themes of loss, memory, retribution and confrontation with unacknowledged and unresolved histories" (10). Haunted houses, then, might be assumed to be places of tragedy, loci upon which painful histories and dark secrets have converged to produce a disruptive spectral echo of the past. This connection with trauma likely explains the kind of structures we commonly imagine to be haunted. Castles, at once sites of political intrigue and domestic spaces, are naturally filled with ghosts. Locations connected to death — cemeteries, funeral homes — are natural habitats for spectres. Sites stained by historical injustices — battlefields, prisons, hanging trees — are also likely candidates for a haunting. Yet, among all of these lively, captivating locales, it is the house that appears most attractive to ghosts. It is here, in ordinary homes, that ghosts are themselves most at home. They sit in rocking chairs, perch on the ends of beds and appear, translucent and pallid, in attics and basements.

American ghosts, in particular, are notorious homebodies. The overwhelmingly domestic character of US spirits is, at least in part, the product of that nation's unique historical character and the contours of its built environment. European settlement in North America is a comparatively recent phenomenon, and so the US lacks the medieval castles and monumental abbeys of the Old World. There was nowhere for its ghosts to go other than down into suburban basements or up into the attics of rural farmhouses. Dale Bailey, one of the foremost scholars of the American haunted house, observes that beyond simple expediency — good old Yankee practically — US ghosts tend to lurk in the corners of ordinary homes because of the symbolic importance houses have accrued in American culture. "The house," he writes, "is our primary marker of class and our central symbol of domesticity, touching upon everything from women's rights (the angel in the house, not to mention the homemaker) to the deterioration of the nuclear family (the broken home)" (8). In a nation bereft of a hereditary aristocracy — though not lacking in social and economic inequality — houses convey status, embody values and attest to the occupant's level of financial success. It's no surprise, then, that the house would emerge as the locus of American haunting. Houses are not just habitations — they are the conceptual nodes where the gossamer threads of history and personal experience are knit together. As the philosopher Gaston Bachelard wrote in his *Poetics of Space*, "A house that has been experienced is not an inert box. Inhabited space transcends geometrical space" (47). Memories and dreams seep into the very foundations of a house, imbuing brick walls and wooden frames with an enduring vitality.

An American ghost story speaks not just to the hopes and fears of those residing within the haunted house, but to the larger socio-political structures in which the household is embedded. A haunting might illuminate the many ways in which an individual family is implicated in systems of patriarchal oppression (as in Charlotte Perkins Gilman's *The Yellow Wall Paper*), White supremacy (Toni Morrison's

Beloved) or economic inequality (Edith Wharton's "All Souls'"). Anthony Vidler, in his treatise on the architectural uncanny, maintains that the most sinister aspect of the haunted house is "not a property of the space itself", but rather a "representation of a mental state of projection that precisely elides the boundaries of the real and the unreal in order to provoke a disturbing ambiguity, a slippage between waking and dreaming" (11).

At the same time, American hauntings are unique because they often lack a ghost, centring instead around houses that are sick, malevolent or imbued with supernatural power. Literary works as diverse as Poe's "The Fall of the House of Usher" (1839), Anne Rivers Siddons's *The House Next Door* (1978) and Mark Z. Danielewski's *House of Leaves* (2000) portray haunted houses conspicuously devoid of ghosts. In these texts, it is the house that haunts its inhabitants. No spectres roam the hallways or rattle chains in musty attics, but the building seems to exercise some entirely malicious will of its own. Occupants die mysteriously, objects move of their own volition, space mysteriously expands or contracts. There is a hopelessness at the heart of these houses, which are not haunted but haunting.

Homesickness — both the sickness of homes as well as the yearning for a lost abode — is a recurring theme in the work of New England (by way of California) writer Shirley Jackson. Jackson knew her ghosts. As a college student, she was obsessed with *Saducismus Triumphatus*, a seventeenth-century treatise on the supernatural that attempted to prove the veracity of witches and earthbound spirits, even asking her friend to steal a copy from the library on one occasion. Yet she also understood the power of houses to bewitch both visitors and inhabitants. She came from a long line of architects, some more successful than others. As she once wrote, "My grandfather was an architect, and his father, and *his* father. [...] One of them built houses only for millionaires in California, and that was where the family wealth came from, and one of them was certain that houses could be made to stand on the sand dunes of San Francisco, and that was where the family wealth went" (quoted in Franklin 13). In many of Jackson's stories, characters, usually alienated young women, search for homes, quiet domestic retreats where they might find warmth and security. Such refuges, however, invariably sour, turn bad and swiftly become prisons in which the young heroines find themselves confined. In "The Lovely House", first published in 1950, an awkward young misfit named Margaret visits a college friend at her beautiful and opulent family home. When she first catches sight of the house, Margaret considers it to be "as lovely a thing as she had ever seen". Nestled amid gently sloping hills and vast gardens, the young guest approaches the house as though it were a beautiful woman, a seductive lover, perceiving with delight, "the long-boned structure within, the curving staircases and the arched doorways and the tall thin lines of steadying beams". The house is likened to a body: its frame, a skeleton; its arched doors and windows, sensual curves. It is alluring, drawing Margaret in, as though she has fallen under some enchanting, soporific spell. However, as she becomes increasingly familiar with the house, Margaret realises that she has fallen prey to its deceptive charms. She is lost and trapped, possibly forever, within an endless maze of mirrors and tapestries, a mise en abyme of eternally receding ornaments and domestic trimmings. The story ends with Margaret enquiring of her hosts, "Surely there will be an end to my visit?" No one answers her question.

This pattern of seduction and entrapment is typical of Jackson's treatment of houses. She conjures up beautiful, lavish manors or cosy, inviting homesteads, only to have them suddenly transform into malevolent, oppressive spaces. The cottage becomes a cage, the home an inescapable dungeon. In her most famous work, 1959's *The Haunting of Hill House*, the novel's shy, awkward protagonist, Eleanor Vance, believes she has found a sense of belonging in the titular Hill House. Having spent most of her life caring for her ailing mother, Eleanor is very much alone in the world until she agrees to join a study of psychic phenomena taking place in a supposedly haunted house. Though the house is depicted as an unsettling space, with its imposing façade and uncanny statuary, Eleanor comes to feel secure, wrapped in an embrace that is simultaneously comforting and suffocating. Ultimately, Eleanor disappears into the house, becoming part of its fittings and fixtures, losing any sense of self she might have once possessed.

The duality of Hill House is, in many ways, reflective of the period in which Jackson was writing and the many dangers the home held for women at that time. In the decades immediately following the Second World War, domestic ideology came to occupy a central position in the American imagination. For many, home and family appeared to offer a gentle salve against lingering wartime trauma. The home was idealised as a secure refuge in an increasingly uncertain world. Motherhood in particular was valorised, and the suburban housewife, safely ensconced in her cosy ranch house and surrounded by state-of-the-art domestic appliances, became an aspirational figure. Yet, although many dreamed of a bucolic existence among the placid streets and uniform lawns of suburbia, others feared the loneliness of such an atomistic existence. Or maybe they were conflicted, desiring the warmth of family life while also dreading the sterility of identical, prefabricated homes. The capacity of Jackson's houses to transform from alluring to oppressive, to be both at once, seems to capture the ambivalence of the post-war period. As with so many American hauntings, Hill House is animated by the dreams, fears and desires of the people who inhabit it, and by the culture that surrounds it. Moreover, like many of the haunted houses that populate US literature, there are no ghosts in Hill House. It is the house itself that is somehow bad, evil, wrong. Dr Montague, the scientist who leads the study in which Eleanor participates, speculates on the sinister force that seems to animate the building. He wonders if the house's malevolent personality was "molded by the people who lived here, or the things they did", or whether it was simply born bad. He goes on to describe Hill House as "disturbed", "leprous", "sick", "deranged". For Dr Montague, a house, like the human mind or the bodies we inhabit, might fall sick, become diseased or degenerate into madness.

There is no Hill House. Rather, there are many Hill Houses. In creating the malign abode, Shirley Jackson cast her net wide. In correspondence, she describes a tenement building glimpsed from a train window en route to New York's Grand Central Station. The structure was ordinary, but, she wrote, something about it seemed "unspeakable… malign" (quoted in Franklin 401). The infamous Winchester House in San Jose, California, located close to where Jackson was born, in the town of Burlingame, likely provided another source of inspiration. Another source may have been a poltergeist case reported in Long Island, New York, in 1958, where an ordinary American family was tormented by supernatural forces in the quotidian setting of a typical suburban ranch house (Franklin 405). There are likely more Hill Houses scattered across the country — it's hard to say for sure. However, what we do know is that a number of the Hill House prototypes can be found in and around Bennington, Vermont, where Jackson moved in 1945 with her husband, the literary critic Stanley Edgar Hyman. Here, Hyman taught at the local college, while

Jackson raised their children and penned unsettling tales of houses possessed by malign forces.

***

The road to Bennington twisted through hills and mountains coated in thick forests. It felt as though the bus was ploughing deep into some dense, primordial wilderness. Wooden stands stood along the roadside selling fresh produce, and renovated barns advertised themselves, usually in big painted letters, as antique markets. The town itself was bright and clean. Full green trees formed canopies over quiet footpaths, as though the brilliant verdancy of the surrounding mountains had somehow trickled down to the streets below. Colourful flower beds erupted from the corners of pavements and the tops of windowsills, bringing life to the staid brick buildings that comprised the town centre.

A popular tourist spot, Bennington appeared deeply aware of its own quaintness. Small shops sold locally produced fudge and maple syrup. A sweet shop had been named "Village Chocolate Shoppe", and a nearby optician bore the archaic name of "Moulton's Spectacle Shoppe". Tourists came here to escape the bustle of modern life, and Bennington presented them with a snapshot of carefully cultivated old-world charm.

In a car park just off Pleasant Street, behind the Green Mountain Christian Centre, I boarded a minibus that bounced and jolted its way further into the surrounding hills to Bennington College. The campus was located at the end of a long road that wound its way through capacious fields overflowing with summertime wildflowers. A young woman on the bus repeatedly turned to her companion and stated, in the same mildly excited voice each time, "They call it the scary path." As in a fairy tale, I looked over on the third occasion and asked her why. "There's nothing there," she responded, "just empty fields all around. Imagine walking here alone at night." She paused to add gravity to her explanation: "People disappear here, y'know." I disembarked near the centre of campus. It was late June and most of the students had returned home for summer vacation. The place looked empty, and the once bright sky had grown heavy with impenetrable, grey clouds. Just before the driver closed the door behind me, I turned around to him: "You're coming back, right?" He nodded. "Two hours. Here at this stop."

What seemed to be the main college building rose above gently sloping knolls and slight, curving pathways, a white bell tower surging upwards to the leaden sky. On either side, recent extensions with huge rectangular windows suggested a newness, a self-conscious modernity, intermingled with the pseudo-colonial trappings of the older structures. In the centre of a rich, green lawn stood the college's traditional student housing, white wooden buildings evincing a Shaker sparseness. Further away from me, past the little cluster of buildings, everything seemed to fall away, and the clean manicured commons vanished into a densely layered imbrication of trees and mountains.

Reflecting on her time at Bennington College in the 1980s, writer Lili Anolik described how this area of the campus, nicknamed "the End of the World", was frequently wrapped in a mist so thick that it was impossible to see your own hands unless they were held right up in front of your face. It was cold but clear when I stood there. Strong winds assailed me from both sides, and I dug a hooded jacket out of my backpack. Apparently, this spot, in the centre of the Bennington campus, was one of the very few places in the world where all four winds converged. Hunters claimed the winds around here were so powerful they could disorientate the most experienced outdoorsmen, throwing them off course to wander, hopelessly lost, in the mountains. It was the middle of summer, but I was chilled to the core.

When Shirley Jackson moved here with her husband in the mid-1940s, Bennington College was one of the most dynamic and progressive institutions in the United States. A women's college, Bennington aimed to provide a world-class education for its girls, albeit in a thoroughly unconventional manner. There were no grades or exams; instead, students wrote lengthy essays, and they were encouraged to pursue independent study, supervised personally by a staff member (Franklin 192). The young women who matriculated at Bennington were granted what was for the time an unusual level of personal freedom. Faculty and their wives were encouraged to socialise with students, and illicit affairs sprang up like weeds. From the point of view of the locals — hardy Vermonters whose familial roots ran deep — the students and faculty alike were perceived as odd, bohemian, potential communists.

Bennington College is surrounded by hills and mountains on all sides — a drop in a rolling green ocean. Rich, dense foliage covers the landscape, and that afternoon, a few slivers of light filtered through the thick clouds, illuminating a vivid spectrum of greens. Walking away from the silent campus, I turned down the trail my fellow commuter had termed the "scary path". Nothing stirred, but on either side of me the earth was carpeted with soft sheaths of grass and busy, abundant flowers. Further from the path, the woodlands stretched, dark and secretive, into the hills. There was something almost magnetic about those woods. They were possessed of a strange allure, like a spell cast in a fairy tale, a little shard of desire penetrating my heart and pulling me into their depths.

In one of my favourite novels by Shirley Jackson, 1951's *Hangsaman*, a young woman disappears, albeit briefly, into those deep, beguiling woods. The story centres on an adolescent protagonist, Natalie Waite, who undergoes a serious psychological break after commencing her studies at a New England liberal arts college that is, perhaps unsurprisingly, little more than a thinly disguised replica of Bennington. Traumatised following a sexual assault and increasingly isolated from her peers, Natalie develops an intense, obsessive relationship with another young woman, Tony. In the novel's climax, the girls run away together, seeking shelter in the woods. Moving through a deserted theme park, along a path flanked by sinister whispering trees, Natalie and Tony find themselves in a secluded grove that seems animated by some indistinct, otherworldly force. Jackson writes evocatively of the uncanny sentience evinced by the trees as they wait, patiently, for the runaways:

> The trees were waiting in the darkness ahead, quietly expectant. [...] Beneath the trees it was not dark as a room is dark when the lights are put out, the artificial darkness which comes when an artificial light is gone; it was the deep natural darkness which comes with a forsaking of natural light. (*Hangsaman* 209).

Jackson's description of the quietly expectant trees and the thick, impervious gloom has echoes of the darkness that enveloped Salem Village in the early months of 1692 — just as the community's children began to complain of spectral harassment — and of the optical illusions that danced in the mountains of Washington Irving's mythic Hudson Valley. In Vermont, as in New York and Massachusetts, the American wilderness is restless, hungry. Rather than the placid, fertile lands that illuminated the fantasies and guided the paths of the first European settlers, the wilds of the North American continent prove themselves time and again to be animated with a dark, destructive agency.

Neither empty nor undiscovered at the moment of its initial colonisation, the wildest regions of the New World assumed a central position in the American imagination. In the fevered dreams of early Puritan settlers, the Devil ranged through thick, tenebrous woodlands. For them, the North American continent was a howling wilderness, a dark realm untouched by the light of the gospel, while its Indigenous peoples were perceived as "children of the Devil". In subsequent centuries, this uneasy relationship with the wilderness remained a vital component of American identity. On the one hand, the natural world was conceived of as a site of renewal and possibility, where new lands are conquered and fortunes made; yet, on the other, the wilderness never fails to threaten us with its dark, ponderous depths. In film and literature, as well as in the endlessly circulating streams of local gossip, remote, sparsely populated regions shelter both the terror of the unknown and the malign forces we must necessarily expel from the midst of our communities.

According to Jackson's biographer Ruth Franklin, *Hangsaman* developed out of the 1946 disappearance of Paula Welden, an eighteen-year-old Bennington College student who vanished while walking along a portion of Vermont's Long Trail hiking path. The story received ubiquitous coverage in local papers, with a host of theories posited to explain the girl's disappearance: a suicide, a hiking accident, abduction, murder, an out-of-town lover. She was never found. Natalie, however, is luckier. In the final pages of Jackson's book, the young protagonist, having briefly contemplated suicide, walks out of the woods, hale and healthy, imbued with a new strength and confidence. Just as the tarot card for which the novel is named — the hanged man — symbolises not death, but transformation, Natalie's journey into the wilderness functions as a kind of spiritual rebirth.

Although Jackson was captivated by Paula Welden's story, hers was not the only unexplained disappearance in the region. Indeed, between 1945 and 1950, five people disappeared from the Bennington area. Decades later, in 1981, a group of hunters also vanished from this part of Vermont. In most cases, no remains were found, and, in all cases, investigators were frustrated in their attempts to discover what happened to the missing individuals. The cluster of disappearances resulted in an area of land encompassing Glastenbury Mountain and the surrounding communities of Bennington, Shaftsbury and Woodford, as well as the ghost towns of Glastenbury and Somerset, being designated the "Bennington Triangle". Alongside periodic disappearances, the triangle has also played host to strange lights and sounds, which some folklorists view as characteristic of UFO activity, while there have also been reports of monsters, wild men, carnivorous stones and spectral apparitions. A quick online search turns up YouTube videos, Reddit threads and podcast episodes devoted to the region's myriad mysteries, each postulating their own explanations for the string of disappearances: serial killers, cults, time warps, interdimensional portals... Perhaps it is the ineffability of the region's darkness that makes it so potent. If we cannot identify or name the evil, its power is stronger. It refuses our attempts to capture it, to pin it down and dissect it.

I couldn't help but hold onto the thought of nameless evil as I turned off the "scary path" and onto a regional road. Following a slight incline, I came to a grey stone building, set back a little behind a field that teemed with purple thistles. The front gables were half consumed by ivy, while on the western façade two parallel windows looked out over the porch like blank, lifeless eyes. Scholars and fans have suggested that this structure, which is now Bennington College's Music Building, inspired Jackson's *The Haunting of Hill House*. It's possible. Early in the novel, she speaks of "evil in the face of a house", describing the eponymous Hill House as evincing "a watchfulness from the blank windows and a touch of glee in the eyebrow of a cornice". The building that glared at me certainly possessed a watchfulness in its blank windows, a malevolent glee in the cornice. Yet, other local houses have also been suggested as potential models for Hill House. The Edward H. Everett Mansion, now part of Southern Vermont College, seems like a distinct possibility, with its imposing turrets and ghostly woman in white (Franklin 402). Rather than mirroring any one house, Hill House, it appears, embodies the many ways that a house can turn on its inhabitants. Crafted from fragments of the Winchester House, the Jennings Building, the Everett Mansion, an unnamed New York tenement, and a haunted Long Island suburb, Hill House is a multifaced entity, a malleable expression of malign domesticity.

Jackson's own home, or at least one of them, is less than half a mile from the Jennings Building, in the village of North Bennington. I followed a quiet country road to the edge of the Bennington campus, passing through a pair of stone pillars and moving along a peaceful tree-lined street. The house that Jackson occupied with her husband and young children, 12 Prospect Street, will be instantly recognisable to anyone who has read Jackson's 1953 memoir *Life Among the Savages*. Most editions of the book feature a colourful illustration of the house with its distinctive Greek-revival style pillars and round upstairs window. Jackson once described the house as looking like an antique Pagan temple replicated in miniature. I stood rather awkwardly on the street, quickly snapping photos with my bulky camera. I wondered if the inhabitants and their neighbours were fed up with intrusive horror enthusiasts photographing their sleepy little street. The Jackson house rose clean and white, like a marble monument, above a rich green garden.

Shirley Jackson's house at 12 Prospect Street, North Bennington

The lawn was overrun by a varied collection of plants and wildflowers, while four tall bushes screened the ground-floor windows from the street and, presumably, the prying eyes of literary tourists.

Life Among the Savages seems, at first glance, very different from the horror stories that many modern readers associate with Jackson (though she was better known during her lifetime by a certain segment of the American population — mostly middle-class housewives — for the humorous tales she published in magazines like *Good Housekeeping* and *Woman's Home Companion*). At the same time, however, there are a number of strange intersections and thematic overlaps that unite Jackson's gothic tales with her humorous domestic anecdotes. In particular, her treatment of homes and houses remained remarkably consistent throughout her career, and the version of the Prospect Street house memorialised in *Life Among the*

Savages unites the allure of home with a pervasive eeriness in much the same way as Hill House. In one passage, Jackson describes 12 Prospect Street as a "good house" that did not "seem to mind when crayon marks appeared on the walls and paint got spilled on the floor". While comforting — this is, after all, a home where cats dozed on rocking chairs and visitors came calling — the house also appears somehow conscious, alive, with a will all its own: "One bedroom chose the children, because it was large and light and showed unmistakable height-marks on one wall" (19). In subsequent pages, Jackson relays how her daughter Jannie spoke about a "faraway voice in the house which sang to her at night" (20–21). The proximity of Jackson's home to one of the many Hill House prototypes, as well as her many playful insinuations that the Prospect Street house was possessed of some preternatural power, induces an odd, somewhat contradictory sensation. The warm, welcoming aura of the home appears undergirded by something dark and cold yet disconcertingly familiar. This, too, is characteristic of Jackson's work; her houses, whether the focus of horror stories or domestic farces, are veritable repositories of the uncanny.

The uncanny, like so many ideas that have dominated twentieth-century thought, is a concept derived from the writings of Sigmund Freud. In his 1919 essay "The Uncanny", Freud attempts to illuminate why certain, familiar things can serve as sources of fear and anxiety. After all, shouldn't we only fear what is different or alien? In doing so, he unravels the linguistic knots of the German word "heimlich", which in the psychoanalyst's native language refers to those things "belonging to the house, not strange, familiar, tame, intimate, comfortable, homely" (2). Yet the same word carries with it a series of more disturbing connotations, as it also signifies that which is "concealed", "kept from sight, so that others do not get to know about it" (3). The multivalence of the term "heimlich" thus allows it to encompass that which is safe and familiar while also incorporating everything hidden, secret and repressed. In this way, Freud notes, "heimlich is a word the meaning of which develops towards an ambivalence, until it finally coincides with its opposite, *unheimlich*" (4). Translated directly from German, "heimlich" is rendered as "homely", while "unheimlich" — which we often call "uncanny" — is expressed as "unhomely". For Freud, then, the home is associated with a very specific mode of terror, whereby the familiar, the intimate and the familial are always haunted by a hidden darkness.

Although codified by an Austrian thinker in the years following the First World War, the uncanny neatly encapsulates the key thematic and aesthetic concerns of the American Gothic, as it has evolved from the colonial era right up to the twenty-first century. American Gothic — whether manifested in film, fiction, television or music — is preoccupied by the power of the familiar, the mundane, the domestic to suddenly shift and expose its own dark, monstrous heart. Jackson's work epitomises the uncanny impulse buried in the American imagination. Her work takes what is familiar, easy, even mundane and exposes the dark, tangled roots underneath. Crucially, she dissects the home, the cultural symbol that, in America, binds together the slack threads of class, race, sexuality and identity to form a single all-encompassing image of security and unity. At least that's what it's supposed to do. Jackson's work is powerful because she undermined the romantic image of the home at the precise historical moment when the nuclear family was at its most powerful, its most culturally pervasive.

***

In her ambitious, trans-historical study of ghosts and

hauntings, Susan Owens explains that, in the course of her research, she "quickly discovered that ghosts are mirrors of the times". Veritable changelings, the spirits that haunt our houses and our minds "reflect our preoccupations, moving with the tide of cultural trends and matching the mood of each age" (9). Travelling across New York and New England, from the placid shores of Lake Erie in the west to the yawning Atlantic in the east, each ghost or spectre I encountered — in story if not in actuality — seemed custom-fit to its era, cut from the cloth of its unique historical moment and hewn from the soil beneath its translucent feet.

From what I had seen, the spirits of Salem and Sleepy Hollow gave form to historical traumas, ruptures in the nation's mythic narrative of innocence, liberty and justice. Huddled close to the Eastern Seaboard, where the first European settlements were raised up beneath the flash of steel and the deep sonorous drone of canon fire, these spirit-haunted regions speak to a past that refuses a clean and final burial. Further inland, on what was once the westernmost frontier of the United States, the ghosts of New York are far more loquacious creatures. They have their moments of mischief, certainly, blowing through old mansions and shuttered museums like strong winter winds, but overall, they are chatty, welcoming. They speak of tomorrow and the promise of the future, a better world in Summer-Land or here on earth once we rid ourselves of prejudice and injustice. In true hauntological fashion, all of these spirits, across New England and New York, emerged in moments of crisis, of a break in the chronological order of things. They speak of the past, haunting us with memories of what was, but they also embody a future never realised, hopes that remain unfulfilled.

As the evening darkness began to paint the already heavy sky a deeper shade of blue, I wandered back to Bennington College. The driver and his minibus returned. I clambered into one the back seats. As darkness fell, the only light for miles seemed to be the LED controls at the front of the bus. The driver hummed along to the radio all the way back to town. He deposited me outside a small diner that smelled like layers of cooking grease, but whose warm orange glow beckoned me inside. At a table by the window, I watched as the night blotted out the last traces of Bennington, its mountains and its deep, rustling forests.

2. BURIED DEEP IN THE DEEP SOUTH

Winter passed and caterpillars began to cross the road again. [...] So I slept a night, and the next morning I headed my toenails toward Louisiana and New Orleans in particular. New Orleans is now and has ever been the hoodoo capital of America. Great names in rites that vie with those of Hayti in deeds that keep alive the powers of Africa.

— Zora Neale Hurston, *Mules and Men*

Richmond, Virginia

I awoke in a small house in rural Henrico County, just a few miles outside of Richmond. On both sides of a rarely used country road, houses sprang up from thickets of grass and foliage; lawns disappeared into dense woodlands. Further along the quiet road, tall rows of corn crowded, like furtive conversationalists, in fields that reached up to the battered edges of the tarmac. I sat on the front steps of my temporary home, watching strange clusters of insects pass over the yard. My surroundings hummed with life: butterflies, squirrels, the occasional stray cat that approached me tentatively, shaking droplets from its matted fur. The rain-slick pavements had just begun to dry off, sending faint coils of steam snaking upwards into the thick, humid air.

It was late June, and New England had been warm. The days slipped by with a balmy, golden glow illuminating their edges. In Virginia, however, the heat was different. It was humid, sticky, and your breath stopped in your throat, forced back by gulps of warm air. To walk outside was to feel as if you had suddenly been immersed into a hot bath. The heat here was tangible, with a viscous texture that enveloped your body and seeped into your pores. Everything felt so alive, vivified by the warm, wet air, like plants in a greenhouse. Foliage grew in abundance, insect life trilled in a continuous, low-level hum. I imagined that nothing could die here, that the earth, so damp and moist, would never allow flesh to desiccate or bones to crumble, that whatever was buried here would invariably push back up through the clammy soil.

Ghosts are a pervasive presence in the Southeastern United States. Ectoplasmic tendrils twist in the night air and wispy figures entwine themselves among the tress like strings of Spanish moss. Abandoned plantations and decaying gravesites give up their ghosts eagerly, offering their spirits to the deep, indifferent night. In Tananarive Due's short story "Ghost Summer" (2015), a little boy looks forward to visiting his grandparents in North Florida precisely because of the ghosts that crowd their home after dark. He later learns that the ghosts, spirits of murdered Black children, were victims of the racism that continues to deform not only the South, but the entire United States.

Yet, for all the spectres that hang in the humid Southern air, it is the fleshy corporeality of the embodied dead that most powerfully animates the imagination here. Ghosts may flit by, but vampires, the undead and victims of live burials are the most formidable incarnations of the Southern Gothic. In the stifling, oppressive heat of the South, monsters are unlikely to be free-floating spectres. Instead, they most often appear as weighty, tangible bodies, dragged down by the burden of history, yet refusing to rest in their graves. From the grotesque tales of Edgar Allan Poe to the romantic, erotically charged novels of Anne Rice and Charlaine Harris, the Southern Gothic imagination appears preoccupied with the restless dead, interred bodies that rise again from the damp earth and refuse the silence of the grave. Moving beyond the thrills of supernatural shockers, the Southern fixation with burial refused or delayed also creeps into more canonical works. In William Faulkner's 1930 novel *As I Lay Dying*, a poor Mississippi family struggles to bury their matriarch. Placing her coffin in a wagon, they brave injury, impediment and natural disaster before eventually reaching their destination, the town where the deceased woman wished to be buried. By that point, eight days after her death, the corpse has begun to fester, and the curious locals who approach the wagon are forced to do so with handkerchiefs covering their noses.

The Southeastern United States is characterised by a subtropical climate. In the summer, thunderstorms sweep in from the Atlantic Ocean or swirl up in warm currents from the Gulf of Mexico. Rich mud, caked thickly along the banks of the Mississippi, and primeval swamps generate noisy, buzzing life in abundance. Things grow quickly, lavishly sprouting tendrils, buds, petals, vines. The gauzy purple flowers of wisteria plants hang placid as bluebells while their thick vines wrap around tree trunks in twisted choking knots or crash through the foundations of houses, pulling up boards, cracking walls. Spanish moss clings to the branches of oak and cypress trees, drifting in the breeze like ragged burial shrouds.

Much of the Southern United States is coloured by the inescapable presence of swamps and wetlands. The dark, viperous underside of the "genteel" Antebellum South, the swamp was a tenebrous reflection of the region's concealed horrors. Anthony Wilson observes that during the pre-

Civil War period, when the Southeastern states grew rich on the trade in cotton, tobacco, rice and human bodies, the region's planters saw themselves as a civilising force engaged in a perpetual struggle against the raw, animalistic swamp. Expelling noxious fumes, fowl stenches and clouds of mosquitoes, it was viewed as a breeding ground for diseases such as yellow fever and cholera, afflictions that, at the time, were understood to arise from "bad air". The swamp sheltered life that was thought to be treacherous. It was primordial chaos, a liminal space that disrupted the neat topographical division between land and sea.

The swamp might be best understood in terms of living death. Its swarms of insects and slime-covered reptiles, its dark waters and dense soil speak of death and decay. Yet, if the swamp signifies death, it is an impermanent, restless death. The swamp is decay that generates new life, effluvia fertilising generations of plants, animals and insects. Describing the inhabitants of the Great Dismal Swamp that stretches between southern Virginia and North Carolina, eighteenth-century surveyor and writer William Byrd II lamented their "cadaverous complexion[s]". The vapours that rise from the swamp, he observed, "infect the air for many miles round and render it very unwholesome for the bordering inhabitants. It makes them liable to agues, pleurisies, and many other distempers that kill abundance of people *and make the rest look no better than ghosts*" (quoted in Giblett 117, emphasis added). Death here is really a kind of undeath. If the miasma of the swamp is thought to bring death, the deep, fathomless waters and rich, syrupy soil promise vibrant, albeit cryptic, life. Things buried here might refuse death, stumbling back to the world of the living like zombies. Decayed matter may engender new life, but that growth might be wrong, twisted, corrupt — like the Spanish moss that interlaces the gnarled fingers of old-growth oaks.

The Southern preoccupation with the undead body was first and perhaps most viscerally evoked in the work of Edgar Allan Poe, the father of the detective novel and modern science fiction, as well as the progenitor of the American Gothic. Poe's short stories, the literary form he pioneered, evinced an intense obsession with undeath. What is buried always makes a return, clawing its way up through the earth with bloody, broken fingers. In his 1844 tale "The Premature Burial", the narrator imagines being consigned alive to the tomb and contemplates the "unendurable oppression of the lungs — the stifling fumes of the damp earth — the clinging to the death garments — the rigid embrace of the narrow house — the blackness of the absolute Night". For Poe's unlucky narrator, it is not the inevitability of suffocation that renders live burial intolerable, but the sticky solemnity of the grave and the damp, oppressive soil.

Poe was a Virginian. He may have been born in Boston and buried in Baltimore, but the city of Richmond was his childhood home, and it was to this home that he returned in the months before his death. As J.W. Ocker writes in his biography-cum-travelogue *Poe-Land*, it is "the state of Virginia that truly bookends his life" (261). It was here that Poe first knew loss, as his mother, the actress Elizabeth Arnold ("Eliza") Poe, was carried away by tuberculosis, the disease that would later claim both his stepmother and his wife. He also passed much of his childhood in Virginia. After his mother's death, Poe was taken in by the wealthy Allan family — who gave him his middle name — and was instilled with the values and attitudes befitting a young Southern gentleman. Yet his relationship with Richmond was also complex, fraught with familial and class tensions. He was part yet not part of the Allan family; he moved among the merchant classes — the nouveau riche who were encroaching on the territory of the old Southern aristocracy — but he was not truly one of them. An unwanted spectre, Poe slipped quietly between the diffuse strands of Richmond society.

Today, Richmond plays host to what Poe fan and literary traveller H.P. Lovecraft would have called "homes and shrines of Poe". Certainly, Richmond houses a collection of sombre monuments, testaments to the sorrow and loss that haunted Poe throughout his life. The quiet green graveyard that encircles St John's Church, an unassuming white-steepled house of worship, is the last resting place of Poe's mother. Shockoe Hill Cemetery, meanwhile, holds the remains of Poe's guardians, John and Frances Allan, as well as the bodies of Jane Stith Stanard — the inspiration for his poem "To Helen" (1831) — and Sarah Elmira Royster — Poe's childhood sweetheart and, later, his fiancée. Other monuments, however, speak to his life and work, memorialising Poe as someone who walked the city's streets, ate in its taverns and gazed at the busy thoroughfare from his desk behind high office windows. The Allan residence, where Poe lived with his guardians, has been long since demolished, but it is commemorated by a plaque on the corner of 5th and Main Streets, while the home of Sarah Elmira Royster still stands as a private residence.

Richmond's pre-eminent temple of Poe, however, is likely the Poe Museum, located at 1914 East Main Street. It doesn't look like a museum, more like a quaint cottage seated just off to the side of a red-brick pavement, its wooden shutters closed against the pervasive Southern heat. The museum is housed in a building referred to as the Old Stone House after the stone walls that have endured almost three centuries and outlasted countless rulers, governments and regimes. Poe never lived in this house. However, as the oldest residential building in Richmond, it is a structure he would doubtless been aware of. Built in the mid-1700s, the Old Stone House would have been familiar to Poe from both his youth as a junior honour colour guard escorting the Revolutionary War hero General Marquis de Lafayette on a tour of Richmond, as well as simply from passing the building as he walked down Main Street to his workplace in the offices of the *Southern Literary Messenger*. It became a museum to Poe in the early part of the twentieth century, when an organisation of literary enthusiasts came together to create a monument to him. They failed in that endeavour, but established a museum in the writer's honour, turning the little stone cottage — which at the time was rented by a pair of historic preservationists — into a veritable reliquary of Poe ephemera.

Over a short email correspondence, I had arranged to meet Chris Semtner, the museum's curator, for a conversation about Poe's time in Richmond. When I introduced myself to the young interns staffing the entrance, they asked me to wait in the gift shop while they went to find Chris. Poe seems to be one of those historical figures whom we, as a culture, have welcomed into our hearts in a way that both amplifies and softens his gloom. We turn the morbid preoccupations that characterise his literary work into a pervasive devouring misery, assuming that he was swallowed whole by his sorrow. But we also imagine that he simultaneously possessed the kind of warmth that might easily translate to a stuffed toy or a caricature on a fridge magnet. Poe is somehow both a dark, tortured artist and a jovial cartoon character. I am not immune to thinking of him as the cuddly uncle of Gothic literature. I bought a little Poe finger-puppet — all exaggerated forehead and conspicuous moustache — that now sits, affixed with a small magnetic strip, on the side of a filing cabinet I never use.

Chris found me perusing postcards in the gift shop and led me out the back door to the Enchanted Garden, a little green oasis bordered by red-brick buildings and crafted from fragments of Poe's life. The garden, Chris explained, was inspired by Poe's poem "To One in Paradise" (1833). It recreates, in rich detail, the poem's vivid images of "A green isle in the sea, love/A fountain and a shrine/All wreathed with fairy fruits and flowers". As in the verse, a stone fountain occupies the centre of the garden, while an immense hackberry tree leans over as if to touch it. At the far end of the garden stands a brick structure vaguely reminiscent of some ancient temple. Beneath the roof of this reconstructed shrine sits what Chris, referencing "The Raven" (1845), described as a "pallid bust" of Poe. This bust, Chris informed me, is actually a copy. The original plaster bust was stolen from the museum grounds in 1987. A few days later, the museum's then director, Dr Bruce English, received a phone call, at midnight appropriately enough. The caller, who didn't identify themselves, requested that English read Poe's "Spirits of the Dead" (1827) over the telephone. After Dr English complied and read the poem, the caller confessed that the bust was on the other side of the James River, in a biker bar called the Raven Inn. The story goes that a man in a cowboy hat strolled into the bar, placed the bust on the counter and ordered two drinks: a beer for Poe and something stronger for himself. When the man left, Poe remained in the bar with his beer and a paper bag bearing the words "Spirits of the Dead". The original bust is now displayed safely in the museum's reading room, while the shrine houses a copy.

As we chatted, Chris and I were joined by two of the museum's most popular employees, a pair of black cats named Pluto and Edgar. The cats, Chris told me, were found on the grounds by the museum's gardener in 2012. Edgar apparently displays many of the personality traits of his namesake, while Pluto was named for the titular feline in Poe's "The Black Cat" (1843), a horrifying tale in which a man murders his wife and walls her body up in the basement

One of the Poe Museum cats, Richmond, Virginia

only to be undone by the cat he had inadvertently buried alive alongside her. At the climax of the tale, the cat's cries alert the police to the location of the body; its "informing voice", the murderous narrator observes, "had consigned me to the hangman". I bent down to stroke the cats, who purred gently and nuzzled against my body. Pluto, Chris pointed out, has a conspicuous white patch on his chest that mirrors, uncannily, the "indefinite splotch of white" that distinguishes his fictional counterpart. According to Chris, the cats find a great deal of joy in their daily routine at the museum, taking pleasure in greeting guests and even dressing in little bow ties for the weddings the museum regularly hosts. Their presence also testifies to Poe's love of cats. In an 1840 article about the relationship between instinct and reason, Poe notes that he is the "owner of one of the most remarkable black cats in the world". Relating the cat's habit of carefully opening the latch on the kitchen door, he observes that "the black cat, in doing what she did, must have made use of all the perceptive and reflective faculties which we are in the habit of supposing the prescriptive qualities of reason alone". Poe, it seems, was awed by the intelligence of the cat, going so far as to suggest that there is little separating the natural instincts of animals from the reason of man.

After convincing me to bid farewell to the cats, Chris brought me upstairs to the reading room. Comprised of four buildings in total, the museum feels a bit like a maze, a warren of Poe memorabilia. Everywhere, fragments of the author's life line shelves, peer from frames or burst from cabinets. Among the museum's Poe keepsakes, visitors can find his childhood bed, a silk waistcoat, a pair of socks, his desk from the offices of the *Southern Literary Messenger* and even a lock of hair cut from the author's head after his death. The reading room is lined with volumes by Poe and about Poe. There are monographs on his use of imagery, psychoanalytical readings of his work and texts on Poe and American literary history. There are also translations of Poe's work from around the world — volumes in French, Italian, Mandarin and Russian. Chris was an avid Poe fan, capable of spontaneously reeling off lengthy — and apt — quotations, and seemed genuinely proud as he described how visitors travelled from all over the world to visit Poe's hometown. I glanced at the shelves crowded with translations and thoughts on Poe from across the globe and wondered about the author's own peripatetic existence. He had lived in Richmond, but the cities of Boston, Baltimore, Philadelphia and New York can also claim him. As a child, he had even spent time in Britain.

"Poe moved around so much," I observed. "Do you think he retained some of Richmond when he left? Did the South stay with him?" Chris nodded and proceeded to explain that Poe was deeply influenced by his Southern youth, often in unexpected ways. In the years following the Revolutionary War, many of the city's major planters manumitted their slaves, and so by the time Poe was a young man, the city had a large free population of colour. Poe, it appeared, spent time with African American servants and workers, talking to them about their folk traditions. Some of his stories, Chris continued, bear striking similarities to tales derived from the African diaspora: "I found a folktale that was similar to 'The Black Cat', of this woman who died: they found the Black Cat in there screeching." Poe's story "The Gold Bug" may also contain elements borrowed from Black oral culture: "There's something called the walking man where — it's similar — they would put a beetle inside of a bottle. And whichever way the beetle points, they would turn the bottle that direction, and they keep moving. And that's how you were supposed to find buried treasure."

Poe's positioning within the context of the Antebellum South has always been a source of controversy and debate among scholars and literary enthusiasts. When we look to Poe's correspondence, his many essays, we find mostly silence on matters related to race and slavery, while his fiction appears to offer only contradictions. He often relies on racist caricatures or grotesque images of "savage", "uncivilised" Black bodies, but — as Chris notes — he also created characters of colour who appear as noble, heroic figures. Other works — such as "The System of Doctor Tarr and Professor Fether" (1845) and "Hop-Frog" (1849) — have been read by scholars as subtle critiques of chattel slavery. His guardians, the Allans, owned slaves, and in one letter, Poe berates his foster father for allowing him "to be subjected to the whims & caprice, not only of your white family, but the complete authority of the blacks". However, the print library of the Poe Museum also holds what Chris calls a "strange document". The artefact in question is a bill of sale for twenty-one-year-old male slave, sold by Poe's mother-in-law, Maria Clemm, in 1827. As a woman, she was unable to sign the document himself, so Poe stepped in. The curious part of all this is that the enslaved man was sold to his own relatives for $42, at a time when a young, healthy slave would typically fetch around $1,000. Chris speculated that this "sale" was in reality an act of manumission. Because slave owners in Maryland needed permission from the legislature to free their slaves, many circumvented this complex legal process by simply selling slaves to free family members for a low price. "That was a loophole," Chris added. Considering the dearth of direct commentary on Poe's part, we may never fully understand his position on slavery. His thoughts on the matter become simply another haunting lacuna in a sad history of absences and occlusions.

I was also interested to know whether, beyond the specific socio-political context of antebellum Virginia, Poe's work might have been shaped by the landscape of the South, its unique topography and at times oppressive climate. I explained to Chris the thoughts I had been having about the sticky, humid South and its damp earth, about how such rich, vital soil might never allow a body to rest peacefully. "Poe certainly thought differently about the natural world," Chris responded. In the nineteenth century, when Poe was penning his macabre tales, there was a growing enthusiasm for nature. Northern artists, like the Hudson River School, were portraying the American landscape as inspiring, sublime, awesome. Americans were considering the benefits of being outdoors, immersed in the beauty and revivifying power of nature. By the end of the century, Yellowstone would be declared America's first national park, lauded for its wild beauty and protected from the encroachment of industry. Poe's visions of nature, while frequently beautiful, more often than not veered towards the grotesque. In 1827, he published a poem entitled "The

Lake", an ode to the dark beauty and sublime power of the Great Dismal Swamp. As Chris pointed out, this is an unusual nature poem: "He talks about the black waters, and it's smelly, dismal." Later, when I tracked down the full text of the poem, I understood what Chris meant. The natural world described by Poe is not lush, joyful or even particularly inspiring. Instead, "The Lake" portrays the Southern swamplands as suffocating, poisonous even. The speaker, who is imbued with a poetic soul and capable of imaginatively transforming the dankest morass into a bucolic paradise, finds only death and decay in the swamp:

> Death was in that poison'd wave
> And in its gulf a fitting grave
> For him who thence could solace bring
> To his dark imagining;
> Whose wild'ring thought could even make
> An Eden of that dim lake.

The viscous, sticky materiality of the swamp is a pervasive presence in the author's work. In tales such as the perennially horrifying "Facts in the Case of M. Valdemar" (1845) bodies dissolve into an amorphous goo redolent of the sticky sludge of the swamp. In other works — "The Black Cat" and "The Tell-Tale Heart" (1843), for instance — corpses secreted in the bowels of basements or beneath floorboards rise once again to the surface, resisting their burial and clinging to life like the vibrant matter of the swamplands. In "The Fall of the House of Usher", the incestuous madness of the titular family is reflected, literally, in a stagnant mountain lake. As Anthony Wilson notes, "While a tarn is not technically a swamp [...] the images of pestilential vapors and miasma [...] could not fail to evoke a sense of the Southern swamps that had become so laden with rhetorical significance" (58). The Usher's mountain lake — which reflects only "ghastly tree-stems" and the "vacant and eye-like windows" of the family's ancient home — incarnates the corruption, the fatal languor, of the Southern aristocracy, as well as the futility of humanity's attempts to exert control over the natural world.

Poe's vision of death as a restless state, one defined by a vital materiality that resists entombment, is perhaps best encapsulated in the figure of Lady Madeline Usher. Having been interred alive, trapped in a cataleptic slumber, she breaks free of her tomb and appears at the chamber of her brother/lover with "blood upon her white robes, and the evidence of some bitter struggle upon every portion of her emaciated frame". However, she is only one member of a whole gruesome pantheon of undead women who appear in Poe's fiction: Madeline, Berenice, Ligeia, Morella — they all refuse death, clawing their way out of the grave to torment the men who loved them in life. While much has been made of Poe's preoccupation with beautiful dead women — with critics diagnosing this literary obsession as a symptom of his own grief following the loss of his mother, foster-mother and wife — I think the grim vitality of the swamp may also have had a role to play in the development of this motif.

Having grown up in the South, knowing how life thrived in unexpected — sometimes disturbing — ways in its humid air and damp earth, Poe refused to treat matter as an inert object. Rather, informed by the looming presence of the swamp in the Southern imagination, he dwelled on the slimy viscosity of the material: Valdemar dissolving into an oozing, yet still sentient mass of liquefying viscera; Madeline stirring in her mouldy, oppressive tomb. The swamps that surrounded him in his youth were still thought at that time to be vectors of disease, spewing clouds of polluted air and generating sickly life in their hot, sticky cauldrons of mud. In his poem "Dream-Land" (1844),

Poe imagines such mires as superabundant not only with natural life, but with supernatural entities as well: "By the grey woods,—by the swamp/Where the toad and the newt encamp,—/By the dismal tarns and pools, Where dwell the Ghouls".

Poe's understanding of restless death and clamouring materiality existed in startling contrast to dominant nineteenth-century conceptions of mortality, which were centred on visions of peace and elaborate systems of memorialisation. As the US turned away from the dour, apocalyptic Puritanism that still stirs the bones of Salem, ideas around death began to change. Death was no longer conceived of grimly, in terms of rotting flesh — the grinning skull of the memento mori — but was instead rearticulated through practices of mourning and memorialisation. Lost loved ones were just that, lost. They had moved on to an ineffable realm, remote from our earthly concerns, but this loss would only ever be temporary. Grieving family members and parted lovers would be reunited one day in Paradise.

Death also became cleaner in the nineteenth century. While it never achieved the level of sanitisation we associate with the modern American funeral industry (with its caskets instead of coffins and heavily made-up "loved ones" displayed like wax sculptures), there was a concerted effort on the behalf of clergy, officials and the burgeoning funeral industry to reframe mortality in a more salubrious manner. Burials moved out of city centre churchyards and into tranquil, pastoral cemeteries. Mass-manufactured funeral goods — including ready-made mourning garb, stationary and even mourning tea sets — transformed death into a commercial enterprise (Frisby 46). Judith Pike notes that the advent of garden cemeteries and funerary sculptors enabled nineteenth-century Americans to repress the visceral, corporeal aspects of death, to think of it only in emotional and spiritual terms. Alongside new burial practices, technological advancements, such as the 1839 invention of the daguerreotype — which allowed families to capture images of lost loved ones for posterity — and the later development of embalming technologies, further allowed mourners to deny the gruesome physicality of death by preserving an idealised image of the deceased (Pike 172). Poe's vengeful revenants, beautiful dead women reduced to madness and fury by the oppressive darkness of the grave, challenge the sanitisation of death, the fetishisation of the peaceful porcelain corpse. Moreover, the gore and viscera that attend such resurrections are redolent of the swamp, a reminder of the mad irrational mire upon which our ostensibly civilised society rests.

***

After I said goodbye to Chris and left the Poe Museum, I wandered through the Shockoe Bottom neighbourhood towards where the city's canals feed into the James River. Poe's workplace, the offices of the *Southern Literary Messenger*, once stood in this area, on the corner of 15th Street and Main. It's long gone, the periodical having ceased publication in 1864. However, it's likely that when Poe was employed by the magazine, in the 1830s, he was able to glance out his window and watch the neighbourhood's primary commercial enterprise as it flourished — busily, monstrously — just a few feet away. Between 1830 and 1865, when the American Civil War came to an end, Shockoe Bottom was the second-largest slave market in the United States. In only thirty years, approximately 350,000 people were bought and sold — torn from their families and communities, reduced to the status of livestock — in the jails and auction houses of Richmond. While slaves were traded in almost every town and city in the American South, Richmond was a particularly important hub for the industry. Slaves purchased here were, more often than not, transported further south, resold in New Orleans and forced into gruelling labour on the sugar and cotton plantations that buttressed that region's thriving economy. However, in contrast to New Orleans, where slave auctions played out as immense public spectacles in the city's most fashionable hotels, in Richmond, the trade was hidden away in a low-lying riverside neighbourhood.

Today, Shockoe Bottom appears even more secluded. Perhaps because I was practically the only person wandering its cobbled streets on an oppressively hot July afternoon, the whole neighbourhood — no more than eight blocks — seemed abandoned. Red-brick buildings whose signage told me that they housed bars and nightclubs seemed utterly desolate. High above my head, the concrete curves of elevated highways and the metal frames of bridges snaked among the rooftops. Shockoe Bottom had something subterranean about it, as if the entire area had been reluctantly reclaimed from the riverbed, as if that river might someday choose to take it back. There is nothing left of the jails and auction houses of the nineteenth century, no structure or mouldering pile of bricks that might speak to the sad history of Shockoe Bottom. The pens where thousands of men, women and children were imprisoned as they awaited sale, the auction rooms where they were displayed on blocks — their limbs, teeth and skin inspected by potential buyers — the businesses that sprang up like little parasites to profits from the trade, they're all gone now. After the Civil War, these buildings became warehouses, dealing in tobacco rather than human lives. Later, the construction of railway lines and highways resulted in layers of dirt and detritus further obscuring the physical markers of Richmond's slave trade. Whatever ruined memorials might have testified to this shameful history were simply buried and later paved over to become car parks.

The memory of the slave trade and its role in Richmond's history exists now in a series of statues, plaques and memorials, erected in recent years to attest to a horrendous moment in US history, a moment that was neither a blip nor an anomaly, but an integral part of the American past. The first enslaved Africans arrived in the lands that would become the United States in 1619, on the shores of Hampton, Virginia, and Black Americans remained enslaved for over two hundred years, until the 1860s. African Americans spent more time in chains than they have since spent free. I followed the Richmond Slave Trail, a historical walk, marked with bronze plaques that guide visitors from the Manchester Docks, where slaves transported from Africa would have first set foot on American soil, across the river to Shockoe Bottom and further inland to the Reconciliation Statue that commemorates the horrors of the Middle Passage and the transatlantic slave trade. For some reason, I walked the trail backwards, moving from the buried markets of Shockoe Bottom, along Mayo Bridge — shuddering with traffic and thick with exhaust fumes — and back towards the docks, where ships offloaded their human cargo. At one point, I thought I had gotten lost. I wandered through a car park, past a water treatment plant and what I took to be an abandoned mill or factory, its windowpanes shattered, its red-brick walls covered in graffiti that appeared to creep upwards, growing along the side of the building like ivy. A few cars crawled past me on the gravel pathway, and I half expected someone to yell at me for trespassing on private property.

Aside from the plaques I encountered sporadically along the trail, I knew I was in the right place when I passed a shrine with a sign that read "The Untold RVA: 11:11 Portal. In honour of Richmond's self-determined ancestors — upon whose shoulders we stand." On one side of the sign stood a large black picture frame, crammed with monochrome

Ancestral monument, Richmond, Virginia

photographs: Black men and women smiling in the bowler hats and high-collared dresses of a century past; tired men in straw hats and work clothes; unreadable images faded by the relentless Southern sun. On the edge of the frame sat a series of statues and ornaments: Rotund women dressed in white head scarves, small children playing with drums. Flowers and beads decorated the case. Rusted tools, nails and stones were scattered on the bottom ledge. Below that, a wire grill — bearing the words "We give thanks here with fruits + flowers + candles" — was filled with painted pebbles and burnt-out candles. On the opposite side of the sign, there was a framed list of instructions, explaining how to activate ancestral blessings. I later learned that this was just one of several markers placed around Richmond by the organisation Untold RVA in an attempt to educate both locals and tourists about the city's Black history. There was something profound and meaningful in this little monument, a more intimate history of loss and separation than could ever be conveyed by civic plaques. The small personal objects spoke to unbreakable affective bonds, to memories passed on over generations.

Later that day, I found myself wandering through another car park — Richmond is rife with them. Beyond the cracked concrete, a vast carpet of grass stretched out peacefully, undisturbed. It was ringed by a fence, an ironwork boundary that no one crossed. A gate swung open on one side, and I had already walked through by the time I realised that I was standing in a graveyard. The little green pasture was a graveyard and so was the car park lined with rows and rows of unassuming hatchbacks, hulking pickups and cumbersome SUVs. The innocuous little patch of green had, at one time, been designated as Richmond's "Burial Ground for Negroes". Operational between the 1700s and the early part of the nineteenth century, the site had been the final resting place of both free and enslaved people of colour. The land set aside for this burial ground was poor, unsuitable for construction and prone to flooding. When free people of colour petitioned for a new burying place in the 1810s, they complained that after heavy rains, coffins were regularly carried away by the current of the Shockoe stream. Today, the burial ground is invisible. Like many of the relics that should testify to Richmond's historical entanglement with the slave trade, it was paved over and forgotten for well over a century.

The burial ground, because it held Black bodies, was functionally invisible. Its boundaries were never officially recorded. It appears on only two contemporary maps and garnered scant mention in a few books from the period. Significant portions of what many historians now believe to be America's largest African burial ground lie beneath the north- and southbound lanes of Interstate 95. Every day, an indifferent procession of lorries and cars passes over these forgotten graves. Over the course of a century and a half, the site housed the Richmond City Jail, a dog pound and a car park. In 2011, a section of the burial ground was dug out from beneath the concrete. Part of the car park was removed and replaced with the tranquil green memorial in which I now stood.

On one edge of the plot, just bordering a rich thicket where bright fuchsia flowers and withered berries wrapped around tree trunks, a painting was affixed to a series of wooden panels. The words "African Burial Ground" were bordered by a thick chain. Above the writing, coffins were shown stacked, lying atop one another — top to bottom — a honey-combed latticework of death. In one coffin, a Black body was folded in upon itself, arms clasped close to a skeletal chest. A smaller body, that of a tiny infant, clung to the waist. A halo hovered overhead. In other coffins, skeletons held each other close or vanished into the darkness of rotting earth. The coffins, piled in neat rows, recalled nineteenth-century engravings of slave ships packed with bodies, human chattel stuffed into every nook and cranny. On stone markers, wilted flowers crumbled in the afternoon sun and small Pan-African flags peaked out from piles of pebbles. One stone commemorated "the Hero Gabriel", a reference to the leader of a planned slave revolt that was betrayed and ultimately crushed by the state militia. Gabriel was hanged close to the burial ground, and according to one sign, blanched and faded by the sun, the stones that formed the gallows platform were later used in the construction of a nearby overpass.

The burial ground is an uncertain, liminal space. It speaks of a past that has been obliterated, paved over and forgotten, and a future that has yet to be written. Local officials have been engaged in heated debates about the site. At one point in the 2010s, plans were afoot to develop the area bordering the burial ground into a baseball stadium and commercial complex. While this proposal was eventually overturned, the city of Richmond remains

Offerings in the African Burial Ground, Richmond, Virginia

unsure of how to memorialise its shameful past, and so the burial ground remains, largely obscured by highways and car parks, covered over with centuries of dirt, brick and concrete. The only visible reminder that this was ever a cemetery in which the city's Black population, both free and enslaved, mourned its dead is a single, striking patch of greenery that interrupts the seemingly endless flow of multi-lane highways.

The distinct environmental, historical and literary themes that tied together my time in Richmond — the uncanny revivifying powers of the swamp, Poe's vengeful undead brides and the burial ground forgotten for centuries — are powerfully, inextricably interconnected strands of the American story. All three speak of a desire to forget, to bury some troubling facet of ourselves or our history in the soft, inviting soil of some remote forest or swampland. The refusal of history's violence and our own cruelty is a key component of the human narrative. We want to believe that we are always moving forward, away from the horrors of the past. Crucially, in the American context, such acts of burial and repression commonly express a desire to forget a history characterised by slavery, racial violence and systemic disenfranchisement. The nation wants to believe that the events of the past have been ameliorated by the forward march of time, grasping vaguely towards what sociologist Victor Ray terms "the narcotic mythology of America's racial innocence and steady progress". Yet, in true Gothic style, such horrors can never rest. They drag themselves up from the grave; they shatter the crumbling, weed-strewn concrete of anonymous car parks; they return from the sludgy depths of the swamp to confront us with our own evil.

Eatonville, Florida

On the afternoon of 3 July, I boarded a train for Jacksonville, Florida, a short stopover on a journey that would bring me even further down into the Deep South. The train was three hours late. As I queued at the ticket counter, a ruddy-faced man in wraparound sunglasses berated the ticket agent for the delay, as if this young woman were somehow responsible for the sluggish Southern transit system. "We're supposed to be the best country in the world," he snarled, "and we can't even make the trains run on time." I would soon learn, as I travelled further from the densely populated Northeast into the Deep South and the far West, that whatever makes the United States "the best" in the minds of its citizens (or *some* of its citizens), it certainly isn't the transit system, which outside of large cities and occasional cross-country lines is practically non-existent. People like my fellow commuter in his firmly secured shades might express a belief in American superiority, but I could never locate a real-world correlative to that ardent faith. In its neglected transit networks, I felt I could detect an essential callousness, an indifference towards or even a contempt for its citizens that characterises much of the American experience. If you can afford to buy and maintain a car, if you are healthy enough or young enough to drive without an impediment, you are golden. You can zoom down those vast open highways that television and Hollywood cinema have taught us all to regard as the ultimate symbol of freedom. However, if you are poor, disabled or otherwise incapable of assuming responsibility for your own transport, you are on your own. In Ireland, I'd always felt that the failure of our public infrastructure was largely due to a lack of funding, governmental incompetence and, of course, corruption. But in the US, it seemed like a product of contempt. America loves a success story; America loves a strong, self-motivated individual, but it has nothing but disdain for the poor and vulnerable, who it seems to regard as a needy homogenous mass.

When the train finally pulled into the Richmond Station, hours late and without any kind of explanation for the delay, passengers shuffled aboard. Most were families, laden down with young children, picnic coolers and pillows — they were in it for the long haul. It was the evening before Independence Day, and it seemed as though everyone else on the train was travelling to spend the holiday with friends and family. I was the only rootless, friendless voyager, travelling not to join in barbeques and eat grill-blackened hotdogs as roman candles exploded over pitch-black summer lakes, but to delve further into the dark heart of the South.

I passed a single night in Jacksonville, falling asleep early in a rented room and waking precisely at midnight to the sound of fireworks popping overhead, brilliant fronds of colour blazing in the heavy Southern night. The next morning, I boarded one of the innumerable buses that travel

Spanish moss in Jacksonville, Florida

daily between Jacksonville and Orlando, before taking an Uber the remaining six miles to my destination. Most of my fellow travellers were weary locals, heading further south for work or family. However, just before the bus pulled out of the station, a group of young German tourists piled into the seats behind me. They were all, each one, startlingly blond and tan and healthy. They passed the entire journey shouting across the aisle at one another, passing beers back and forth when they felt the driver wasn't looking. By the time the bus slithered along a curved off-ramp and plunged into the dense forest of electronic billboards, hotel chains and outlet malls that signalled our arrival in Orlando, the raucous Germans had fallen asleep. At one point, I thought I glimpsed the rounded tops of Ferris wheels and the peaks of roller-coasters cresting over the highways. We were in Disney country after all.

Eatonville was intensely, overwhelmingly green. Palm trees and palmetto plants lined every street. Longleaf pine trees brushed the sky. Brilliant pink and purple flowers, interlaced with tenacious vines, wound themselves through the gaps in chain-link fences. In the grass yards of wood-panelled bungalows, sturdy oaks dripped with spidery strands of Spanish moss, and pink oleanders bloomed on hedgerows. Along every roadside, a veritable jungle of fecund plant life exploded from ditches; snakes slithered in the undergrowth. A pale-yellow water tower emblazoned with the town's name rose above the roofs and treetops. In every bush and thicket, choruses of cicadas hummed, a noisy, persistent drone.

The overpass, part of the I-4, which bisected the town's main road, was adorned with a sign that read, "Historic Eatonville — The Town that Freedom Built." "Freedom" tends to be a fairly ubiquitous word in the US. Along with its synonyms "liberty" and "independence", it graces national holidays, local festivals, the sides of buildings and billboards advertising shopping centres. In Eatonville, however, the allusions to "freedom" etched on road signs, commemorative plaques and municipal buildings signify something more substantial. The small town, which has since been subsumed within the sprawling Orlando suburbs, was founded in 1887 by emancipated slaves who had migrated to the wild "frontier" region of Central Florida in the first decades after abolition. That year, twenty-seven African American men signed a charter of incorporation, transforming what had been a small Black settlement adjacent to the town of Maitland into Eatonville, named for the White landowner who helped the town's founders acquire some of the land on which the community still stands. Two years later, the town issued a call welcoming Black families seeking to escape the violence and discrimination of the Jim Crow South. The local newspaper, the *Eatonville Speaker*, lauded the town as "all colored, and NOT A WHITE FAMILY in the whole city".

In this way, Eatonville became, with much pride and perseverance, the first incorporated Black town in the United States. The process by which the town developed into a self-sufficient community is particularly impressive when one considers how, in the US, segregation and housing inequality are woven into the nation's legal framework. As the scholar Richard Rothstein explains, the racial segregation that endures even into the twenty-first century "is not the unintended consequence of individual choices and of otherwise well-meaning law or regulation but of unhidden public policy that explicitly segregated every metropolitan area in the United States". Discriminatory policies embedded in legislation, restrictive covenants, selective lending and ingrained practices such as redlining have ensured that not only are historically Black communities underfunded, they are often literally severed from their more affluent, usually White, neighbours by impassable multi-lane highways, wide boulevards and a general lack of reliable public transportation. In Jacksonville, the majority-Black neighbourhood I stayed in had been designated a food desert because it didn't have a single grocery store in walking distance. This was a pattern I had noticed throughout my travels along the East Coast and which I would see replicated across the length and breadth of the nation: poorer communities often lacked the most basic amenities necessary to sustain life and raise healthy families. In neighbourhoods whose residents were neither White nor wealthy, you might find a few scattered fast-food restaurants, perhaps the occasional liquor store where, along with a six-pack of beer and a few scratch cards, you could also pick up a bag of potato chips and other starchy snacks, but there was never a simple shop where you could buy bread, vegetables or dairy products that weren't infused with nauseating neon hues.

Eatonville struggled into being despite policies of this kind, and on more than one occasion faced the prospect of almost total obliteration by racist municipal orders and zoning laws. However, if Eatonville is known by outsiders, it is not for its historical position, but for its folklore. The town is a repository of stories, a lively cauldron seething with tall tales. In Eatonville, wily animals — Br'er Rabbit along with his Fox and Gator brethren — roam the orange groves and swamplands, playing tricks and outwitting one another in games that seem at once frivolous and laden with meaning. God and the Devil bicker, trying to one-up each other, competing for souls and power. It was here, amid the high grasses of Central Florida that the Devil asked God for a Christmas gift and God told the Devil to "take the East Coast", allowing the prince of darkness to huff and puff his storms all the way up the Florida Peninsula. It was here too that the folk hero John defeated "Ole Massa", or Old Master, winning prestige or wealth and always humiliating his master in the process. Walk in the graveyards of Eatonville under cover of darkness and you might encounter Raw Head — a two-headed doctor, or conjure man, who possesses the power of Moses and whose bald head sweats blood. In the same burial grounds, beneath a phalanx of gnarled oak hung with spectral swathes of moss, you could run into High Walker, another powerful magic worker, who has the ability to imbue desiccated skeletons with life, commanding the clacking, clattering carcasses with the words "Rise up bloody bones and shake yo'self."

These stories, if they flew far beyond the town limits of Eatonville, settling in the homes and hearts of readers thousands of miles away, were disseminated largely thanks to the efforts of anthropologist, author and (occasional) hoodoo priestess Zora Neale Hurston. Hurston, who was born in Notasulga, Alabama, at the end of the nineteenth century, moved to Eatonville with her family when she was around three years old, and from then on claimed both the town and its rich culture of storytelling as her own. As a child, she would linger by the porch of Joe Clarke's store, trying to imbibe the outlandish tales passed between the local men who wiled away their days beneath the shade of its wooden beams. The stories she heard there, in the course of what she described as "lying sessions", crystallised her view of the world as essentially animated by wonder and mystery.

She would later recall that when she eavesdropped on these vivid folktales, "God, Devil, Brer Rabbit, Brer Fox, Sis Cat, Brer Bear, Lion, Tiger, Buzzard, and all the wood folk walked and talked like natural men" (quoted in Boyd 46). The stories Hurston treasured as a little girl often served an explanatory function, elaborating on how different religious sects came to be, how Black people acquired their colour, how cats and dogs came to despise one another, how the alligator came to have such a wide grin. Other stories were simply humorous tales — a man drowns in a flood, and once he reaches heaven, makes the mistake of complaining about the deluge to none other than Noah himself. Still others were expressions of rebellion. These popular tales featured an archetypal folk hero, sometimes named John, other times named Jack and generally thought to be embodied in the magical plant High John the Conqueror. In one story, John exploits Ole Massa's greed and tricks his oppressor into drowning himself in a river. While John generally manages to manipulate situations to his liking — he is, after all, a consummate trickster — Bruce Dickson, Jr observes that these particular yarns "were remarkably devoid of fantasy and that John, himself, was only a little larger than life" (422). Likewise, John was a "multidimensional character", who could be put to a wide range of different uses; he could be a hero or a villain, a victor or a clown. Yet, in every case, regardless of John's eventual fate, such stories serve as acts of resistance in which the entire community comes together to challenge the power of racist political and economic systems, but also to laugh and joke and find joy even in the most difficult of times.

Some of the most interesting stories shared on the porches of Eatonville feature the Devil as a central character. Sometimes he is a villain, a foil for the hero John, who beats him in a test of wits or strength in order to win a lucrative prize. In other tales, the Devil is himself a trickster, outsmarting God. Most intriguingly, the Devil is rarely found sweltering amid the fires of hell. In Black folklore, he often appears as neighbour, a man who lives down the street in his own house, frequently with a wife and children. Hurston would later explain that in African American folk traditions the Devil is "not the terror that he is in European folk-lore", but is instead re-imagined as a more mischievous figure (*Mules* 248). In this way, Hurston elaborates, the Devil can be understood as an "extension" of the Black storyteller "while God is the supposedly impregnable white masters, who are nevertheless defeated by the Negroes". In Eatonville, Hurston explains, "even the Bible was made over to suit our imagination" (*Mules* 3).

Eatonville and its neighbouring communities are scattered across a series of lakes that saturate the landscape like the remnants of some great flood. On my first morning in Eatonville, I walked to Maitland, the next town over. I would later be told that the distance between the two communities is so meagre that if you were standing on Eatonville's main street, you would simply need to "breathe twice and take a left and breathe one more time you'd be in Maitland". I went as far as Lake Lily, a tranquil body of water covered over by a thick mantle of water lilies and surrounded by wooden walkways that traversed thick, sticky patches of marshland. Clouds of white ibises and boisterous assemblies of herons congregated on the shore. I stopped briefly to chat with an elderly man who was diligently pushing a geriatric Chihuahua in a pram. A small electric fan clipped to the edge of the basinet wafted a continuous stream of cold air in the animal's sweet, wizened little face. "She's goin' on fourteen years," the man explained, adjusting the pram's shade so I could steal a better look.

***

That evening, as I walked to the offices of the Association to Preserve the Eatonville Community, the colour drained from the sky. The bright blue firmament that during the day seemed to promise infinite warmth and comfort had turned an ominous steel grey. Electricity sang in the powerlines above my head, but it also hummed in the air around me. Thunder rumbled far off in the distance, a low stertorous groan.

In the association's blissfully air-conditioned boardroom, which sits on top of Eatonville's Zora Neale Hurston National Museum of Fine Arts, I met with Angela. A founding member of the Association to Preserve the Eatonville Community, and a driving force behind the town's cultural renaissance, Angela is a soft-spoken older woman with a sharp, somewhat intimidating, intellect. She wore a white linen scarf neatly tucked about her head and a light, summery pantsuit. Angela's family have lived in Eatonville since the 1930s. Her father helped to build the town's first elementary school, and her mother studied under the great African American philosopher W.E.B. Du Bois. Each member of the family excelled in education, dedicating themselves to public life and community work. Even now, Angela's deep, abiding love for her community shone through in every word and gesture.

Angela was welcoming despite her natural reserve. We chatted for a while in the boardroom, but she soon suggested we go for dinner instead. We drove to an Indian restaurant a few towns over, in an area that was rapidly gentrifying. The identical black awnings that hung from the façades of identical restaurants testified to the speed at which the town was becoming both homogenised and unliveable for its residents. "You have to fight gentrification," Angela explained. "They can only gentrify land if they can take it." Eatonville, it seems, was battling similar incursions and had been ever since the town was founded. Outside development companies eye its ample tracts of land while municipal bodies envision the little town transformed into a five-lane highway, an endless stream of traffic belching fumes as tourists tear through on their way to Disney Land or Universal Studios.

Over our meal, Angela told me about the history of Eatonville, which she said grew out of "the failed Reconstruction era". Immediately after the Civil War, laws were implemented to protect newly emancipated Black Southerners, including the promise of freedom from discrimination for all, regardless of race, ethnicity or previous condition of servitude. However, these protections were swiftly and systematically dismantled. Following the 1876 election of Rutherford B. Hayes as president and the concomitant withdrawal of federal troops — previously the guarantors of Black freedom — the infrastructure of segregation began to be assembled in the South. Within a few short years, the Supreme Court decision Plessy vs. Fergusson formalised the dictum of "separate but equal" and paved the way for segregation in everything from public transport and schools to restaurants and theatres. The town of Eatonville grew in response to the entrenchment of segregation, an all-Black community that could exist outside of racial hierarchies and discriminatory structures.

In the introduction to her 1935 book *Mules and Men*, over half of which is comprised of folktales gathered in and around Eatonville, Hurston describes her hometown as "the city of five lakes, three croquet courts, three hundred brown skins, three hundred good swimmers, plenty of guavas, two schools, and no jail-house"(4). Growing up in the heart of a small Black community, as a child Hurston was entirely unaware of the racism that permeated the segregated South, and it was not until she later moved to the larger city of Jacksonville that she was exposed to such forms of prejudice. She later recalled that "Jacksonville made me know that I was a little colored girl" (quoted in Boyd 60). "Eatonville," Angela observed, "was like a cocoon." Hurston's childhood was far from idyllic, but in that tiny, fledgling community, she could see — as biographer Valerie Boyd explains — clear evidence of "black achievement"(60).

She could look to the town hall and see Black men writing the laws that governed the community. She could see Black women running schools and presiding over the town's spiritual life. Her classmates and teachers were all Black, as were her neighbours and friends. Hurston grew into a staunch individualist because her earliest memories were coloured by a world in which race could not fetter personal ambition.

Despite eventually moving north to pursue her education, Hurston never managed to shake off the dust of that Florida swamp town. In her autobiography, *Dust Tracks on a Road*, published in 1942, she claims to have retained "the map of Dixie on my tongue". When she was later asked to collect African American folktales for the Federal Writers' Project — an initiative created during the Great Depression to provide work for unemployed writers — Hurston returned to Eatonville because it was there that mythic figures like John and Ole Massa, High Walker, Br'er Fox and Br'er Rabbit, even the Devil himself, seemed most real.

Such folktales bear within themselves the marks of history, speaking to both sorrow and joy. They carry hopes and express fears; they contain a mischievous spirit and the spark of revolution. As Henry Louis Gates, Jr writes in a recent anthology of African American folktales, stories of this kind are important because they have succeeded in "preserving the unique traces of a cultural legacy that reached back through enslavement to Africa". For many enslaved peoples and their descendants, folklore, songs and oral literature became a survival strategy, kindling hope by allowing both the storyteller and their listeners to imagine a different word, to dream up other ways of being. Black folk traditions encompass a range of diverse narratives and motifs: from flying Africans who break free of their New World chains and soar back across the ocean, to witches and "Boo Hags" who slip out of their skin by night, crawling down chimneys and slipping through keyholes to torment their sleeping victims.

That peculiarly Southern motif of burial refused also manifests in a startling array of guises in African American folklore. However, in tales collected by Hurston and other folklorists, the essence of this motif is transformed. Unlike Poe's tales of terror, Gothic nightmares where that which was once consigned to the grave returns to wreck a terrible vengeance, the stories Hurston gathered in and around Eatonville are more playful, even mischievous in their imagined resurrections. As Gates and folklore scholar Maria Tartar elucidate in a co-authored essay, in African American folklore "long-dead ancestors, spouses, friends, and foes are animated in the nocturnal hours". However, they are rarely malignant, "alarming more than harming" shocked witnesses.

In the story of High Walker and Bloody Bones, for instance, a conjure man possesses the power to raise the bones of the dead. He walks through graveyards, directing the scattered remains to rise from the earth, come together and shake themselves. High Walker takes pleasure in having dominion over the dead, until one set of bloody bones tricks him into making a bet with his master that ultimately results in the hoodoo man's death. There is horror in the story — the bloody bones are the remains of a man who sold his soul to the Devil — but also humour, as the skeleton promises High Walker that his smart mouth will be his undoing. In the grand tradition of the folktale, this warning comes to fruition.

Similarly, in her portrayals of the swamplands around Eatonville, Hurston conjures a vital, fairy-tale world filled with danger but enlivened by wonder and magic. Where White Southerners imagined the swamp as a foul crucible, churning deadly pestilences and generating streams of polluted air, their Black neighbours often conceived of its dank, silent waters and gloomy, cypress-shaded depths as a sanctuary. From the late seventeenth century until the abolition of slavery almost two centuries later, runaway slaves escaped into the dense tangle of Virginia's Great Dismal Swamp, forming maroon enclaves on its remote islands. Other escapees may have simply hidden temporarily in swamps as they travelled north. In Hurston's most famous novel, 1937's *Their Eyes Were Watching God*, an elderly woman called Nanny describes how, after being raped and impregnated by her master, she fled with her infant child into a sodden, snake-infested swamp. The swamp is an undeniably terrifying place for Nanny and her baby. She describes the environment as something living, the trees and plants imbued with a terrible sentience: "De noise uh de owls skeered me; de limbs of dem cypress trees took to crawlin' and movin' round after dark" (18). However, Nanny knows that what awaits her back at the plantation is far more terrible than the rattlesnakes and the dense, treacherous wetlands. Indeed, the swamp, despite its horrors, also provides some care and succour for Nanny and her baby girl, Leafy, whom she swaddles in moss and cradles in the limbs of a tree.

In *Dust Tracks on a Road*, Hurston writes of the swamps that surrounded Eatonville and its neighbour Maitland in a way that evokes both wonder and terror. "The terrain," she notes, "swarmed with the deadly diamond-back rattlesnake" and "huge, centuries-old bull alligators bellowed their challenge from the uninhabited shores of lakes" (12). When the town of Maitland was hewn from swampland at the end of the nineteenth century, it was, Hurston alleges, necessary to carry a lantern at night "to avoid stumbling over these immense reptiles" in the newly laid streets (12). In Eatonville, likewise, "bears and alligators raided hog-pens" and "wild cats fought with dogs in people's yards"

(34). Yet, for all the dangers posed by these terrible beasts, there is a magic to Hurston's portrayal of a town carved out of the wild swamp. Her tone remains light and jovial, so the rattlesnakes and alligators that slither or crawl from the deep mire to materialise in the streets of Eatonville recall nothing so much as their folkloric counterparts, mythic animals like Br'er Fox, Br'er Gator and Br'er Dog.

For many White authors writing at the end of the nineteenth and the beginning of the twentieth centuries, the swamp was a source of disease, its rich mud and slimy, effluvial waters embodying the unruly defiance of nature. In Hurston's work, though, the swamp is a powerful revitalising force. Anthony Wilson notes how in Hurston's 1934 debut novel, *Jonah's Gourd Vine* — a loosely fictionalised account of her parents' migration to Eatonville from Alabama — the swamp functions as a vital nucleus of Black resistance. Wilson explains that in the novel, "Hurston contrasts the swamp, and the spiritual community it enables and preserves, not with white civilization, as tradition would dictate, but with African American progress" (138). In an age of rapid modernisation and migration, as many African Americans were moving — both geographically and culturally — away from their Southern roots, Hurston portrays the swamp as an increasingly endangered, yet eternally generative, reserve of Black tradition and resistance.

Resistance and the preservation of Black culture are central to Zora Neale Hurston's literary and anthropological work. During our conversation, Angela described how, in her work as a folklorist, Hurston would repeat the stories she heard over and over again to ensure that she had them right. Likewise, she often stressed in her writing that Black Americans, although sold into slavery on a distant continent, were never passive victims, broken by the dehumanising system that held them. Rather, they retained the religious beliefs, mythic archetypes and cultural practices that endured the Middle Passage alongside them. In a 1929 letter to her mentor Franz Boas, Hurston expressed her conviction that the conversion of African slaves to Christianity was never fully realised and that Black Americans held close to the spiritual systems of their ancestors: "Is it safe for me to say that baptism is an extension of water worship as a part of pantheism just as the sacrament is an extension of cannibalism? Isn't the use of candles in the Catholic church a relic of fire worship?" (Quoted in Young 14).

Angela went on to tell me that it was this spirit of resistance that engendered Eatonville's largest cultural event, the ZORA! Festival. Organised in five-year cycles, with a unique theme guiding each year, the festival honours Hurston as one of the most important American writers of the twentieth century, while also celebrating Black art and culture. Thousands of visitors attend the festival each year to enjoy public talks, museum and gallery exhibitions and musical performances. Roads are closed and the streets come alive with a profusion of stalls and booths selling crafts and serving food. Angela explained that the festival emerged out of Eatonville's ongoing struggle for survival. The community was split in two when the town was bisected by a flyover in the 1960s, and it was threatened with almost complete obliteration in the late 1980s when the state began to formulate plans to turn its main street — Kennedy Boulevard — into a five-lane highway. If the plan had come to fruition, the highway would have hollowed out the soul of this strong, vibrant community. Angela is, and was, acutely aware of the devastating impact this project would have had on the town, and characterises the proposed development of the highway as an extension of a colonialist mentality: "Eatonville is the largest undeveloped parcel of land in Orange County. And if you are familiar with what the colonial experience is, or what the imperialistic system is, in order for you to develop you have to build infrastructure, and the infrastructure necessitates to improve the quote-unquote improved roads." This kind of infrastructure, Angela explained, is called a "community-busting highway". Rather than bringing any kind of material or economic benefits to Eatonville, a road of this kind would have simply torn the town in half, destroyed the municipal park and clogged the centre with more than ten thousand additional cars each day.

Unfortunately, the practice of running dangerous, polluting highways through Black neighbourhoods, often for the specific purpose of destroying them — physically and psychologically — is by now well documented. Similarly, federal interstate highways were often used to buttress segregation, creating a seemingly insurmountable barrier between affluent White neighbourhoods and their impoverished Black equivalents. "So at any rate," Angela continued, "the decision-makers and opinion shapers had never heard of Zora Neale Hurston. For them, Eatonville was just a little something that can be dispatched." Yet Angela and her Eatonville neighbours refused to let their community be destroyed in this way. The festival they established, and which continues to this day, was created as part of a wider resistance to the proposed expansion of Kennedy Boulevard. Like the stories, songs, jokes and folktales Hurston collected, the festival exemplifies how art and literature can become powerful tools in the fight against oppression.

After a year spent collecting folklore in Eatonville, Hurston headed west, to New Orleans. She was drawn to New Orleans because this eclectic city of hanging baskets and wrought iron balconies, this precarious, flood-prone metropolis hugging the banks of the Mississippi, has long been considered the "hoodoo capital of America" (*Mules*

183). I was pulled to New Orleans for much the same reason. In my mind, the Crescent City thrummed with magic and mystery. An intoxicating admixture of French, Spanish, African and Caribbean cultural strains, New Orleans is the city of carnival, the bacchanalia of Mardi Gras encapsulated in the ubiquitous phrase, "*Laissez les bons temps rouler*" (let the good times roll). It is also the city of the dead — its cemeteries lined with rows and rows of elaborate mausoleums — and the city of Voodoo, replete with awesome tales of the great priestess Marie Laveau and her powerful enchantments. Like Hurston, I left Eatonville to trace a route that brought me from the rural swamplands of Bloody Bones and High Walker to the chaotic pageantry of New Orleans.

***

A few miles outside of Tallahassee, the Greyhound bus on which I was travelling joined US Route 98 as it meandered west along the Gulf of Mexico. I was leaving Eatonville for Mobile, Alabama, and going from there on to New Orleans. Exiting highways bounded on all sides with towering billboards — prolife billboards, anti-immigrant billboards, billboards advertising personal injury lawyers and local gun shows — we found ourselves travelling through seaside towns like Panama City, Destin, Miramar and the curiously named Mary Esther. Each town we passed through was identically pastel-hued. Traffic moved at a lazy crawl through main streets packed with holidaymakers eating ice-cream cones and clustering outside seafood grills. Shops decorated with tropical motifs sold tie-dyed swimsuits, body boards, goggles and flippers. Coral-coloured stalls dispensed candy and fudge. Children pointed and cried, imploring red-faced parents for inflatable turtles and colourful sand pails.

Highrise buildings towered above white sandy beaches, their balconies facing the azure sea. We passed by water parks and fairgrounds where blond, freckled children shrieked on Tilt-A-Whirls. Motorboats gleamed in commercial lots that sold nothing but motorboats. This was not the South I had known. In Jacksonville and Eatonville, rows of palm trees were usually interspersed with ancient, gnarled oaks draped in a gauzy film of Spanish moss. In such cities, insects trilled in thick, vine-covered bushes and lizards darted from one hiding place to another. These beach towns — Emerald Beach, Pelican Beach, Gulf Beach — seemed so clean, so pristine. The beaches were as white and pure as new snow. The animal noise and thick secretive foliage I had come to associate with this part of the country had been supplanted by a sparse, carefully cultivated tropical island.

After half a day curled up on sticky polyester bus seats listening to the college kids behind me sharing stories of drunken adventures, we finally crossed the vivid blue expanse of Mobile Bay and saw the city rise up out of the flat green wetlands. In the distance, its skyscrapers gleamed like fractured shards of crystal.

In Mobile, I spent two nights sleeping in a small wooden bungalow on Church Street — where the immense thunderstorms that arrived each afternoon on their journey north from the Gulf of Mexico shuddered the very bones of the fragile little house — then departed for New Orleans on yet another early morning bus. When I arrived at the Mobile Greyhound station, sometime around 4:00am, I found it already crowded with people. A convenience store was open and selling hot food. Families crowded around boxes of fried chicken or shared soggy hamburgers. Single travellers dozed using backpacks for pillows. By the door, waiting for the conductor to announce their departure, a young blonde woman stood

Cemetery in Mobile, Alabama

holding on to two small children. The whole family, all three of them, looked utterly worn down. The children wore dirty, ill-fitting clothes that were torn and stretched around the neck and arms. The youngest child, a little girl, sobbed quietly, her tears forging a glistening path down her grimy face.

When I was kid, our house contained very little. We slowly accumulated furniture, mostly gathered from auctions of second-hand goods that my grandmother assiduously attended. She found two beds, a dresser and some end tables in that way. Our living room, which was covered with squishy, chequered linoleum that always seemed as if it were about to swallow my small, stockinged feet whole, consisted for a time of nothing but an old couch and a TV set placed on top of a fridge. For a long time, we didn't have a washing machine, a telephone or a shower. My mother had to wrestle me into the bathroom one a week to wash my hair using a pink rubber hose attached to the sink. Naturally, we didn't have a car, but back then, before the Irish economy blossomed in the late 1990s, that wasn't so unusual. My mother and I took the bus everywhere: to the seaside on summer afternoons, into Cork City to buy school supplies, rattling down the roads of West Cork to visit relatives.

Today, I still take the bus a lot. Growing up without a car, I never learned to drive. With increased car ownership, the services in Ireland are getting worse, but you will still encounter a broad spectrum of people on the bus. When I return to my childhood home at weekends to visit my mother, I encounter teachers, nurses, shop assistants and call centre workers on my regular route. In the US, bus stations speak to the growing fissure that continues to split the nation ever more deeply along the lines of race and class. Frequently located in the most impoverished sections of cities, bus terminals here are like holding-pens for the poor, the disabled, drug addicts, the mentally ill — all those people for whom the American dream was an elusive phantom, a wavering spectre in the night.

Part of the problem in the US, of course, is distance. Travelling between major cities in Ireland might take two or three hours, but in America, overland journeys might take days. Anyone who had the choice would drive their own car or, with the growing number of low-cost airlines, fly. During my time in the US, I took two domestic flights, and it felt like I had stumbled into another world. Everyone was so middle class, so clean and healthy. The other part of the problem is that much of the infrastructure in the US, which was developed in the post-World War II period, was built with car owners in mind. The structures necessary to support efficient transit systems simply don't exist, and so, those who need to rely on public transportation are left behind.

New Orleans, Louisiana

On my first day in New Orleans, I spent an hour trapped in the famous Café Du Monde. Sitting at the far end of the city's French Market, the café is in a large, high-ceilinged hall that extends onto the street with white-and-green awnings shading a cluster of outdoor tables and chairs. Inside, chairs click loudly against tiled floors and customers file past the counter, ordering from a menu that has changed little over the course of almost two centuries: black coffee, café au lait, beignets, orange juice. Glass panels provide an unimpeded of view of staff in papery white hats folding dough and deep frying the mountains of pastry that are consumed on the premises every day.

The sky was already beginning to crack open as I walked down St Peter Street and turned onto Decatur. The afternoon thunderstorms were beginning again, the overpowering heat that weighed upon the early part of the day giving way to torrents of hard, hot rain. Once inside, I settled down with a saucer of beignets — fried choux pastry — piled high with powdered sugar and a café au lait served in a spongy Styrofoam cup. Famously, the coffee here is infused with chicory, and this creates a rich, albeit somewhat bitter, flavour. The thunderclaps grew louder, and the rain became heavier, falling in thick sheets, sharp and swift, like a knife slicing air. A jazz band that had been playing outside on the street hurried into the café, struggling to keep their instruments dry. Shaking off the drops of rain that still clung to them, the band began to play, loudly, joyfully, drowning out the thunder with crashing cymbals and raucous trumpets. Customers stood up, swaying to the music and clapping along in time. Some took out phones and began to film. When the rain eased and the heavy clouds began to dissipate, the band members moved from table to table, collecting tips in their hats.

Jazz is the beating heart of New Orleans, the pulsing rhythm that drives the city. Brassy notes circulate on street corners; in bars across the Vieux Carré, piano keys pound out jerky, staccato tunes. Tourists pass up and down the neon-soaked pavements of Bourbon Street, brightly coloured cocktails in hand, listening to melodious strains of clarinets and trumpets waft through the air.

Like so much of what makes New Orleans unique, jazz has its roots in the traditions of the city's African diaspora. The first slave ships to dock in New Orleans brought captives from Benin, but throughout the period of initial French control of the region, the majority of enslaved peoples were brought from Senegambia. From these initial arrivals came a style of "melismatic singing and stringed instruments" that were, according to Jerah Johnson, "crucial forerunners of blues and the banjo" (quoted in Vincent and Lindsey 163). Under Spanish rule, many of the slaves imported to New Orleans came from the Congo, and their music was characterised by hand-drummed polyrhythms that would later form the basis for jazz.

For around a hundred years, between the mid-1700s and the 1840s, African music reverberated through the streets of the Vieux Carré. Under the *Code Noir* that governed French colonial territories, slaves were forbidden to work on Sundays or on Catholic holy days. Many gathered in Congo Square, a tree-encircled corner of what is now Louis Armstrong Park, just on the edge of the French Quarter. Seizing a rare opportunity to sing and dance, to renew friendships and even conduct business, they made music from bells, drums, gourds and banjo-style instruments, as well as with violins and tambourines

(Vincent and Lindsey 164). Although these meetings were eventually curtailed as New Orleans became increasingly Americanised following the 1803 sale of Louisiana to the United States, the deep, resonant rhythms of jazz, or what would become jazz, still echoed through the streets, pouring through open doors and cascading from rooftops and high windows.

If jazz is the heart of the city, then Voodoo[1] is its soul. Fragments of this much-maligned and poorly understood religion are scattered across the city. "Haunted history" tours promise to follow in the footsteps of mythical Voodoo priests and priestesses, framing the practice as a supernatural oddity in the vein of the city's legendary ghosts and vampires. Bars and nightclubs bear the grinning skeletal visage of the deity Papa Legba. Tourists can buy "Voodoo doll" kits and shot glasses featuring cartoonish "African fetishes" in the souvenir shops that line Canal Street. There's something almost carnivalesque in how tourists, especially those visiting from other parts of the United States, engage with this carefully packaged version of Louisiana Voodoo. It's almost as if the journey into the deepest part of the Deep South has freed them, at least temporarily, from whatever conventions had previously constrained them. Middle-class mums from the Midwest buy "Voodoo dolls" to bring home to their families and

---

1 Language becomes tricky here. Historians and anthropologists are generally hesitant to use the term "Voodoo" (Newman 2). An Americanised spelling of the Haitian "Vodou" that emerged during the US occupation of that nation (1915–1934), "Voodoo" has acquired negative and wholly racist connotations of sinister magic (Morrow Long, *Spiritual Merchants* 37). However, because there is no other way to clearly distinguish between Haitian Vodou and the Louisiana variety, many writers reluctantly use the word "Voodoo".

friends; Christian college girls delight in rifling through the dressed candles and bagged herbs that crowd the shelves of botánicas. Whatever laws of decorum, conventionality or faith previously governed their lives seem to have been suspended, even inverted, for the length of their holiday.

Yet, while a sensationalised version of Voodoo is often presented to tourists for easy consumption, beneath — perhaps even intertwined with — this colourful simulacrum, a sincere and ardent faith still flourishes in the city. Glimpses can be caught in the *vèvè*, sacred symbols that both represent and invoke deities, drawn on walls across New Orleans, as well as in the scattered offerings — coins, photos, feathers, stones — embedded in the ancestor tree that stands in Congo Square. Even in the shops and museums of the French Quarter, whose bright neon signs act as a beacon for wandering tourists, there are flickers of something more meaningful. Shuffling along the aisles of one overcrowded Voodoo supply shop close to Jackson Square, I caught snippets of a reading taking place in a curtained room off to one corner. A male voice was telling a female client, "Don't be messing with that broke-dick energy." At the counter, a tall Black woman, who wore her hair wrapped in an elaborate headscarf that recalled the colourful *tignons* of the colonial period, stopped me to chat about my hair. "Where'd you get them curls?" she asked. I told her that my naturally curly hair had succumbed to the Southern humidity and was now impossible to control, becoming bigger and frizzier than ever before. She paused upon hearing my accent, and like most Americans, asked with sincere curiosity where I was from. She nodded slowly when I explained that I had come from Ireland and was working on a book. "Come take a look at this," she said, indicating with a gesture that I should come closer. After a few seconds spent rummaging through a drawer, she produced a small card that bore a familiar image: St Patrick, Ireland's patron saint, stood solemnly on a patch of emerald-green grass, a crozier in his hand and a snake under foot. "It's Damballah," she stated, "the serpent spirit. He made the world. His wife is Ayida Wedo, the rainbow." She handed me the card. "Take that home and give it to your mama. He brings peace."

I wasn't surprised to find St Patrick in a Voodoo shop on the mouth of the Mississippi. I'd read about Voodoo, and I was aware of its inherent plasticity, the myriad ways in which it changed shape, adapting itself to different social and religious contexts. This is a survival strategy, and Voodoo is a religion of resistance. Voodoo, despite the Hollywood mythos of sinister rituals and blood sacrifices, is a religion born out of the trauma of the slave trade and the refusal of enslaved Africans to abandon their traditional beliefs. Louisiana Voodoo, or Mississippi Valley Voodoo, is related, through a complex web of diasporic movement and exchange, to both West African Vodun and Haitian Vodou. In centuries past, the Ewe and Fon peoples of the Senegambian region maintained a view of the world as created by either a single God or a pair of Gods who are typically conceived of as distant and remote from their worshippers. These Gods can be neither implored nor commanded. However, a lower pantheon of deities or spirits called *voduwo* are more approachable. The singular form of *voduwo* is *vodu*, and so the term "voodoo" can be traced to a word meaning "spirit". The deities that comprise this more accessible pantheon are worshipped directly — receiving prayers and offerings from the faithful — and they are thought to regularly intervene in human affairs. Closer to the earthly sphere, there are a range of different spirits, including ancestral spirits and the in-dwelling spirits of natural features such as rivers, streams, trees, stones and mountains. To enlist the aid of the spirits, the Fon created charms called *gbo*, which must be "fed" with liquor, oil, mixtures of flour and pepper and even blood in order to maintain their potency. The Yoruba people, also located in Western Africa, worshipped a similarly stratified pantheon of spirits and deities, while the central African Kongo people imagined that such spirits could inhabit objects called *minkisi*, through which they might be put to work by believers.

When members of these diverse African nations were captured and sold into slavery in the Americas, they carried their beautiful, elaborate spiritual systems with them. In Cuba and Brazil, Yoruba slaves brought the seeds of what would become Candomblé and Santería (also known as Regla de Ocha or Lucumí). Louisiana Voodoo and its close cousin Haitian Vodou grew out of an eclectic mixture of Fon, Yoruba and Kongo elements, as patterns of slave importation shifted over time in the French colonial territories. Voodoo, a religion characteristic of the lower Mississippi Valley, has a history analogous to that of other African faiths imported to the New World. It contorted itself to the exigencies of Euro-American Christianity, borrowed elements of Indigenous traditions and, in doing so, was transformed into an essentially syncretic, endlessly dynamic religion. As in Haiti, Africans arriving in Louisiana mapped their existent spiritual universe onto the Catholic faith that awaited them and to which they were forced to convert.

Indeed, Catholicism was an ideal receptacle for the West and Central African faiths arriving on the shores of the New World. Recalling the complex hierarchies of the Fon, Yoruba, Ewe and Kongo peoples, Catholic cosmology is comprised of a single, fundamentally unknowable creator God and an elaborate litany of saints through whose intercession one might receive help and guidance. In this way, the major *loa* (spirits or deities) of both Haitian Vodou and Louisiana Voodoo have been syncretised with a range of Catholic saints. Papa Legba (sometimes Lébat), who serves as the intermediary between humans and other loa, corresponds to Saint Peter, bearer of the keys to Heaven. Erzulie Freda, the loa of love, beauty and riches, is often blended with Our Lady of the Sorrows. Damballah, the serpent, is of course St Patrick, while his wife, Ayida Wedo, is Our Lady of the Immaculate Conception.

When Zora Neale Hurston arrived in New Orleans in the late 1920s, she noted that "Hoodoo, or Voodoo, as pronounced by the whites, is burning with a flame in America, with all the intensity of a suppressed religion. It has its thousands of secret adherents. It adapts itself like Christianity to its locale" (*Mules* 183). For Hurston, Voodoo was a uniquely metamorphic faith, capable of sustaining itself by incorporating elements of its environment, masking its intentions and kindling an indissoluble core of strength in its practitioners. Prior to Emancipation, Louisiana Voodoo, alongside related folk-magic practices (like Conjure) that thrived in other parts of the slaveholding South, functioned as a form of resistance against the abuses of chattel slavery, a means of retaining an essential core of selfhood in the face of overwhelming horror.

In her study of the African American Conjure tradition, Yvonne P. Chireau observes that, for slave owners, the dilemma posed by Black religio-magical practices "lay not in the question of direct efficacy — that is to say whether such practice 'worked' against them — but in the ways that the slaves utilized these beliefs to challenge their authority" (17). Similarly, for many White observers, particularly those who profited from chattel slavery, Voodoo and related practices were associated with the ever-present threat of slave uprising, a fear that became increasingly pronounced after the Haitian Revolution, which began in 1791 with a Vodou ceremony and culminated in the creation of the world's first Black republic.

For a time, though, Voodoo thrived quite openly in New Orleans. In the early part of the nineteenth century, the city was 30 percent White, 34 percent free people of colour, and 36 percent enslaved people (Ward 33). The *Code Noir* that governed the lives of slaves in the French colonies, although reinforcing the brutal racism inherent in the system of chattel slavery, did grant a freedom of movement unknown to their counterparts in Anglo-American parts of the South. The sixty articles that comprised the code regulated everything from marriages and burials to punishments permitted, but it also included the provision that all slaves should be baptised and educated in the Catholic faith. It stipulated that slaves should be fed, clothed and cared for when sick, and it also forbade slaves from working on Sundays and holy days. Additionally, because it was easier to manumit slaves under the *Code Noir*, New Orleans retained a vibrant, free community of colour. Although their movements and activities were still curtailed — they could not vote or marry a White person — free people of colour participated in the life of the city in unique ways: they opened and ran schools, managed businesses, attended social gatherings and could live wherever they chose. This tenuous and heavily circumscribed freedom, along with the intermingling of enslaved and free people of colour, enabled Voodoo to flourish in the city, at least briefly.

Perhaps the pre-eminent symbol of Voodoo's unique hold over New Orleans is Marie Leveau, the legendary priestess. She is everywhere in the city, her shadow cast upon its streets, her name and image adorning shops, restaurants and museums. She is usually portrayed as a light-skinned woman of colour, smiling cryptically, her hair wrapped in an elaborate tignon, a colourful scarf that became a symbol of defiance for Black women during the French colonial period. Statues and paintings bearing her visage crowd every gift shop and spiritual supply store in the city. At the

Island of Salvation Botánica on Claude Avenue, a towering, nine-foot papier-mâché statue of Marie presides over the entryway. Huge and vivid, she resembles nothing so much as a beautiful, elaborately decorated float awaiting the annual Mardi Gras parades. Floral patterns adorn her dress and her colourful scarf coils into snakelike tendrils atop her head. A large python wraps itself around her shoulders. Candles blaze and flowers erupt in a brilliant profusion at her feet. In front of the statue, there is a small wooden pew where the faithful can kneel and pray. A basket stands ready to receive offerings. Bringing gifts to Marie, whether here or at her tomb in the St Louis No. 1 Cemetery, is believed to bring good fortune.

The city fixates on a single, unitary image of Marie Laveau, the bewitching, exquisite Voodoo Queen. In reality, however, there were likely two Maries: Marie the First and her daughter, Marie the Second, both free women of colour. In an act that reflects either a form of proto-feminist self-assertion or her Catholic devotion to the Virgin Mary (perhaps both), Marie the First named all three of her daughters Marie. Consequently, it becomes increasingly difficult to disentangle the complex genealogical threads of the great Voodoo Queen. The first Marie was born in 1801, when Louisiana was governed by the Spanish and just two years before it was sold to the United States. She died in 1881. Marie Eucharist Heloise, Marie the Second, was born in 1827 and probably passed away in the early 1860s. The first Marie Laveau was described in contemporary newspaper reports as "head of the Voudou sisterhoods" and "mother of the Voudou orders" (Ward 61). These distinctly feminine appellations were appropriate as, according to the Laveaus' biographer Martha Ward, Voodoo is an essentially matriarchal faith, with traditions passed down from mother to daughter. The priestess, as the religion's central figure, is imbued with the power to welcome the loa into her body or call them forth to her altar. She is a healer and spiritual guide who presides over births, marriages and deaths. In addition to her Voodoo work, Marie the First was a fever nurse during the many epidemics that plagued mosquito-ridden Mississippi, and a member of numerous benevolent societies that cared for the poor and the sick throughout New Orleans. She was a Catholic who, as Ward puts it, "attended Mass at the cathedral on Sunday morning and danced to possession with a great snake in Congo Square that afternoon" (20). These two facets of Marie's faith were not incompatible; indeed, they were closely interwoven, and one of her most ardent supporters was Père Antoine, the priest who presided over St Louis Cathedral. Her daughter, Marie the Second, worked as a hairdresser for the city's wealthiest residents, a calling that some scholars posit was intertwined with her spiritual practice. Others dismiss the popular belief that Marie the Second took on her mother's mantle as "Voodoo Queen", claiming that Marie Eucharist's early death makes this inheritance unlikely.

Biographies differ, and even the most informed scholars have stumbled across glaring omissions and disturbing lacunae in the history of Marie Laveau. Her life and the lives of her daughters remain obfuscated by centuries of myth and misinformation. Nevertheless, I decided to travel in Marie's footsteps, faint as they are, through the streets of New Orleans. I wandered along St Ann Street early in the morning as the sun was still shielded by thick grey clouds and municipal workers were just beginning to hose off the pavements following the previous night's revels. On the intricate wrought-iron balconies that wrap around the street's two-storey buildings in a loving embrace, freshly risen residents watered the thick, leafy plants that sprouted from prodigious collections of hanging baskets. Droplets of water trickled down to the ground below, falling on me like a gentle rain.

Towards the end of the street, where St Ann meets Rampart, stood a small collection of wooden cottages. Each was painted in a bright, candy-coloured hue: yellow, blue, mint green, salmon pink. Their vivid wooden shutters were still closed against the early morning chill, and I noticed that some of them had been painted in a very distinct shade of blue. This colour, I later learned, was haint blue, and it owes its origins to African American Gullah communities who traditionally inhabited the coastal plains and islands around Florida, Georgia and the Carolinas. It was believed that painting a porch or shutters in this particular shade would deter haints, or evil spirits, from crossing the threshold, either because the blue evoked water, which they feared, or because it reminded them of Heaven.

Painted an unassuming violet, there was little to distinguish the house at 1020 from its richly hued neighbours aside from a small bronze plaque informing visitors that Marie Laveau lived at the site — in a now demolished older cottage — for almost sixty years. During those years, visitors described seeing rooms decorated with elaborate altars, blazing candles and the requisite images of saints. One elderly woman, who as a child played with Marie's granddaughter, recalled that the little cottage "had so many candles burning... I don't see how that house never caught on fire", and described how Marie owned a large statue of Saint Anthony, which she turned upside-down in the backyard when performing rituals (quoted in Morrow Long, *Priestess*).

A few feet away, across Rampart Street, a gleaming white archway marked the entrance to Louis Armstrong Park. Inside the park, a two-dimensional bronze jazz band was frozen mid-stride as they marched towards the Municipal Auditorium. Off to the side, encircled by a ring of oak trees, stood Congo Square. Although now shrouded by the silence of a mid-week morning, the square was once the loud, bustling centre of Black life in New Orleans. In the antebellum period, Congo Square not only became the birthplace of jazz, it also pulsated with rhythmic drums and ecstatic dances that defined Voodoo ritual. It must have taken Marie Laveau mere moments to cross the street from her little cottage on St Ann Street to the carnivalesque swirl of Congo Square. In the centre of the assembled crowd, she would dance, intertwining her body with that of an immense snake. The music swelled, drums pounded, and colours swirled. Other women joined in and danced alongside her as the rhythm intensified. Today, the spirit of Marie Laveau lingers in Congo Square. As late as the 1930s, the faithful still flocked to the square, where they would make offerings to the departed priestess by pouring milk into holes in the ground (Anderson 16).

About a mile away, just a short walk along Rampart Street and a hasty turn on to St Roch Avenue, I found another site connected to the legend of Marie Laveau. St Roch Cemetery, dedicated in 1875, was named for a medieval European saint who cared for plague victims. His chapel, which stands at the end of a long row of marble and stone mausoleums, has long been venerated for its healing powers. The piles of abandoned back braces and prosthetic limbs that hang from the crumbling plaster walls of the vestry testify to the efficacy of the saint's interventions. Marie the First apparently called upon Saint Roch while nursing yellow fever victims, while her daughter, Marie the Second, allegedly met clients at the St Roch Cemetery, dispensing gris-gris charms beneath the towering crosses of its grandest tombs. Saint Roch, who died in prison after five years of incarceration, was apparently sympathetic to prisoners, and so the second Marie would meet victims of carceral injustice and their desperate relatives on grounds consecrated in his honour.

St Roch Cemetery, New Orleans

I turned on my heels, travelling back down Rampart and along the tree-lined streets of Esplanade Avenue, bordered by perfect white houses, their porches held aloft by thick Doric columns like the frosted layers of wedding cakes. At an intersection where another dense New Orleans cemetery met the desolate, cracked forecourt of an empty petrol station, I arrived at Bayou St John. Legend and local gossip claim it was here that Marie Laveau — perhaps both Maries — presided over elaborate Voodoo ceremonies on the feast of St John the Baptist. Throughout Europe, bonfires blaze throughout the night of 23 June, St John's Eve. In my usually quiet little city in the southernmost part of Ireland, it's not unusual to hear sirens scream through the streets to quell out of control fires, usually set by teenagers. In the New Orleans tradition, St John's Eve sees fire unite with water in a comingling of powerful elemental forces.

In my imagination, the bayou had acquired the characteristics of some dense, unexplored swamp. I imagined cypress trees cracking at their base to reveal dark, fathomless hollows, alligators half-submerged in cloudy waters and thick veils of Spanish moss parting like curtains to reveal hidden mysteries. In reality, the bayou that slithered from Lafitte Avenue in Tremé all the way up to the great oceanic expanse of Lake Pontchartrain was a calm blue creek, along whose banks children rode bicycles and families walked their dogs. Just where the bayou twists towards NOLA City Park, an iron footbridge, painted a mesmerising sky blue, crosses the water. It is here that St John's Eve is once again celebrated by both Voodoo initiates and curious visitors. I had missed it this year, arriving in the Crescent City in early July. A few weeks prior, the bridge would have been crowded with tourists and locals dressed in white. The highest of Voodoo holidays is now commemorated with a head-washing ceremony where participants gather to engage in a ritual cleansing and leave gifts for Marie.

Later, I caught a bus and headed back downriver to the busy French Quarter. Evening was spreading its dark cloak over the city streets, and the shadows lengthened into sharp, menacing talons. On Basin Street, just across from a church where, for over two centuries, locals have left gifts and petitions at the feet of Saint Expedite — a plaster Roman soldier mistakenly identified as the patron saint of urgent causes based on the francophone instructions on a shipping crate — a high white wall marks the perimeter of the St Louis No. 1 Cemetery. Inside, rows of mausoleums form complex geometric patterns. Elaborate tombs with vaulted roofs line the pathways, stone counterparts to the wooden cottages that border the nearby streets. Extravagant monuments to the city's wealthiest citizens tower above their more humble neighbours, and statues of saints stretch their hands out over the rooftops. Burial niches extend along each wall forming checkerboard patterns as they recede into the distance. Atop tombs and vaults, tiny plaster angels kneel in supplication, and here, in the heart of the great city of death, stands the tomb of Marie Laveau. The tomb is a high stone structure with a marble face that must once have gleamed proudly in the afternoon sun. The engraving on the façade gives little indication of the mythic stature of its most famous resident, simply reading "*Famille Vve Paris née Laveau*", the family of the Widow Paris born Laveau.

Until very recently, it was possible to wander the streets of this vast necropolis, to meander between its tombs and vaults as though you were strolling city streets. However, in the past few years, the city has limited access following a spate of vandalism, including a bizarre incident in December 2013 when a mysterious nighttime caller painted Marie Laveau's tomb a strange shade of pastel pink. Locals speculated that it was an attempt, perhaps on behalf of a disciple, to obscure the decades' worth of graffiti that had accumulated on the surface of the tomb. As far back as the 1930s, observers recorded a ritual whereby those who trusted in the power of ancestral spirits would knock three times on Laveau's tomb before leaving a gift of flowers and fifteen cents in change for the queen (Anderson 19). Over time, this seems to have evolved into a related ritual that involved marking her tomb with a row of three X's. For a while, the mausoleum was an elaborate scrawl of graffiti: names, symbols, hastily scribbled prayers. At its feet, gifts were piled high: flowers, candles, Mardi Gras beads, beignets from Café Du Monde, holy statues and pictures, even a few hair pins reflecting the popular belief that it was Marie the First, rather than her daughter, who worked as a hairdresser. Today, the tomb is a far more sober monument. The graffiti has been washed away and the only gifts that remain are two vases of carefully arranged flowers positioned tidily on either side of the structure.

The days of ecstatic dances in Congo Square died long before the first Marie. After the Haitian Revolution, Louisiana's slaveholders became increasingly concerned about the possibility of slave uprisings and Voodoo's power to embolden any revolutionary sentiments stirring among the city's Black population. Christopher L. Newman suggests that during these tentative years following the establishment of the Haitian Republic and Louisiana's absorption into the rapidly expanding United States, Voodoo disturbed White Americans because, for the enslaved peoples of New Orleans, this powerful, passionate faith "represented what a true liberation force could look like" (13). As the nineteenth century progressed, the new state of Louisiana began to place more and more restrictions on its Black citizens, including legislation limiting the movement of slaves in and out of New Orleans. Media representations of Voodoo worked to quell its subversive power, as newspaper articles described, in salacious detail, human sacrifices, cannibal feasts and interracial orgies that never happened.

By the time Zora Neale Hurston arrived in New Orleans in the late 1920s, Voodoo had gone underground. Yet, like anything buried in the vital, clamorous soil of the South, it refused to lie still. Voodoo thrived surreptitiously in hidden corners of the city. Practitioners still gathered behind the locked doors of cottages or out on the bayou, but their rituals were more subdued, secretive. This, too, had been my experience. I had tried to contact a number of practitioners in hopes of securing an interview and learning more about the faith as it exists today. However, many adherents, especially those who did not participate in the city's tourist industry, remained reticent, unwilling to share the secrets of a precious faith with a stranger.

Hurston spent four months living in Algiers, a neighbourhood located on the western side of the Mississippi River and from whose raised banks it is possible to observe the sun set behind the twin spires of the St Louis Cathedral. During that time, she worked alongside a number of Voodoo priests, conjurers and two-headed doctors — so called because they possessed the power to look both ways between worlds. During her initiation, she fasted, prostrated herself before altars and entered ecstatic trances. Later, she describes assisting practitioners with rituals to retain a lover, influence a court hearing and quell a wagging tongue. She also details a ritual intended to kill: a statue of Death was adorned with a black crown, a black cat was buried alive alongside a black chicken and black candles were burned for ninety days. The object of the ritual, Hurston notes, did indeed die after three months.

Fantasy and reality, it seems, enjoy a somewhat antagonistic relationship down here in the broiling depths of the South. If Voodoo has been buried, secreted away in the warm embrace of the unfathomable swampland, it does — like all things interred in the dark, effluvial Mississippi mud — return in surprising, even unsettling ways. Voodoo has become irrevocably bound up with the city's identity as both a historic site and a popular vacation spot. As such, this complex, secretive spiritual system has become increasingly entangled with the plastic world of keychains and novelty shot glasses. However, this doesn't mean that Voodoo has vanished, nor does it signify a hollowing out of the practice.

In her study of tourist engagements with New Orleans Voodoo, Elvira K. Katić observes that tourist destinations typically comprise at least three different levels of authenticity: "the front room that presents a certain façade to the public, the true back room where this façade is created, and the false back room that is shown to the public, to satisfy the desire of many sightseers to catch a glimpse of the 'truth' behind the 'playacting'" (16). The Voodoo supply shops and museums of the French Quarter engage in precisely this kind of layering: a gift shop brimming with multicoloured voodoo dolls, bottled love potions and bumper stickers inevitably gives way to quiet room, screened from prying eyes behind a gauzy patterned drape or an endlessly clacking beaded curtain. Within, the walls may be painted a serene sky blue, evocative of the haint blue that adorns the cottages near Congo Square. Framed portraits, purportedly depicting Marie Laveau, hang on the walls. Others depict nude figures dancing around bonfires, their limbs interlaced with the scaly bodies of gargantuan pythons. Shelves groan under the weight of wooden figurines, bowls, baskets, shells, stones, snakeskin only recently sloughed off.

Vèvès inscribed on walls or emblazoned on banners invoke powerful loas like Damballah and Papa Legba. In every corner, altars bloom with eclectic displays. Candles drip frozen streams of melted wax onto silky table clothes. Statues of saints line up in solemn processions: The Blessed Virgin, Saint Brigid, Saint Michael the Archangel crushing a devil underfoot, Saint Anthony (the same one my elderly relatives swear will recover any lost object if you light a candle in his honour). Offerings of coins are scattered at their feet, dollar bills stuffed into crevices. Bottles of liquor sit full and undisturbed; cigarettes are left intact and unsmoked, gifts for the loa. Yet this is always only ever the false back room, a staged "authenticity" that panders to the tourist's desire for the real. Somewhere else, hidden entirely from our prying eyes, another room guards its secrets.

***

On my last night in New Orleans, I decided to find out what it is that lures streams of tourists, most from other parts of the United States, down past the Mason Dixon Line to the sweltering, secretive South. Hoping to grasp the essential allure of this strange, ornate city, I joined one of the innumerable ghost tours that trickle through the streets of the French Quarter every evening after sundown. Never in any other city had I seen so many signs and flyers, brochures and coupons advertising ghost tours. New Orleans has standard haunted history tours, vampire tours, pirate tours, Voodoo tours. Any kind of macabre manifestation you can name, New Orleans has a tour dedicated to following it through the dusky streets. In fact, New Orleans has so many tour groups meandering along its footpaths and lurking in its alleys that the city has several ordinances dedicated to managing their behaviour and mitigating any potential disruption to locals.

My group was led by Ariadne Blayde, a friend of a friend who I had reached out to before leaving Ireland. We arranged to meet outside the gift shop where her tour began. I arrived early and milled about with the other tourists who had begun to congregate on the footpath. Some were families — parents and children in identical uniforms of shorts and T-shirts — others were college kids sipping colourful drinks through twisty straws. I knew Ariadne as soon as she arrived, though we had never met before. She was tall and slender, with long blonde hair falling over her forehead in neat, symmetrical bangs. She wore leather boots with thick heels and a PVC cap. She handed me my ticket with a smile, and I joined the line of tourists as we twisted through the back streets of the Vieux Carré.

Ariadne moved through her stories as the group meandered along side streets enfolded in shadow. We began in a narrow alleyway that runs alongside St Louis Cathedral, and ended somewhere on the banks of the silent, dark

Mississippi. She told us of vampires brought from the Old World to the bustling docks of Louisiana; of sadistic slave owners and their monstrous crimes; of tragic lovers and children carried away by cholera, yellow fever, dysentery. At one point, she explained that a particular haunted house is known to be plagued by strange floating orbs, ghost lights that hover just above the rooftops and only become visible, after the fact, in photographs. I snapped pictures as darkness claimed the city and the streetlights began to cast their amber glow. An older man asked to see my pictures and was convinced that he could see inexplicable lights floating above the rooftops.

When the tour ended and the tourists drifted away, Ariadne and I decamped to one of the French Quarter's many bars. Even though it was only around 10:00 pm, the little hole-in-the-wall bar was almost empty. Lamps hung low over a long wooden bar, and the bottle-filled shelves that stood behind glowed in the half-light like votives on an altar. A few patrons nursed their glasses at wobbly high-top tables. In the corner, a jukebox radiated a tenuous, flickering light. The machine kicked into life, playing the first few bars of a Fleetwood Mac song just as we pushed open the heavy wooden door. Seated in a corner next to the window, Ariadne told me about her journey to New Orleans. A Northerner by birth, she studied theatre and history in college, moving to the Deep South to teach. Instead, she found herself working as tour guide, a job she is truly passionate about.

Ariadne is also an award-winning writer, and her most recent book, *Ash Tuesday*, is a novel about New Orleans tour guides. Structured around the stories they tell as they lead tourists through the French Quarter, the book explores the power of story, of myth and folklore, to structure our lives and inform our understanding of the world around us. In Ariadne's novel, New Orleans emerges as a richly layered city, densely and often disturbingly stratified. The novel's narrator describes the sickly tension between the glossy surface — the New Orleans of Mardi Gras's colours, exotic smells and flavours, boisterous jazz bands — and the dark, sticky morass that seethes just beneath that intoxicating façade. "The houses are termite-infested," she writes, "and for every fancy cocktail there's a pile of vomit in the gutter and that music, that rat-a-tat, is a thread pulsing back to this city's original sin, those days when the enslaved gathered in Congo Square to beat out on drums an identity that had been stolen."

New Orleans is viscous, fluid, unstable, an extension of the swamplands out of which it was hewn. A soupy brine churns beneath its quaintly cobbled streets, occasionally pushing centuries-old bones to the surface. They pop up, it seems, with a reliable regularity when residents and developers break ground on new projects: houses, backyard swimming pools, patios. In fact, Ariadne said with a smile, this is precisely why New Orleans began to construct above-ground tombs in the late 1700s. New Orleans has over forty cemeteries, a lot for a city of its size, but a testament to the inhabitants' long battle with the swamp, with the ever-present shadow of death and disease. The city streets lie, on average, at least six feet below water level, caught between the tumultuous Mississippi and the huge watery reaches of Lake Pontchartrain. In the early days, the heavy storms that blow in from the Atlantic caused the waters to rise, floating rotting corpses up from their burial plots, while the intense Southern heat combined with the gases that invariably emanate from decomposing bodies to blow the slabs off the tops of graves. The dead had to be contained in massive above-ground tombs, sealed off from the corrupting vapours of the swampy earth, or baked in hot stone until nothing fleshy or tangible remained.

New Orleans Cities of the Dead

This may be why New Orleans has long been captivated by tales of the living dead. In her book, Ariadne has one of the tour guides tell the tale of the Ursuline vampires, the first such revenants to make their home in the New World. In the early 1700s, when New Orleans was still being settled by the French — who called it La Nouvelle Orléans — a group of young women were brought from France to be married off to the rough, taciturn men who built the city. Presumably, these lonely settlers were elated by the prospect and dreamed of ripe, buxom brides. However, when the ship carrying this precious cargo finally docked, it disgorged a procession of gaunt, sickly girls who brought nothing with them but small caskets containing, they said, all of their worldly possessions. The girls were to be cared for by the sisters of the Ursuline order until they were ready to be dispatched to their new husbands. The legend, which has since sprouted multiple variants, usually tells of how the caskets were stored in the attic of the convent, but when the nuns went to fetch the girls' belongings, they found the caskets empty. Tour guides and visitors speculate that these pale young women, shipped to the New World as brides-to-be, were in actuality vampires, and that they slept in those empty caskets during their long ocean voyage.

Other vampires have also made their homes along the banks of the Mississippi. After collecting our drinks at the bar, Ariadne and I planted ourselves at a cosy, corner table, where she told me about the Comte de St Germain. A handsome enigmatic Frenchman who was born in Europe in the 1700s, the Comte may have lived in New Orleans as Jacques St Germain in the early part of the twentieth century. Some speculate that he was an alchemist, brilliant and immortal, while others maintain that his home near Rue Royale was empty of all food and dining utensils, containing only wine bottles filled with human blood. That story struck me as familiar, and I mentioned to Ariadne that St Germain reminded me a great deal of the aristocratic French vampires who haunt New Orleans in Anne Rice's Vampire Chronicles. As in the legend, Rice's vampires live in decadent homes, eating from empty plates and drinking from wine glasses filled with blood.

From the second half of the twentieth century through to the early years of the new millennium, the vampire has becoming increasingly at home in New Orleans and, indeed, in Louisiana as a whole. Jewelle Gomez's 1991 novel *The Gilda Stories* follows a Louisiana slave who is transformed into a beautiful, immortal vampire in the 1850s, while Poppy Z. Brite's *Lost Souls*, published the following year, centres on a coven of queer vampires who prowl the bars and clubs of the French Quarter. Charlaine Harris's Sookie Stackhouse novels (2001–2013) chart the romantic entanglement between a young woman and centuries-old vampire in the fictional town of Bon Temps, Louisiana, and eventually became the basis for the popular television series *True Blood* (2008–2014). It's likely that the proliferation of New Orleans vampires has much to do with the popularity of Anne Rice's immensely successful series, which began in 1976 with *Interview with the Vampire* and concluded with 2018's *Blood Communion*. However, all of these works are diverse in terms of both narrative and thematic concerns. Gomez's and Brite's novels use vampirism as a means of exploring sexual desire, family connections and the experiences of marginalised groups in America. Conversely, Harris's series not only shudders with intense erotic longing, it also expresses a deep longing for a romanticised vision of the Antebellum South: the story's brooding, vampire hero fought for the Confederacy against what one character terms "the War of Northern Aggression".

I asked Ariadne if she had any thoughts on the ubiquity of (fictional) Louisiana vampires. She responded by suggesting that the monsters had been engendered by the essential eclecticism of the state, with New Orleans in particular constituting a rich crucible of European, Caribbean and African cultural strains. "Plus," she said with a laugh, "New Orleans is a beacon for weirdos and misfits. All the strange people from all over the country come here." I couldn't help but agree. New Orleans seemed like a city ripe for vampiric outbreaks. The diverse cultures that intermingled here likely brought their own tales of the undead to the city, while the epidemics that regularly devastated the city provoked new concerns about the porous boundary between life and death. Moreover, the history of New Orleans appeared to parallel that of the vampire. I wondered, also, if Ariadne's tales of skeletons pushed to the surface by floodwaters and centuries-old carcasses dug up in the incongruously domestic space of backyards might have played a role in the swift dissemination of the vampire myth. After all, New Orleans was a city where bodies could not be buried in the earth for fear that the powerful tides of the Mississippi or the churning swamp might return them to the surface.

The potent magic of the swamp is certainly at the heart of Anne Rice's astounding debut novel, *Interview with the Vampire*. While it is a novel about grief — she wrote it after the tragic death of her five-year-old daughter — and a deeply philosophical study, one that ponders the meaning of a life freed from the bonds of death, it is also a book that considers, often uneasily, the power of nature over humanity. The novel's protagonist, a French planter named Louis, is transformed into a vampire in the eighteenth century, when Louisiana was still very much a wilderness. The plantations that ring the city of New Orleans seem constantly at war with the swamp's incursions. In his recollections of his life as a human, Louis describes the swamp rising in the distance, "the moss-hung cypresses floating against the sky", "a chorus of creatures" and how monstrous wisteria plants "tore the shutters off the attic windows" of his home (Rice 6). In an early part of the novel, Louis and his companion Lestat hunt slaves in the swamps that border his plantation, the dense mire becoming a site of death and transgression.

As in Poe's tales of burial refused or Hurston's wondrous stories of vital life thrumming in the rich, fecund wetlands, Rice paints the swamp as possessed of a soul of its own. Its obscure waters and thick, resonant mud are so utterly possessed of a sinister vitality that nothing consigned to the swamp could every deteriorate or crumble to dust. When Lestat is murdered by Claudia, a vampire child adopted by the pair, Louis helps his daughter to dispose of the body in the swamp. Wading out into its depths, Louis releases the body, where it sinks "beneath the slimy surface" (138–9). Yet life swarms, busy and tenacious, in the swamp, and whatever is interred here will invariably return. A few nights later, Lestat does return, pounding at Louis's door like Poe's maddened Madeline Usher. The swamp has restored him, but his skin remains a "mass of scars", a testament to the death from which he has returned (157).

***

Ariadne returned me to my accommodation — a backyard cabin near the tranquil waters of Bayou St John — in her red Mini Cooper. We drove with the top down, and the scent of night-blooming jasmine hung in the heavy, gelatinous air. When I opened the rickety wooden door and entered my little flat, my eye was caught by something moving, fast and green, in the top corner of a high wall. A lizard, a small emissary from the viscous swamp, had found his way inside.

There's a well-known photograph, a Gothic artefact from the 1940s, called *Elegy for Moss Land*, which I think sums up the uniquely haunted quality of the South. The photograph was captured and then manipulated by Clarence John Laughlin, who in his book *Ghosts Along the Mississippi* collected images of decaying Southern plantations, the ghosts of the title. In *Elegy*, a double exposure captures the image of an old plantation superimposed over a dense marshland and a bent, gnarled cypress tree hung with moss. Here, Laughlin articulates the two central nodes of the Southern Gothic imagination: the horrors of a history marked, indeed defined, by slavery, and the pervasive, looming presence of the swamp. Both resist burial and refuse the silence of the tomb. The swamp remains unmoved, eternal, as it gestates swarming, teeming life. The legacy of slavery still shapes America even as school boards and lawmakers throughout the region seek to bury its horrors in the deep caverns of history.

Yet, while these swampy regions seem obsessed by the gruesome return of what has been buried, such horrors cannot be confined to the South. They are not the property of these lands alone. The US's popular imagination frequently attempts to banish its historical horrors to the South, framing the whole region as a sticky container for degeneracy, excess and the racism it doesn't want to recognise in itself. In an essay titled "The Grotesque in Southern Fiction", Flannery O'Connor, a writer whose tales of sudden, brutal and inexplicable violence are often viewed as exemplary of the region's literary output, laments that "anything that comes out of the South is going to be called grotesque by the Northern reader, unless it is grotesque, in which case it is going to be called realistic" (40). The South, for many, is a repository of horror, a grotesque realm still deeply entangled with slavery, racism and segregation. However, to view the South in this way, to attempt to consign the spectre of racism to one region, is misguided and ultimately impossible. The legacy of slavery, of discriminatory housing and civic policies, of police violence and carceral injustice has shaped the entire nation. It can't be buried in the swamp. It inevitably claws its way back.

3. MONSTERS AND MUSHROOM CLOUDS: DESERT GOTHIC

Like something from another life. Serene, quiet, yet strangely evil as if it were hiding its secret from Man.

— Tarantula

Up Through Texas

Somewhere between Baton Rouge, Louisiana, and Austin, Texas, we shed the last vestiges of the yawning, sucking swamp. The gnarled, moss-shrouded oaks began to thin out and the landscape flattened into wide plains that stretched out into a seemingly infinite horizon. After the thick, dense foliage and clamouring animal life of Florida and Louisiana, I felt the scarcity of Texas so much more acutely. When I stepped off the bus during one of the many breaks in our journey — a fast food restaurant, the forecourt of a petrol station, changing vehicles in a car park — I was struck by the dryness of the air. It was desiccated, bone dry, a parched white skull. I spent a single night sleeping in an Austin suburb where warm orange lights glowed in windows and bicycles glided along in silent cul-de-sacs. Open garage doors revealed poker games in progress, and the smell of barbeque circulated on a cool dusky breeze.

Cicadas hummed around me, a low continuous chirp, but I never found evidence of living creatures here, just abandoned, empty shells clustered beneath trees like tiny, shrivelled mummies.

The next leg of my journey took me from Austin to Dallas, a three-and-a-half-hour bus journey that stretched as vacant and quiet as the landscape itself. Clouds hung low in the endless sky, casting their flying-saucer shadows over a brown and brittle landscape. We passed fields, brown and flat aside from the occasional tree surrounded by scrub grass. The blanched wood of rotting barns and abandoned farmhouses flaked off beneath an oppressive glaring sun. A derelict school bus sat alone by the roadside, its rusted carcass crumbling to red dust. As we trundled towards the gentle granite slopes of Texas Hill Country, I couldn't help but notice that meat was everywhere. Cows and sheep grazed in fields that disappeared into the horizon, their numbers increasing the further north we drove. Signs dangling from sturdy wooden posts announced the entrance to cattle ranches, and billboards advertised steakhouses with pictures of great sizzling slabs of meat.

I thought of the spectre of undeath that haunted the Deep South I had left behind, the sense that the moist, lively earth would never allow a body to rest in peace but would instead return it, dark and twisted, to the land of the living. Here, there was a similar sense of burial refused, of death intruding on and intermingling with life. It resided in decaying farms baking in the persistent heat, in blanched cow skulls hanging from gateposts while their still-living counterparts stood, passively chewing, by the roadside and waited for death.

If a single Gothic text links the sticky, fecund swamps of the Deep South to the dry, arid plains of the Southwest, it is likely Tobe Hooper's 1974 horror film *The Texas Chain Saw Massacre*. The movie opens with images of graverobbing, with disinterred bodies transformed into grotesque sculptures that boil beneath a huge, red sun. Elsewhere, tarmac blisters and bubbles, the air thick with heat and pregnant with menace. It is a film about decay, chaos, the apocalypse, and nothing that dies ever stays buried. The cannibalistic family at the heart of the film make sure of that. They dig up corpses, robbing the dead and turning their bodies into gruesome works of art. They stalk the highways and dirt roads of precisely this part of Texas — Hill Country — looking for victims, for food. They turn healthy living bodies into meat, which they consume, and craft their bones into furniture.

The Texas Chain Saw Massacre is a film about the end of the world. The plot follows a group of five young people as they venture into this remote, desolate part of the Lone Star State. As they drive along its wide, straight roads, a radio news programme drones in the background, portending catastrophe. It describes natural disasters, violent crime, inexplicable acts of brutality, the dying days of the Vietnam War, the Watergate scandal and solar flares wreaking havoc with communications systems. The world these young people know is falling, irrevocably, into chaos. It is August 1973, and the American economy — so brilliant and promising in the first decades after the Second World War — is collapsing. There is an embargo on the sale of oil to the United States, and queues at petrol stations stretch for miles. Capitalism is devouring itself and sucking on its own bones.

On a smaller scale, too, communities are hollowed out by a creeping economic stagnation. The kids' road trip takes a turn for the worse after they pick up a hitchhiker who captures their images on a polaroid, smears the picture with blood and then sets fire to it, as though performing some strange, arcane ritual. He explains that generations of his family had worked in the regions' slaughterhouses.

His grandfather, father and brothers had wielded the heavy sledgehammers whose swing brought death to countless sad-eyed cows. However, as new technologies reduced the need for human labour and economic decline set in, these jobs vanished. What was the family to do but continue the only work they knew and loved? How were they to eat without finding another source of meat?

The Texas Chain Saw Massacre is undoubtedly a film that investigates the ethics of meat consumption, and it does so in an environment where signs of the meat industry are virtually inescapable. Hooper's film consistently reframes meat as the characters' knowledge of its source begins to shift. In an early scene, the youthful travellers stop at a barbeque joint and buy some meat for their journey. It's good "down-home" cooking. Later, when Sally, the only surviving member of the group, returns to the same place, she looks at the slowly roasting meat with horror, realising that it is not cow but human flesh turning in that brick smoker. Yet, while the film might question the morality of meat, it also imagines economic inequality and the exploitation of the working classes in terms of consumption. Robin Wood, one of the pioneers of horror film criticism, suggested in the 1970s that the film's cannibals were not simply monsters but victims of economic exploitation, conditioned by their degrading industrial slaughterhouse work to become ravenous killers.

The landscape of Hooper's film suggests the omnipresence of death in such a disgusting, sickening way that the under his lens the whole region becomes a legible text written over with teeming signs of economic deprivation and social collapse. Houses crumble on the roadside, devoured from within by gnawing masses of spiders and the forward march of time; roadkill festers on the highway, and the cannibal family's home, with its chairs of bone and lampshades fashioned from skin, becomes a veritable monument to mortality. The ubiquity of death, the endless leering shots of corpses and skeletal remains, extends the resurrectionist horror of the Deep South upwards into the arid plains of Texas.

From Dallas, I caught an evening bus to Amarillo, falling asleep almost as soon as I climbed onboard. When I awoke, dusk had covered the land with a misty, purplish hue. The highways were strung with powerlines that often pulled the eye in strange directions, down odd, under-explored dirt roads, up to the silent porches of farmhouses. In faraway fields, giant wind turbines turned in a great nauseating ballet. The last splinters of light were extinguished, and darkness pressed down on the plains. We moved silently along US Route 82, passing through sleeping towns all bearing strangely personal first names: Seymour, Lorenzo, Mabelle, Benjamin. Turning onto Interstate 27 in the town of Lubbock, we came alongside the small agricultural community of Happy, Texas — "The Town without a Frown." Nothing was visible except for hundreds of lights that blinked in the darkness: the red lights of lorries, the bright yellow glow of petrol station forecourts, distant amber sparks that recalled the warmth of living-room firesides. Neon signs shone in the darkness, lighthouses in a black ocean.

The next day, Amarillo was deserted. No one walked the streets, which were wide and open to the sun's merciless glare. The flat-roofed commercial buildings that comprised the city's main agricultural style seemed to ripple in the thick, heavy air, their brown bricks baking in the heat. A few SUVs lumbered in and out of drive-thru banks and coffee shops, but I seemed to be the only person walking the streets. Located right in the centre of the Texas Panhandle, the town of Amarillo was founded along the newly laid railway lines that facilitated US expansion across the North American continent. Its name — the Spanish word for yellow — was derived either from the golden soil that cakes the banks of the nearby creek or from the profusion of yellow daisies that grow wild in the region. For a time, the city thrived as a hub for rail transit and later grew rich on petroleum and natural gas.

From the 1920s onwards, Amarillo was a main stop on the mythic Route 66, the 2,400-mile road that linked Chicago to Los Angeles. Pieced together from existing roads and routes, US Highway 66 was the main thoroughfare travelled by Depression-era migrants fleeing the apocalyptic winds and parched soil of the Dustbowl for the orange groves and blue waters of California. In the post-World War II period, as automobile ownership grew and the economic boom gifted more and more Americans with disposable income, 66 became the preferred route for tourists, who piled their growing families into the backs of Cadillacs and station wagons as they set out to see the country. John Steinbeck, who wrote about migrants travelling West to the promised land, christened the route "Mother Road", imagining the highway as a nurturing caretaker wrapping herself around the hulking body of the continent. Others referred to Route 66 as America's Main Street, the meeting place where all pathways converged, friendly and warm, in the great American night.

For a time, the road was an artery, pulsing with the lifeblood of a newly mobile, car-obsessed America. However, in 1985, Route 66 was officially decommissioned, replaced with a series of anonymous four-lane interstates that bypassed the towns that had once relied upon the heavy traffic for their main industries. The little towns withered away. In Amarillo, a section of Route 66, once a busy channel ferrying streams of traffic across the state of Texas, has been designated "US Route 66 Sixth Street Historic District". Across the United States, fragments of the once-thriving highway have been fenced off in this way, so that if you travel far enough into the West, you will encounter multiple disembodied sections of it frozen in time. It's a strange sight, all of these slivers of the great road — once a promising symbol of modernity, hope and freedom — trapped like insects in amber, barely living exhibits in a museum.

In Amarillo, the preserved section of Route 66 began somewhere around South Georgia Street, where flat single-storey commercial units opened out onto a massive building that appeared part Spanish revival, part medieval castle. This was the Nat. Originally the Amarillo Natatorium, it had been constructed in the early 1920s as a public swimming pool. It was later renovated and turned into a ballroom, and later a nightclub that catered to the lively crowds that poured into the city along Route 66. In the summer of 2022, when I pushed open the heavy wooden doors and entered the cool, faintly mouldy main hall, the huge building had been transformed into an antiques market where different vendors set up stalls selling everything from mannequins and dusty victrolas to faded leather cowboy boots and decades-old board games. Traces of the Nat's former life could still be deciphered behind the shelves that bulged with ancient cameras and the walls lined with velvet paintings depicting uncanny wide-eyed children. The old stage served as a dais on which a varied collection of antiques was displayed: a globe showing countries that no longer exist, a rusted stop sign, the ubiquitous Texas cow skull.

Little snapshots of the street's history as the hub of a great transit root could be seen painted on the walls of half-deserted buildings. Colourful murals depicted cowboys, wagon trains and Cadillacs barrelling down highways bordered by cacti and blooming yellow daisies. Dozens of former petrol stations that had once fuelled the stream of westward migration now stood empty or had been transformed into cafés. One eatery sat at the far end of a rusted forecourt. Letters had fallen off the tall sign that soared into the air above the hot, cracked asphalt. Inside, huge plastic menus listed equally massive breakfasts: eggs, bacon, pork chops, hash browns, grits, gravy, dollar cakes, biscuits, fries, ham. Each one was named after an iconic American automobile of the past: the El Camino, the Cadillac El Dorado, the Ford Thunderbird. Across the street, the former Shamrock Gas Station had been converted into Moe Dogs Grill, though it still retained its green-tiled façade. Beneath the forecourt awning, a light-blue Studebaker rusted quietly in the sun. I met no one on the silent, sweltering streets aside from a group of bikers gathered outside a bar that promised "Live music and mayhem", and a small black cat methodically torturing a lizard by the roadside.

There were no buses in Amarillo, so I took a taxi to the intersection of Interstate 40 and Hope Road. I stepped out onto the dusty shoulder surrounded by miles and miles of flat, brown earth. Brushstrokes of white cloud lay low in the sky. On the other side of the road, a huge head bowed, silhouetted against the afternoon sun. I dodged the sporadic traffic and stood beneath the giant fibreglass figure that loomed over the plains. Clad in blue denim jeans, a yellow shirt (for Amarillo, the yellow city) and a comically large white Stetson, the behemoth that towered above me was the "Second Amendment Cowboy". An iconic roadside attraction, the cowboy was originally a muffler man — a huge piece of novelty advertising produced in the 1960s — that had stood outside a local steakhouse for about a decade before being purchased by new owners. Today, he stands next to an RV park and right in front of a souvenir shop that sells Route 66 memorabilia and plays loud Christian rock. A plaque in front of the cowboy recites the Second Amendment to the United States Constitution,

Cadillac Ranch, Amarillo, Texas

the guarantor of the right to bear arms. The cowboy is a strange, almost parodic figure. His owners clearly intend him to stand as an embodiment of American self-

Second Amendment Cowboy, Amarillo, Texas

sufficiency: the mythic cowboy of the Texas plains, always armed, but brave and heroic, judicious in his choices and beholden to some higher morality. Yet there is something inherently ridiculous about the figure. His chiselled jaw is

Rusting Car, Old Route 66, Amarillo, Texas

just a bit too square. His bright blue jeans and yellow shirt make him appear like a cartoon cutout, somehow misplaced in the vast brown expanse of North Texas. Three pastel Cadillacs, tilted at odd angles and containing mannequins styled after three equally mythic American heroes — John Wayne, Willie Nelson and Elvis — flank the cowboy. It was odd, yet not entirely surprising, to see the stony-faced cowboy and his earnest plaque crassly entangled with such flat symbols of consumerism, mass-produced luxury and hyperbolic masculinity.

Leaving the cowboy behind, I crossed the road and headed east along the side of the interstate, walking in the dry, dusty earth and brittle grass that border the asphalt. Out on the horizon, I spotted a series of metal fins emerging from the earth like the shoots of rusty blossoms. This was *Cadillac Ranch*, an art installation created in the 1970s to celebrate the golden age of American automation. The piece was created by an artistic collective called the Ant Farm, and its patron was the eccentric helium tycoon Stanley Marsh 3 (a man who found the Roman numeral "III" too pretentious). The installation is a romantic, nostalgic evocation of the days when cars filled with hopeful travellers and curious families surged west along Route 66. The Cadillacs, which are half buried in the soil, all face west, pointing towards the promises of the California Coast. Over the decades, however, the buried Cadillacs have come to symbolise something else. Route 66 was already dying in the early 1970s, and the monument to the great American automobile became a quirky roadside attraction, an anomaly bordering I-40, one of the great interstates that hastened its demise. Tourists come with cans of spray paint — which you can buy at the Second Amendment Cowboy souvenir shop just down the road — and mark the cars with initials, scrawls or colourful symbols. The graffiti, in fact, has become a part of the artwork, attesting to the generations of travellers who have stopped here.

The ranch was bustling when I walked through the gate. Families unloaded themselves from SUVs; groups of teenage girls in identical shorts and T-shirts wandered between the cars. Some college-aged boys laughed as they sprayed their initials on a Cadillac. A middle-aged woman with a sharp grey bob stopped me and said she had seen me walking alone along the road earlier. She was a teacher from Illinois and had decided to spend the summer travelling solo along the old Route 66 in an RV. "It's so wide, so open!" she exclaimed. "You just feel this sense of possibility. Anything is possible here!"

***

Texas is indeed vast and open. When you look out over the plains, your eye is immediately drawn to the furthest point on the horizon. There seems to be an immense, yawning emptiness that the imagination immediately fills up, populating the landscape with free-floating fantasies of what could be. Yet the emptiness of Texas — and of the West more broadly — is deceptive. Its history is not (as some of the more heroic renditions of American history would have it) one of eternal, timeless vacuity.

Though only three federally recognised tribes remain in the state of Texas, prior to European colonisation a large number of distinct Indigenous populations inhabited the region. Decimated by disease and government-sponsored violence, the mythic empty West was created through an aggressive campaign of ethnic cleansing that opened the region to Euro-American settlement. As with the first colonies carved out of the deep forests of New England, the expansion of the United States into the West was dependent upon a constructed notion of empty space, a vessel to be filled with the dreams of advancing settlers.

In 1862, congress passed the Homestead Act, seizing almost three hundred million acres of land from Indigenous populations and redistributing it to White settlers lured West with the promise of 160 acres of land each. Homesteaders were required to live on their plot for a period of five years, cultivating the land and "improving" it. The myth that sustained the push westward was grounded in a largely illusory vision of acres upon acres of vacant land primed for colonisation. Perhaps the most famous representation of this fantasy is John Gast's 1872 painting *American Progress*. The image is ubiquitous now — a staple of textbooks and history classes — but in the late nineteenth century it was even more pervasive. While few Americans saw the painting on display, thousands — if not millions — pored over reproductions of the image, which depicts Columbia — symbol of American liberty — leading the nation westward from the smoky metropolises of the East Coast to the sparse plains of the new territories. She bears the "Star of Empire" upon her forehead and in her arms she carries a schoolbook, emblematic of the "civilising" force of education. She passes over the land, draping telegraph wires — a symbol of technological advancement — behind her. Trains, covered wagons, stagecoaches and farmers pushing ploughs all follow in her wake. The land that stretches out before her is vast and untamed. The only figures who occupy this space are small groups of Native Americans — one band, roughly sketched, fading into the distance, and another fleeing in terror before the might of American progress. Alongside the frightened Indians, a bear turns back to snarl at the encroaching settlers, while a herd of buffalo retreat into darkness.

There's a stunning digital recreation of this image, a gif produced in 2021 by Diné (Navajo) artist Klee Benally entitled *The Dark Mark of Manifest Destiny*. In this glitchy, static-choked piece, the dark spectre of death hovers menacingly in the air in place of the luminous Columbia. Benally's work renders explicit the massive destruction wrought by Euro-American colonisation and excoriates the absurd fantasy embedded in Gast's original painting: the

West was never empty, it was never a waiting receptacle for the American dream. Rather, it was made empty by a systematic programme of colonial incursion and destruction. Not only were numerous Indigenous tribes annihilated, wiped out by diseases to which they had no immunity, massacred and forcibly relocated, but the environment itself was devastated by American forces as they marched across the continent.

Beginning in the 1820s and continuing into the latter part of the nineteenth century, US government policy sought to eradicate the Plains peoples by first eradicating the buffalo, the basis of both their diet and economy. Primarily enacted by the army as well as commercial hunters, the "Great Slaughter" resulted in the almost total eradication of the buffalo, with tens of millions killed and the entire population reduced to only a few hundred by the 1880s (Dunbar-Ortiz 142). Hunters only valued the animal's hide, so when buffalo were slaughtered, the rest of the carcass was simply left to putrefy in the stultifying heat. The bones, meanwhile, would be taken and shipped to the East Coast. Attempting to articulate the scale of the slaughter, a Kiowa woman named Old Lady Horse described how, in the wake of the White hunters, "there would be a pile of bones as high as a man, stretching a mile along the railroad track" (Dunbar-Ortiz 143). The land itself was also ravaged. The tall grasses native to the Plains region were destroyed, ploughed into submission or over-grazed by the cattle who replaced the vanishing buffalo.

The image of the West that endures in the popular imagination is one of emptiness, flat and expansive. As most of us picture it, the Texas Plains meld imperceptibly with the desert landscape of New Mexico, Arizona, Nevada and Utah, the land becoming increasingly hostile and lifeless as it unfolds into the far West. Out in this hot, arid land, the world itself seems parched and bone dry. Indeed, it is the image of bone — bleached white and pure — that perhaps most fully embodies both the history and the topography of the region. Cattle skulls hang on doors and gate posts all across Texas; fragments of animal bones — mandibles, shins, ribs — lurk in scrub grasses and nestled in the cool spaces between rocks.

My first thought travelling up through Texas had been of bones. I recalled *The Texas Chain Saw Massacre*, a film practically built from bones, in which the living room of an outwardly innocuous Texas ranch house becomes a grotesque charnel house, littered with fragments of discarded skeletons. Something in this image of pervasive, omnipresent death seemed to evoke Old Lady Horse's description of mountains of bones piled along the railway lines, as though the horrors of the twentieth century, the apocalyptic thunder of a distant war and the festering of a stagnant economy had been built atop the bones of earlier horrors. There is a violence that underpins the dream of the West. Its openness and apparent vacuity merely mask the centuries of bloodshed that created the illusion of emptiness.

Albuquerque, New Mexico

The painter Georgia O'Keefe once described bones as "symbols of the desert". To her, these sun-bleached artefacts, snatched from the thirsty sands of the New Mexico wilderness, encapsulated the duality of the American desert. "The bones," she claimed, "seem to cut sharply to the center of something that is keenly alive on the desert even tho' it is vast and empty and untouchable — and knows no kindness with all its beauty" (quoted in Pounders 20). O'Keefe, who painted dozens of images of the enchanted New Mexico landscape, clearly grasped the complexity and the apparent contradictions of the

American West. Although she described the desert "as vast and empty", she also understood that it was "keenly alive". There is always something moving out there in the dust.

If the American Gothic is, as I have been arguing throughout this book, essentially metamorphic, moulding itself to the contours of history and topography, the horror evoked by the desert draws from the landscape's apparent dichotomy: at a glance, the desert is dead. It is parched sand, dry and desiccated — the moonrock surface of some lifeless satellite — but, once you look closer, scrutinise its rocky outcroppings and secret, shady places, the entire desert becomes an ocean teaming with life. Philosophers and mystics often frame the desert as the locus of ascetic practice, a harsh, unforgiving environment in which to scourge the soul and excoriate the ego. The desert is sublime, in the sense theorised by the eighteenth-century philosopher Edmund Burke. Its immensity shatters our conceptions of time as well as of space. The desert is terrifying in its vastness, transcending all limits and boundaries. It causes us to hesitate in wonder and awe, but it also freezes us in terror. As Burke elucidates, such sublime vistas evoke a profound astonishment, a "state of the soul in which all its motions are suspended, with some degree of horror" (quoted in Morley). Yet, even in the midst of such a petrifying, eviscerating power, there is a liveliness to the desert that is difficult to express. Maria Del Pilar Blanco describes this vibrancy in terms of the "semiotic 'thickness' of the desert", a density that pulsates in the "heart of an ascribed emptiness" (67).

On my first morning in Albuquerque, the most densely populated city in the state of New Mexico, I hopped on a city bus and travelled east towards the Sandia Mountains. The peaks rise high over the flat basins of the Rio Grande and at sunset come alive with shifting reddish-pink hues resembling the rosy flesh of the watermelons that give the mountains their Spanish name. As the bus rattled along yet another fragment of the old Route 66, the road took on the characteristics of a busy supermarket aisle. Signs jostled for attention, billboards and neon adverts crowded both sides of the street like shelves bursting with brightly coloured goods. Motels, motor lodges, diners, fast-food restaurants, sushi places and pet stores flanked the long, straight road as it ploughed towards the distant mountains. Fashioned from adobe (a kind of mud brick made with earth, water and organic matter like grass, straw or even dung), all of these familiar enterprises became strange, appearing as though they had just been hollowed out of the earth itself.

A few stops beyond Downtown Albuquerque, the suburbs began to thin out in the foothills of the Sandia Mountains. Crossing the street after disembarking from the bus, I saw the crushed body of a snake lying in the centre of the road, its silvery black scales glistening in the sun. I followed the road to where the asphalt disappeared

Rusting cars outside an abandoned motel in Albuquerque

into sandy mountain trails. Everything appeared silent and still, the foothills a skeletal desert landscape. Nothing moved, and in that moment, the only life that surrounded me seemed to be parched thickets of scrub grass, the barbed spines of cholla cacti and low-lying clusters of prickly pears. Yet, despite the silence and the bone-dry earth, signs warned of life. A wooden placard informed unwary hikers that rattlesnakes could be found in the mountains, but that they would not attack unless threatened. Other posted signs listed mountain lions as local predators. I strolled along the pathways that threaded through the base of Embudito Canyon, where the earth was cast in shadow and cool, grey rock formations shielded me from the sun. As I walked, life unveiled itself. Birds chirped in the distance and butterflies flitted past. Cactus wrens nested in sharp, spikey cholla gardens. The trail took me higher into the mountains, where the plant life became increasingly dense. Tall spruce and fir trees, verdant and lush, replaced the arid cholla cacti that rose out of the earth like the clawed hands of the dead. Turning my head quickly, I glimpsed the long tails of desert lizards whipping through the dust as they darted between rock formations.

There is an uncanniness to the desert, an eeriness that sharply diverges from the architectural uncanny of the haunted houses I had encountered in the thickly forested hills and valleys of New England. Here, in the desert, the uncanny has less to do with Freud's concept of home as the site of repressed horror, and everything to do with an earlier formulation of the uncanny: Ernst Jentsch's 1906 framing of the phenomenon as an essential, ontological uncertainty. Jentsch is mentioned in Freud's later and much more famous essay "The Uncanny", when the renowned psychoanalyst first considers and later dismisses his predecessor's theories. Freud's vision of the uncanny is grounded in repression, the unease that emerges when things that should have remained secret and hidden come to light. Jentsch, however, attempts to pin down, to diagnose, the uncanny as rooted in a profound, disturbing uncertainty. Jentsch explains that in German, the uncanny (or *unheimlich*) signifies that someone "is not quite 'at home' or 'at ease' in the situation concerned, that the thing is or at least seems to be foreign to him". The word, he notes, "suggests that a lack of orientation is bound up with the impression of the uncanniness of a thing or incident" (8). To perceive the uncanny is to not quite know where one is, or what one has been confronted with. Jentsch goes on to observe that the most profound sense of the uncanny arises from "doubt as to whether an apparently living being really is animate and, conversely, doubt as to whether a lifeless object may not in fact be animate" (11). Thus, humans are innately disturbed by wax figures, mannequins and automatons. Our more recent fascination with zombies and the living dead might also be related to uncertainty's power to evoke the uncanny.

The desert embodies precisely this mode of uncanniness. Its initial silence, perhaps only disrupted by a sharp wind shifting the sands, suggests death. On first glance, it is a dead landscape, a scorched and still panorama where nothing could possibly survive. Yet, once you look closer, leaning into the tangled cactus patches, peering under rocks and beneath the shady patches of dry grass, everything comes alive: snakes, lizards, birds, insects, spiders. The desert offers up its own brand of rich, abundant life.

***

The uncanny vitality of the desert is perhaps most powerfully expressed in the profusion of "Big Bug" films that invaded cinemas in the 1950s and early 1960s. In these movies, giant arthropods, rendered immense through creative combinations of scale models, huge puppets and compositing, crawled out of the desert to wreak havoc on unsuspecting towns. Born of the atom, these gargantuan insects and spiders grew to inconceivable sizes in the irradiated sands of nuclear test sites. Dragging their grotesque bodies across the landscape, they demolished powerlines, devoured livestock — sucking the meat from their bones — and threatened to annihilate entire communities.

These creatures, emerging from the dry expanse of the desert, embodiments of clamorous, hungry life, can be read as the uncanniness of the desert writ large (literally). In the 1955 film *Tarantula*, a group of scientists who are using radioactive isotopes to accelerate the growth cycles of animals inadvertently unleash a huge spider upon a small community named — presumably in honour of a series of nuclear tests carried out in Nevada in the 1950s — Desert Rock. The spider, while a monstrous incarnation of nuclear anxiety, the terrors of a post-Hiroshima world, is also a creature native to these desert regions, where it burrows beneath the earth to hide from predators. In *Tarantula*, the arachnid's monstrous transformation speaks to the unsettling liveliness of the desert. Rather than an arid wasteland, the desert sands play host to an abundance of lifeforms that defy human understanding.

Early in the film, the characteristically strait-laced hero, Dr Matt Hastings, tells his romantic interest, "lady scientist" Stephanie, that everything that ever walked, crawled or swam on the face of the earth first set its footprint in the desert. For him, the desert is a primordial crucible whose imagined emptiness conceals a dark and threatening cornucopia of life. He describes the desert as alien, ancient and unknowable, "like something from another life. Serene, quiet, yet strangely evil as if it were hiding its secret from Man."

Desert biomes and their lifeforms are, in the American popular imagination, intimately bound up with such atom-age terrors. After all, it was here, in the moonrock landscape of the New Mexico desert, in an area that sixteenth-century Spanish explorers called *Jornada del Muerto* (Journey of Death), that the first atomic test took place. In a remote section of the Alamogordo Air Base, just before dawn on 16 July 1945, the successful completion of the Trinity test heralded the birth of the atomic age. Scientists, who had spent years racing against Nazi Germany to develop nuclear weaponry, had to wait for the desert rains of monsoon season to clear before attempting to detonate the device, codenamed "the Gadget". You can watch videos of the explosion on YouTube. They are silent, flickering in black and white, like an old home movie. There is a small explosion in the distance, a fiery sphere expands and then turns in upon itself. It disappears, swallowed by a brilliant white cloud that glows, rich and translucent, in the early morning darkness. The cloud expands, as if before a terrible thunderstorm, extending upwards and outwards, assuming the mushroom shape that has become perhaps the most readily identifiable icon of the nuclear age. William L. Laurence, the only journalist present at the test site, described Trinity in language that evokes both creation and destruction, genesis and apocalypse:

> And just at that instant there rose from the bowels of the earth a light not of this world, the light of many suns in one. [...] Up it went, a great ball of fire about a mile in diameter, changing colours as it kept shooting upward, from deep purple to orange, expanding, growing bigger, rising as it expanded, an elemental force freed from its bonds after being chained for billions of years. (9).

Watching the sky split apart, torn asunder by the immense, towering conflagration, Laurence could only understand the test in transcendent, spiritual terms. Trinity was monstrous, powerful, cruel, spectacular and divine. It was, when all was said and done, a new God for a new world: "One felt as though one were present at the moment of creation when God said; 'let there be light.'" (9).

The Trinity site was chosen to host the inaugural detonation of the nuclear age because, like the vast Western plains carved up by Euro-American settlers, it was understood to be empty, dead, lifeless. It was ripe for colonisation and cultivation, an empty space in which the dreams and nightmares of scientific advancement could play freely amid the barren sands and silent dunes. The scientific and military personnel responsible for selecting the test site regarded the New Mexico Desert "as relatively empty, and they valued that undeveloped space for its apparent capacity to buffer people from the dangers associated with making and testing nuclear weapons and storing hazardous wastes" (Hevly and Findlay 4). However, as Andrew G. Kirk observes in his study of the communities and landscapes impacted by nuclear testing, "Deserts aren't like the greener and wetter parts of the world where nature is right there not requiring much attention to be noticed and remembered" (13). In the desert, one needs to look closely and listen carefully, to give the arid surface of desert sands time to reveal the richness of life within. Indeed, as Kirk goes on to explain, the scientists who participated in the Trinity test would have spent years living in and around the New Mexico desert. They would have been aware that the area teemed with life, both human and non-human. The site of the Trinity test had once been the ancestral lands of Mescalero Apache nation, and the reservation on which its displaced peoples now lived was located less than fifty miles from where the bomb was detonated. Dozens of families — mostly Indigenous and Hispanic ranchers — lived within twenty miles of the test site. Those who lived closest to the test site had their properties seized. Some were paid a small sum to evacuate their homes, others were simply forced off at gun point.

Radiation travels; it is invisible and insidious. It is carried in the wind, in the rain. It settles in the earth, buries itself in the deepest parts of flesh and bone. As Joshua Wheeler notes, radioactive material unleashed in the wake of the Trinity test spread far beyond New Mexico, with fallout even damaging a batch of x-ray film at a Kodak factory in Indiana. For the communities that lived downwind of the Alamogordo site, fallout had a more devastating effect. Most nearby ranches were inhabited by poor families who drank the rainwater that collected in basins or cisterns. They ate vegetables grown on their own plots of land and raised animals who grazed on that same land. Although data is scarce, owing to either a refusal to acknowledge the health implications of fallout or a lack of interest, the region has seen a startling increase in a number of illnesses in the decades following the test. High rates of cancer, thyroid disorders, auto-immune diseases and other chronic illnesses have been attributed to the tests. In the 1950s, in the afterglow of the Allied victory in World War II and the emerging tensions of the Cold War period, information was tightly controlled, and for many it was difficult to acknowledge that the miracle weapon that had brought the conflict to a close might have a dark side. Moreover, in the years immediately following the Second World War, a hopeful utopianism accrued around the bomb. Scientists speculated on the positive, peace-time applications of nuclear power, while brightly coloured animated films, produced primarily for children, unveiled a new world where radioactive isotopes could be used to increase crop yields and eliminate hunger, where atomic-powered trains and planes traversed vast distances in record time, where homes were warmed by the glow of cheap, efficient atomic energy. Such promises of the radiant future that unfurled before the eyes of war-weary Americans superseded — at least initially — some of the uncertainties surrounding the atom. Although accounts of the bomb's devastation and the horrific effects of radiation had already begun to emerge from Japan, where the first wartime deployments of the atomic bomb had devastated the cities of Hiroshima and Nagasaki, it was easier to forget these accounts of scorched flesh and violent sickness, to look to the horizon and see a world of ease and plenitude.

The science-fiction films produced in the 1950s can be understood as a dark reflection of the era's early nuclear optimism. In films such as *Them!* (1954) and *Tarantula*, the inchoate fears that proliferated around nuclear weaponry were reified in the bodies of gargantuan arthropods. Certainly, many critics have dismissed the "Big Bug" films of the 1950s. Richard Hodgens frames these films as empty, hollow spectacles, arguing that "a twelve-ton, woman-eating cockroach does not say anything about the bomb simply because it, too, is radioactive, or crawls out of a test site" (quoted in Tsutsui 241). Yet there is something essentially uncanny in how these films represent their monstrous antagonists. The immensity of the creatures, their furious, fitful liveliness, seems to embody the repressed vitality of the desert. These creatures are eco-Gothic monsters par excellence; their outsized forms looming over vast, alien stretches of desert appear to enact nature's revolt against humanity's scientific hubris.

In both *Them!* and *Tarantula*, the sublime cruelty of the desert is emphasised in the opening scenes. *Tarantula* begins with wide, panoramic shots of desert sands, parched scrub grasses, powerful winds whipping across the dunes. The desert is possessed of a peculiar magic. The film's doctor protagonist quips in one early scene, "The desert, it gives people wonderful ideas!" — as though the strange, arid topography was somehow capable of possessing the human soul. *Them!* likewise opens with images of the beautiful, blasted desert. Joshua trees stand still, like sentinels on roadsides, and sand dunes lurch towards the horizon like some otherworldly ocean.

In *Them!*, atomic tests in remote desert regions birth a colony of gargantuan irradiated ants, who emerge from their subterranean colony to menace first a small rural town and eventually the city of Los Angeles. Crawling up from their colonies deep in the bowels of the earth, the gargantuan ants embody all of nature as they seek revenge against human arrogance. Like the eponymous spider in *Tarantula*, they devour the flesh of their victims, both bovine and human, reducing them to little more than discarded shards of bone, the rounded enclosure of a rib cage, a few enervated tibias.

The history of nuclear testing is legible on the landscape of the American West. Some of its traces have vanished, drifted away on the wind or been covered over by desert sands. Before the Trinity test, some scientists worried that the intense heat generated by the Gadget's detonation would interact with nitrogen and cause the earth's atmosphere to ignite. Careful mathematic calculations indicated that this was unlikely, and indeed the worst predications did not come to pass (Rice 49). Nevertheless, Trinity inscribed itself upon the landscape. There is a famous photo, taken just after the test; an aerial shot capturing the aftermath of detonation. A huge area of scorched earth, black and catastrophic, attests to the infernal blast that gave birth to the age of nuclear weaponry. Indeed, the wave of intense heat produced by the blast was so powerful that sand caught up in the 100-million-degree fireball at the heart of the explosion fused into a strange greenish glass that rained down upon the site. Visitors who came to the site after the Second World War, once the Trinity test became public knowledge, were greeted with what *Time* magazine described as a "lake of green jade" that had formed along the bomb crater. Journalists posed for photos holding great chunks of this material, which later came to be known as Trinitite. Tourists slipped it into their pockets on the rare days that the test site was open to the public. Motels, souvenir stands and rock shops across northern New Mexico sold the mineral as a fun curiosity.

Trinitite is radioactive, but moderately so, and is considered safe to handle. Though, it has since become illegal to take the mineral from the Trinity site, collectors still buy and sell Trinitite, a relic of the distant atomic age. Today, at the test site, fragments of Trinitite can still be found, pushed to the surface by worker ants constructing underground tunnels. Atop anthills, fragments of the green glass glisten deep and mysterious as the ocean. Further west, in Nevada, dry desert lakebeds are riddled with craters from the hundreds of underground nuclear tests conduct in the region between the 1960s and the 1990s. There are also man-made monuments to Trinity and the advent of the nuclear age. At the test site, which remains closed to the public — except for two days a year, a Saturday in April and another in October — there is a stone obelisk bearing the words "Trinity Site — where the world's first nuclear device was exploded on July 16, 1945." It says little else, remaining steadfastly silent about environmental impacts, illness or the destruction that followed. My schedule didn't allow me to visit in either April or October. However, I was able to see another of New Mexico's monuments to the atomic age, the National Museum of Atomic Science and History.

From the roadside, the museum was rather inconspicuous: another low-lying building almost obscured on one side by clusters of thirsty-looking scrub grasses. At a glance, it might have been another megastore, with its simple white façade and front-facing car park. Looking closer, though, other details came into focus. Half obliterated by the glare of the sun, its bright white casing narrowing and vanishing into silvery morning light, stood a single missile flanking the left-hand side of the building. Further down, towards the entrance, another pair of missiles appeared primed and ready to launch. These towering weapons, long-since demilitarised, stand as a testament to the apocalyptic tensions of the Cold War period.

Inside, where the high ceiling of the main atrium slopes down to the more confined space of the gift shop, I met one of the museum's curators, James Stemm. A grey-haired, middle-aged man with a warm and welcoming energy, James reminded me of the sort of kind, enthusiastic primary school teacher I wished I'd had as a child. He told me that the museum opened — in its original incarnation as the Sandia Atomic Museum — in 1969. At the time, the Cold War had chilled somewhat. After the Cuban Missile Crisis of the early 1960s, when the world appeared to be on the brink of nuclear war, but before the renewed posturing of the Reagan era, the late 1960s represented a period of relative calm, a brief respite from the pervasive threat of annihilation. The museum was established to familiarise Americans with nuclear science, to demystify the atom, which no longer connoted hope and possibility but destruction and terror, and perhaps to allay some of the fears that had grown to monstrous proportions over the previous decade. James explains that the museum was also a way of preserving the region's scientific history. New Mexico, after all, played a crucial role in the development of nuclear arms, and the Atomic Energy Commission felt that rather than destroy decommissioned atomic artefacts, it might be more productive to use them to educate the public.

James led me through the first part of the exhibition, which was centred on the Manhattan Project, the Allied effort to develop nuclear weaponry before Nazi Germany. After winding our way between placards showing black-and-white photos of grim-faced scientists and dense bodies of text mapping the geopolitical context of the project, we found our way to the bombs. In the middle of the busy concourse, where children darted between display cases and dads in Bermuda shorts herded awkward, gangly teens into carefully posed family photos, stood replicas of the two bombs that had been dropped on Hiroshima and Nagasaki, the first and only wartime use of nuclear weapons. Neither was very big, perhaps the length of a tall person lying down, and both looked precisely as one would imagine a mid-century atomic bomb. Little Boy, the uranium-based bomb dropped on Hiroshima on the morning of 6 August 1945, was long and cylindrical. Its body, which fanned out into a tail in the back and tapered to a flat nose in the front, resembled a small metallic whale or a child's drawing of one. The other bomb, Fat Man, was detonated over Nagasaki three days later, on 9 August. Smaller and, as its name suggests, more rotund, Fat Man was painted yellow and black. It looked incongruously like a cartoon bee. Nearby, walled off behind four panes of safety glass, visitors could see a replica of the Gadget, that first bomb detonated in the still hours before dawn broke over the New Mexico desert. The Gadget, James remarked, looks more like a science experiment than a weapon. A bulky, unwieldy thing, it was entirely spherical and reminded me of old textbook images of early satellites. Wires criss-crossed its exterior, looping in and out of the ports that pocked the bomb's surface like craters on the face of the moon. It looked the paraphernalia of a mad scientist — something that in a 1930s Universal monster movie that would pulse with dangerous, life-giving electricity — or the cranium of some wretched cyborg, unwillingly gifted with life.

James walked me over to a photographic exhibition that continued the story of Trinity. On one side of the hall, photographs of the test lined the walls. Clouds coiled in upon themselves, drawing in vibrant strains of red and orange. Pillars of cloud rose out of the earth, stretching into the sky, where the columns coalesced into soft, pillowy mushroom tops. The photographs, James explained, were taken with high-speed cameras. "It's ironic," he remarked. "The explosions seem so beautiful in the photographs." We moved on, following the course of the exhibition to images of Hiroshima and Nagasaki taken in the hours and days after the bombing. Some images recorded artefacts — incinerated bicycles and licence plates, burnt clothes and shoes — while others captured the famous nuclear shadows that for so long haunted the post-war imagination. In the most well-known of these images, you can just make out the blackened space where a man had been sitting on the steps of a bank. He had been waiting for it to open when the bomb exploded. "This person wasn't vapourised," James explained. "The shadow isn't a scorch mark where someone was incinerated." He continued, "It's because the light and the blast are over here," he said, gesturing with his hand, "and this is literally the shadow. And their body protected this part of the concrete from the light."

Nuclear shadows memorialise an absence. They are dark spots where human bodies protected walls and other structures from being blanched by the immense light of a nuclear blast. There is an eeriness to these shadows. They signify the weight, the tangibility of a body that has since been annihilated, a life extinguished. In a short story published in 1950, Ray Bradbury — who was born in Illinois and lived most of his life in Los Angeles, aside from a brief period residing in the Southwest — projected these shadows onto the walls of an ordinary suburban home. In this story, entitled "There Will Come Soft Rains", the last house standing after a prolonged nuclear war has been scorched by an atomic blast. The morbid phantasmagoria that dances on its western exterior wall becomes the only evidence of the once happy family that had resided within: "Here the silhouette in paint of a man mowing a lawn. Here, as in a photograph, a woman bent to pick flowers. Still farther over, their images burned on wood in one instant, a small boy, hands flung into the air; higher up, the image of a thrown ball, and opposite him a girl, hands raised to catch a ball which never came down" (230).

We turned a corner, rounding another series of display cases, and came to a cluster of shelves stocked with brightly coloured boxes featuring cartoonish smiling children, tin ray guns, rickety robots and sleek futuristic cars. It was almost as though a toyshop had somehow materialised in the middle of grim exhibitions on civil defence plans and radioactive fallout. "This," James explained, "is our 'At Play in the Atomic Age' exhibition." Toys, it seemed, were an important conduit for Cold War ideology. While girls growing up in the 1950s were caught in the eternal domestic bind of baby dolls and buggies, learning to emulate their mothers and prepare for lives as the homemakers of tomorrow, boys' toys invariably reflected the scientific and militaristic aspirations of the period. In her study on the politics of childhood in the Cold War period, Ann Marie Kordas illuminates how "toys for male children encouraged them to envision themselves engaging in a variety of 'manly' jobs as adults. The most important of these was the role of a soldier, and toys of the Cold War period designed for boys have a distinctly military theme to them." Toy missiles, ersatz nuclear reactors and brightly coloured "atomic guns" would all have been eagerly unwrapped at birthday parties and on Christmas mornings throughout the 1950s. An "Atomic Geiger Counter" created by Bell Products was another popular diversion. Moulded from bright yellow plastic, this "Geiger counter" only detected iron, but nevertheless sprang to life with a buzzing and clicking reminiscent of the real thing.

Another "toy" displayed nearby resembled a child-sized briefcase popped open to reveal its contents. The top part of the lid featured an image of smiling boy, hair neatly combed in that respectable *Leave it to Beaver* style, peering at an elaborate scientific apparatus. The words "Atomic Energy Lab" were written in a cheerful yellow, and the text below promised that the laboratory "performs over 150 exciting experiments!" The kit included a de-ioniser, a cloud chamber and samples of uranium and other radioactive materials. "After the 1960s," James observed, "these kinds of kits basically became illegal. I mean, this is a bomb in a box."

The exhibitions housed in the Nuclear Science and History Museum, collected under the roof of this low-lying, industrial-style building on the edges of a desert city, speak to the complexities and ambivalences of the atomic age. Replicas of atomic weaponry and monochrome photographs of charred cities sit uncomfortably alongside the rainbow palettes of children's toys. There is, it seems, an ambiguity at the heart of the atom akin to that which resides within the Gothic itself. For so many scholars of Gothic fiction and film, the mode is characterised by an uncomfortable simultaneity of repulsion and desire. We fear the monster, but we are drawn to it; we wish to look away, to cover our eyes, but we still peek through splayed fingers. The Gothic is sickening, abominable and horrifying, but it is also seductive, wondrous and alluring. The atom, at least for a time, appeared to occupy a similarly ambivalent position in the American consciousness. It was terrible yet wonderful; it was destructive yet also infinitely fertile; it might destroy our world, rending our fragile bodies with violent sickness, but perhaps it might banish illness and suffering from the face of the earth.

As I left the museum, turning back onto a boulevard that brought me to other streets whose even, symmetrical layout constructed a neat grid, an even crosshatch pattern scratched into the surface of the desert, I thought about the giant ants and spiders that populated 1950s science-fiction films and wondered about their relationship to this fundamental ambivalence. A warm breeze swept down from the mountains, whose bases flattened to dusty city streets. To me, they were the repressed life of the desert making a gruesome return, the seething vitality that had to be ignored to create a chimera of emptiness. I had also considered them, in typically monstrous terms, as the dark side of America's early fascination with the atom. Yet these radioactive behemoths were a magnification not just of the period's anxieties; they also encapsulated its myriad uncertainties. The philosopher Noel Carroll argues that "along with fission and fusion, another recurring symbolic structure for generating horrific monsters is the *magnification* of entities or beings already typically adjudged impure or disgusting within the culture" (142). Naturally, giant ants and spiders, as well as the gargantuan grasshoppers and mantises that scuttled across cinema screens in the 1950s, lend themselves to this process of magnification: they amplify all that we already consider repulsive. However, such monstrosities are animated not only by a sense of disgust but also by notions of impurity, a disturbing refusal to be situated definitively within our existing conceptual categories. The huge arthropods that populate the "Big Bug" films transcend binaries, evoking both wonder and terror. They are uncanny, sublime; they are wonders of the modern age both diegetically — for the horrified characters in the film — and also for us as spectators. We are transfixed by their grotesque bodies, but also by the power of the atom to create such abominations.

Los Alamos, New Mexico

I passed a few nights in a hostel in Santa Fe where my room had an immense mural of the *Virgen de Guadalupe* painted on the far wall. Her luminous pastel form hovered just above a wooden dresser, her feet balanced delicately on a golden crescent moon. The blankets on my bed were warm, scratchy and woollen. They reminded me of the piles of blankets that covered my grandmother's bed, always wool, always uncomfortable. In the kitchen, we were allowed to cook our own meals with leftover stock donated by a nearby Whole Foods. We could sit with our plates in the courtyard, where some guests crowded around board games while others huddled in corners smoking weed beneath the stars. Chopping vegetables beside a huge gas stove in the kitchen, I met an Englishman who told me that he had come to New Mexico to study philosophy. "Like, in the university down in Albuquerque?" I asked. He shrugged. "No. Out in the desert. It's called the Higher Consciousness Collective." He told me that he had started doing online courses with the collective during lockdown, mostly centred around mindfulness and meditation practice, but he had since progressed far enough that he would need to continue his studies at the group's headquarters. He had certainly joined a cult, but no one likes to be told that they're in a cult, and worse still, no one ever believes it, so I said nothing.

I decided to stay in Santa Fe, not for its vibrant arts scene, its bunches of dried peppers hanging from door posts, nor for its quaint adobe boutiques selling turquoise encased in silver, but rather for its proximity to the remote mesa-top city of Los Alamos. Founded in 1943, Los Alamos was the base for the Manhattan Project, the site where the bomb exploded over the white sands of Alamogordo was born. The region, which bears traces of human habitation dating back to the twelfth century, was occupied by homesteaders, mostly Hispanos, for much of the nineteenth and twentieth centuries. In the 1910s, a ranch school for boys was founded in the area, but in 1943 the school, along with nearby homesteads, was seized by the United States government, which invoked the right of eminent domain to transform the whole area into a massive scientific complex.

Los Alamos was selected for the project largely because it was isolated, far from both large population centres and international borders. The site that would become the city of Los Alamos formed part of what was once the rim of a huge volcano. Now extinct, the volcano would have been, at one point in its history, a huge, belching behemoth, its circumference exceeding fifty miles in width and the expanse of its body stretching to almost two hundred square miles. The city, as it expanded, would come to occupy four mesas that form part of the Pajarito ("little bird") Plateau. In aerial photographs, the four parallel ridges give the impression of long, clawing fingers reaching out from the bowels of the earth. In the 1940s, the secrets of Los Alamos were closely, and easily, guarded. At that time, the only way to approach the top of the mesa was via a single dirt road that climbed thousands of feet to culminate in a perennially surveilled checkpoint. During the war, as scientists raced to uncover the secrets of nuclear warfare, most of the housing was ramshackle: basic wooden prefabs and dormitories, with barbed wire fences snaking along the perimeter of the settlement. Higher-ranking personnel lived in more-comfortable homes on Bathtub Row, so named because they enjoyed the luxury of full plumbing. The secrecy that shrouded the bomb's development necessitated a panoply of code words and doublespeak. Los Alamos was referred to as Site Y and nicknamed "the Hill" by both residents and locals (Hunner 40). Those who lived on the Hill often framed their experiences as an adventure:

they were pioneers, advancing scientific knowledge and "settling" the Wild West. As General Leslie R. Groves, then head of the Manhattan Project, observed, the scientists will "like anything you build for them. Put up some barracks. They will think they are pioneers out here in the Far West" (quoted in Abbott 91).

When the war came to an end, Los Alamos was radically transformed. The secretive wartime project became a permanent civilian facility, the Los Alamos National Laboratory, which even today remains the town's main employer. The simple, hastily erected clapboard houses that had admitted winter drafts and summer dust clouds were replaced by ranch-style houses that reconfigured the military complex into an idyllic post-war suburb. Schools were built, as was a brand-new shopping centre. Indeed, while the media was prevented from reporting on the necessarily secret, and invariably atomic, work being conducted in the laboratory itself, national publications enthused about the safe, clean "atomic utopia" that had been constructed for the residents of Los Alamos (Hunner 44).

Early in the morning, just as the sunrise was beginning to colour the Sangre de Cristo Mountains the blood-red hue that lends them their name — "Blood of Christ" — I boarded a blue-line bus at the Santa Fe Transit Centre. Leaving the city behind, we followed a narrow road that twisted through mountain passes and along the sides of deep canyons and valleys. Small peaks and bluffs rose on either side, forged from great, towering monoliths of red stone. It felt like another world, like the surface of Mars. Tall, scraggly ponderosa pines ringed the roadside like scarecrows. In places, the rockface acquired a gentle, sloping quality that indicated points where the road had been carved out of the mountainside, a sculpture pruned from a block of marble. Yellow signs alerted travellers to the ever-present danger of falling rocks. We shuttled along highways whose cracked asphalt lanes bisected the sovereign nations of the Pueblo communities whose ancestral lands, once extending as far west as Colorado and Arizona, had been reduced to impoverished reservations.

As the road climbed higher along the mesa, traffic began to thicken, and we found ourselves coming abreast of a high concrete wall. Turning left, the bus entered a car park bordered on one side by small white and blue huts: checkpoints. The bus stopped and swiftly emptied. It seemed that every single one of my fellow commuters was disembarking here. Filing off the bus, they were greeted by military personnel in khaki-green fatigues who scrutinised the identification cards presented to them. A helicopter hummed in the distance, and the bus pulled away, leaving me the only passenger continuing on to the town. The others had disembarked at what I immediately recognised as Los Alamos National Laboratory. The early bus had been packed with workers starting jobs in research laboratories as well as in cafeterias, IT hubs and hallways in need of cleaning. The bus crossed a high, steel bridge that connected two of the mesas that formed the central industrial and residential nodes of Los Alamos. From the flat surface of the mesa, a thick covering of pine trees swept down to the canyon floor, thousands of miles below.

Los Alamos may be the brightest, cleanest city I have ever seen. Perhaps it was the silvery morning light or the wide-open streets — foreshortened through a trick of perspective so that the base of the Jemez Mountains always appeared to be just a few short miles away — that created this sense of pure, perfect cleanliness. The layout and design of the city, like many things here, is attributed to J. Robert Oppenheimer, a famous devotee of the majestic New Mexico landscape, who apparently organised the streets so that they cleaved to the natural contours of the mesa rather than adhering to the rigid grid patterns associated with military bases and American cities more broadly. The buildings were conspicuously, overwhelmingly modern. Though some were constructed from the adobe materials characteristic of the region's Pueblo Revival style, most were mid-century modern structures of glass, steel and concrete. Other buildings were newer, blockier, more symmetrical. Nothing appeared older than a century, and the cobwebs of history had been cleanly swept away. Certainly, there are no ghosts in the "Atomic City". Everything was so new that it seemed entirely unmoored from the past.

The clean, antiseptic quality of Los Alamos may be in some part due to the city's affluence. It is essentially a company town. Almost half of its citizens between the ages of eighteen and sixty-five are employed by Los Alamos National Laboratory. The city's population also boasts an unusually high number of advanced degrees (master's and doctorates), and Los Alamos County's median income is one of the highest in the United States. The city is also predominantly White, which is unusual considering that the state of New Mexico boasts a majority Hispano population and a large percentage of Indigenous residents (Slaughter 4). The overwhelming Whiteness of Los Alamos likely reflects the way the city was divided along lines of race and class early in its history. As Carl Abbott explains, in 1949, a new community was built at the base of the mesa; this was a smaller housing project for construction workers (105). Although the project closed in 1957, with the area being redeveloped for private housing, the Indigenous and Hispano populations who provided the majority of the city's support and maintenance work continued to reside outside Los Alamos, in Sandoval and Santa Fe Counties.

I walked through the city centre and out to its more sparsely populated suburbs. The canyons were calling me. Because the mesas are so perfectly flat, it was often impossible to tell at a glance that just beyond the rows of bungalow houses and children's playgrounds the earth fell away into a deep ravine. Behind a small park, I turned onto the Pueblo Canyon trail, following a dirt path that ran alongside a high metal fence with barbed wire protruding from its top. Emerging from a cluster of pine trees, my breath caught in my throat as I found myself balanced on the side of the mesa. Below me the rocks swept sharply downwards to the green base of the canyon, which was thick with trees and a rich covering of grass. Directly opposite me, another mesa rose towards the clouds. I felt as though I was standing on a crack in the earth's surface where the burnt brown rocks had parted to allow in slivers of blue sky and profuse, green life. The path twisted down the side of the mesa to where the rusted body of an abandoned car flaked apart in the midday heat. I wondered if this great, hulking thing had been here when the bomb was being created. Had it crashed — sailed over the side of the mesa, down into the lonely reaches of the canyon — or had it simply been

Pueblo Canyon Trail, Los Alamos

Los Alamos Project Main Gate, once the only entry point to the town

dumped here, like the corroded barrels that occasionally echoed beneath my footsteps. These blemishes in an otherwise pristine, primordial topography were my first tangible clues to the canyon's history, the first indications of how its spectacular, otherworldly beauty simply overlaid a corroded, potentially toxic legacy.

In an article published in the *Guardian* in 2016, Claire Provost points out that "the city is also partly toxic". It has been from the beginning. According to historian Jon Hunner, from 1944 to 1952 the Los Alamos Laboratory released untreated radioactive liquid waste into a canyon that ran alongside residential neighbourhoods. "Children," he writes, "romped through those canyons on their way to school or played among the sands and boulders" (44). Another source suggests that waste continued to pour into the canyon as late as 1964. The area was nicknamed "Acid Canyon", and it forms part of the Pueblo Canyon system where I now kicked my heavy hiking boots along narrow dusty paths. A report published in 2006 by the Amigos Bravos of Taos and Concerned Citizens for Nuclear Safety found a wide range of metallic, chemical and radionuclide pollutants along the Rio Grande and in the canyons below Los Alamos National Laboratory. In a later publication, a newspaper article from 2015 entitled "Los Alamos Will Never Be Clean", Staci Matlock observes that despite its popularity with hikers and cyclists, plutonium and other radioactive particles remain in the canyon. While human beings are exposed to low levels of radiation on a daily basis — from uranium and thorium in the soil and naturally occurring radioactivity in building materials like granite and brick — the Los Alamos canyons have regularly been found to contain higher than acceptable levels of radiation, despite attempts to reduce it by removing contaminated rocks and sediment.

For me, spending an hour or two meandering along the pathways that embroider Pueblo Canyon was unlikely to expose me to a meaningful amount of radiation. However, local communities, particularly neighbouring Indigenous Pueblos, have suffered significant health and environmental effects. Over a period of almost twenty years, the Los Alamos Laboratory conducted implosion experiments in Bayo Canyon that spread fallout, albeit in low doses, over the Pueblo communities whose lands bordered the town (Masco 135–6). Like much of the West during the early period of Euro-American encroachment, Pueblo lands were categorised as "uninhabited", so testing was typically carried out only at times when the wind was certain to carry fallout away from Los Alamos and towards these "uninhabited" areas. Though it remains difficult to map the precise impact of the laboratory's activities on adjacent communities, cancer has become the leading cause of death among Indigenous peoples since the dawn of the nuclear age (Masco 140).

There was a strangeness here, a haunted feeling that hovered around the edges of my perception. The landscape seemed possessed of a distinctly unhomely character, a weirdness generated by the collision of profound, inexpressible natural beauty and a creeping awareness of the largely invisible contaminates that had leeched into this spectacular land. In his work on post-Cold War atomic landscapes, Joseph Masco terms this phenomenon the nuclear uncanny. Starting from the Freudian conceptualisation of the uncanny as "a psychic process whereby sensory experience becomes haunted and untrustworthy", Masco argues that the "nuclear age has witnessed the apotheosis of the uncanny" (28–7). During the Cold War period, when the threat of instantaneous nuclear annihilation cast a sickly shadow over everyday life, this uncanny sensation was grounded in the awareness that, given the swift development of missile technology, less than thirty minutes was all that separated existence and annihilation. At that moment in time, it was entirely conceivable that nuclear missiles could already have been launched while ordinary citizens, completely unaware, went about their lives. In a post-Cold War context, the nuclear uncanny persists in the ongoing awareness of the damage wrought by nuclear fallout and of the insidious, enduring presence of radioactive materials in our environment. As Masco elucidates, "Fear of radioactive contamination has also colonized psychic spaces" (28). He goes on to explain that

> The nuclear uncanny exists in the material effects, psychic tension, and sensory confusion produced by nuclear weapons and radioactive materials. It is a perceptual space caught between apocalyptic expectation and sensory fulfillment, a psychic effect produced, on the one hand, by living within the temporal ellipsis separating a nuclear attack and the actual end of the world, and on the other, by inhabiting an environmental space threatened by military-industrial radiation. (Masco 28).

It was this strange species of uncanniness that assailed me as I weaved between the pine trees and the great, primeval boulders of Pueblo Canyon. Descending the path, the dry faces of rocks grew thick and scraggly with grass and plant life. Pockets of bright yellow flowers flourished in the shady sanctuaries beneath boulders and along the bases of trees. Butterflies glided past me, flapping their wings once or twice before sailing off over the canyon. It was difficult to grasp that in this area, or at least nearby, toxins — including hexavalent chromium, polychlorinated biphenyls and perchlorate — had been found in surface and groundwater. All of these poisonous legacies of the atomic age had for decades percolated throughout the soil and water. Yet, from here, the whole world seemed fresh, newly born. This, of course, is the essence of Masco's nuclear uncanny. "Radiation," he writes, "is colorless and odorless, yet capable of affecting living beings at the genetic level. In this sense, nuclear materials produce the uncanny effect of blurring the distinction between the animate and the inanimate, and between the natural and the supernatural" (30). Here in the West, radioactive materials are the spectres that rove across the landscape. In New York and New England, the ghosts I had encountered were more conventional: spectral horsemen and spirit-haunted séances. Out here, though, the incorporeal echoes of past sins haunted just as powerfully. They were as mean and spiteful as any poltergeist.

Writing about the ghostliness of the nuclear age and its insidious effects on Indigenous communities, Simon J. Ortiz, an Acoma Pueblo poet, describes "feeling a sense of 'otherness'" haunting those Native spaces colonised by the military-nuclear complex (337). It might be, he speculates, "an electric current/coursing in ghost waves through me?" For Ortiz, it was "no exceptional decision that Los Alamos Laboratories were located where they were nor where the bomb would be exploded. This was the remote, barren west after all, and only a few Indians were there" (254).

There is often a chasm, a temporal gulf between exposure to radioactive materials and the manifestation of mutation or disease, as if a past transgression has returned to seek vengeance in the here and now. The invisible, intangible presence of radiation in the soil, air and water — as well as its propensity to travel, windborne, for hundreds if not thousands of miles — engenders an anxiety about the once familiar world we inhabit. About seven miles from Pueblo Canyon, on the other side of a great towering mesa, one can find what Masco terms "a special creature of the nuclear age", *Chrysothamnus nauseosus*, a chamisa plant whose circulatory system pulses with levels of strontium-90 three-hundred thousand times that of an ordinary plant (32). At the base of Bayo Canyon, this dense, rubbery plant — known colloquially as Rubber Rabbitbrush — appears innocuous, even mundane, but it took root atop a nuclear waste treatment site, and mistaking the strontium-90 for calcium, absorbed the isotope into its circulatory system. The truly weird thing about the Bayo Canyon chamisa plants, at least according to Masco, is how healthy they appear; they seem to be thriving. Yet, a strange otherness, a wrongness, will always cling to these lifeforms. They have been transformed, possessed, in Masco's terms, by the nuclear uncanny.

Las Vegas, Nevada

At 8:00am on a Tuesday morning, I stood in the middle of a crowded casino watching flamingos coiling their long peach-coloured legs up into their soft pink bodies. They moved deliberately, gracefully, like ballet dancers flexing at the barre. On every side of their carefully staged habitats

— blue water, red rocks, palm trees, waterfalls — groups of tourists meandered about sipping brightly coloured cocktails festooned with cheerful umbrellas and glittering rings of salt. In the centre of the outdoor area, a fountain ringed by ersatz flamingos gurgled and spit streams of water into the air. A few feet away, a high-rise hotel stretched upwards into the cloud-dappled morning sky. Inside, the casino was its own self-contained universe. Rich carpets stretched from wall to wall, their patterns abstract and elliptical. Huge slot machines, more elaborate than anything I had ever seen, glowed blue, green, pink, yellow, red. They clicked into life, spinning, and spewing slogans, announcing wins. They jingled and clattered, though they consumed bills and tokens rather than coins. Just as I'd seen in movies, there were no windows or clocks, though the news played silently on high-mounted widescreen TVs.

My trip to Las Vegas was one of the few domestic flights I took during my journey around the United States. My train was delayed for more than half a day, and I realised that it would ultimately be cheaper and more efficient to get a refund and book a last-minute flight from Santa Fe's two-room adobe airport. Prior to this, my experience of travel had been exquisitely, sometimes painfully slow. I spent entire days sitting by the windows of trains and buses, watching the landscape as it gradually transformed: the lush green of New England gradually consumed by the clamorous vitality of creeping vines and spectral moss; the dense, sticky swamp drying out into the wide-open Texas plains. Flying was instantaneous. The passenger next to me pulled down the window blind, and before I knew it, we were landing in Las Vegas. The magic, the convenience, of my journey was appropriate to my destination, a city where everything glimmered with a chimerical veneer of enchantment. As I trudged through the arrivals hall, slot machines sang on either side, announcing prizes and playing electric tunes. Later, I would find slot machines in a pharmacy where I was buying shampoo and the woman in front of me was trying to buy cough syrup for her ferret.

Whenever anyone writes about Las Vegas, they always stress its essentially plastic qualities, how fake it is. Vegas is not a place, but a simulacrum of a place, and everything is cheap, mass-produced, crass. Yet, how could it be otherwise? The entire strip looked as though it had been moulded from Bakelite, sculpted from some miracle plastic, sometime in the middle part of the twentieth century. The hotels and casinos seemed like strange formations, coral reefs grown from some unnatural, synthetic substance. In Caesar's Palace, I saw Michelangelo's David shrunk down and placed on top of a fountain. At Luxor, I passed beneath the great body of the Sphynx, smaller now and playing host to innumerable selfie-taking tourists. Like many visitors before me, I felt as though I had stumbled upon a place outside of time, that Las Vegas was somehow freed from the constraints of both geography and chronology. Everything — from the pyramids to pirate ships — existed simultaneously, all available for consumption and enjoyment in this hermetically sealed pocket of pleasure. Las Vegas was a place beyond place, a whirl of spectacle and consumerist delight, frozen forever, a snow globe in the heart of the desert.

Las Vegas has always had an intense preoccupation with spectacle. For a time, in the nineteenth century, the site that would become Las Vegas was a Mormon mission, a way station on the route from Salt Lake City, Utah, to the Pacific Coast. In 1905, the nucleus of the city began to form in a desert oasis along the Los Angeles and Salt Lake City Railroad, and its reputation for hedonism and excess began in the 1930s, when the Nevada state legislature legalised gambling. By the 1950s, Vegas was known for sunshine,

Pinball Hall of Fame on the Las Vegas Strip

casinos and what one journalist referred to as "short-order marriages and six-week divorces" (Hill quoted in Kirk 176).

In 1951, the US Government began testing nuclear weaponry at the Nevada Test Site (NTS), sixty-five miles north of Las Vegas, at a point in the landscape where the Mojave Desert meets the Great Basin. Much as the sites chosen for the Trinity test and Los Alamos National Laboratories were understood to be "empty", the NTS was selected because, for many military and government officials, it was nothing more than "a desolate 1,375 square-mile patch in Nevada" (Anaïs and Walby 955). Yet, like the New Mexico desert, the NTS was not simply an uninhabited wasteland. Aside from local flora and fauna, the area had long been home to the Paiute and Shoshone peoples, whose burial grounds and ritual sites were annexed by the military and the Atomic Energy Commission (Anaïs and Walby 952). Between the early 1950s and the start of the 1990s, 928 nuclear tests were carried out at the NTS. Initially, these tests were above ground, generating immense mushroom clouds that filled the skies and were visible from the pool sides and high-rise balconies of Vegas. Later, with the signing of the Limited Test Ban Treaty in 1963, the tests moved underground, creating a network of craters that riddle the surface of the desert like bullet holes.

During the first years of nuclear testing, Las Vegas was alive with excitement and wonder. The regular detonations promised a new attraction in a city always hungry for entertainment. Sin City casinos hosted "dawn parties", where tourists would dance and drink the night away until, in the early hours of the morning, an atomic blast would illuminate the pallid skyline. North-facing hotel balconies were increasingly in demand as the ideal platforms from which to view the mushroom clouds that billowed up, like primordial steam, from the distant test site. The Las Vegas Chamber of Commerce distributed calendars listing dates and times of planned detonations as well as the best spots from which to view the spectacle. Casinos like the Flamingo, where I began my tour of Vegas, served "atomic cocktails" mixed with brandy, champagne, vodka and a splash of sherry. The bomb was also understood in terms of the sex appeal and glamour that had long been part of the city's allure. Young women, often actresses or showgirls, were selected to perform or pose as "Miss Atomic Bomb" or some variation on that title. In 1952, an actress and dancer named Candyce King was portrayed as "Miss Atomic Blast" in publicity photos released by the Las Vegas Bureau. Accompanying text described the young woman as dazzling the US Marines who participated in nearby nuclear tests by "radiating loveliness instead of deadly atomic particles" (quoted in Nakamura 133).

For a period between the early 1950s and the first part of the 1960s, the NTS averaged around one nuclear detonation per week. During these years, Las Vegas seemed caught in the halcyon swirl of atomic excess. Official publications produced by the Atomic Energy Commission said nothing about the potential health hazards of nuclear testing, suggesting instead that the remoteness of the site and the presumed predictability of wind patterns would protect nearby communities from fallout. In a 1957 pamphlet, whose illustrations included an image of cowboy sitting astride his horse while gazing at a mushroom cloud rising over the desert, the commission explained that "Nevada test fallout has not caused illness or injured the health of anyone living near the test site" (quoted in in Kirsch 238). Rather, because officials were initially convinced that fallout constituted only a minor danger to human life, they worried that any attempt to explain this small risk would confuse the population and potentially cause widespread panic (Hacker 239). Much of the early period of atomic research was characterised by a lack of concern with health and environmental repercussions, and so there is a scarcity of contemporary data about the impact of testing in the area. Nevertheless, surrounding areas, particularly downwind communities like St George, Utah, have been plagued by above-average levels of cancer, thyroid disorders and leukaemia. Similarly, studies carried out in the 1990s showed that military personnel present during NTS tests were more likely to be diagnosed with cancer, particularly nasal and prostate cancers as well as leukaemia. Throughout the 1950s and beyond, local farmers also claimed that their livestock were dying after succumbing to symptoms that looked like radiation injury.

The strange duality of Las Vegas reflects an uncomfortable dichotomy that has threaded its way throughout this book and is broadly indicative of the history of America itself. Idealism and hope are invariably balanced by something darker, a sorrow or a seediness that simmers just beneath the sparkling, alluring surface.

The glamour — not to mention the sense of strength and superiority — that accrued around the bomb was eventually balanced by a fear of its capacity to act upon and transform the human body in unanticipated ways. As Joseph Masco points out, the National Cancer Institute has determined that anyone who lived in the continental United States between the years 1945 and 1963 received at least two rads of iodine-131 (an isotype that can cause thyroid abnormalities) as a direct result of nuclear testing (26). Those who were children in the western part of the US were likely further exposed due to radioactive isotopes present in the region's milk.

There's certainly an uncanniness at the heart of this contrast, the brilliant promise of mid-century childhood in a land of milk and plenty tainted by the threat of contamination and of bodily degradation. While Masco views the atomic age as the apotheosis of the uncanny, we might also understand it in terms of abjection, a peculiar sense of revulsion that hovers at the limits of the thinkable. The concept of the abject in cultural theory was first articulated by philosopher Julia Kristeva in her 1980 book *The Powers of Horror*, where she attempts to capture the elusive tangle of abjection, describing it as a "twisted braid of affects", one that does not have "a definable object" (1). The abject, "the jettisoned object, is radically excluded and draws me toward the place where meaning collapses" (2). It lurks in all those things that must be expelled in order for the Self to delineate the lines of its being and demarcate the boundary that divides Self from Other (i.e., one's own being, identity, values as distinct from — and often in opposition to — those of others), internal from external, human from animal. Abjection inheres in the collapse of boundaries, the realisation that the thin stratum of flesh that separates the vulnerable core of interiority from the external world is porous, easily penetrable. The inexorable creep of radiation, and the attendant threat of transformation or deterioration deep within our cells, bones and organs, might be one of the most upsetting manifestations of the abject. The threat of mutation, of generations sickened and deformed by this invisible force, illuminates the fragility of the Self and the impossibility of severing the Self from the world it inhabits.

Many of the texts already listed here as exemplars of Desert Gothic play out this grotesque scenario, imagining bodies transformed by the invisible omnipresence of radiation. Many of these works, particularly the films of the 1950s, have a reassuring finality to them. With the help of brilliant biologists and upstanding army personnel — an idyllic Cold War marriage of science and the military — the marauding creatures are invariably destroyed, their gargantuan bodies burnt in monochrome conflagrations, the desert released from the brief reign of atomic terror. These stories are always a closed system. Order is restored, and the promise of tomorrow is made manifest in the formation of a romantic union. The scientist or doctor and his love interest are left in peace to look ahead to marriage and children. The nuclear family arises, untroubled, from the ashes of nuclear conflict.

This optimism begins to wither in later years, and subsequent portrayals of nuclear testing and its aftermath emphasise the long-term biological repercussions of the atomic age. One of the most unsettling and perversely violent cinematic treatments of the NTS is Wes Craven's 1977 film *The Hills Have Eyes*. Set in the harsh moonrock expanses of the Mojave, the film, as its title suggests, emphasises the uncanny sentience of the desert landscape. The desert is not simply peopled by a cabal of monstrous, mutated hillbillies; the hills and canyons themselves are imbued with an unsettling liveliness.

The film opens with the Carter family — retired police officer "Big Bob" and his wife, Ethel, along with their children and infant grandchild — taking an ill-advised detour through the dusty roads of Nevada in hopes of locating a silver mine bequeathed to them by a deceased relative. The Carters are, at least in the first reels of the film, a quintessential middle-class American family. Their large cumbersome station wagon pulls a campervan filled with kitschy domestic ornaments: floral table clothes, cheery posters, banal but carefully framed paintings of flowers. Big Bob and Ethel espouse the kind of bland Christian conservatism that appears harmless yet always resists change and transformation. Their two teenage children are blond, tanned and healthy. Their daughter and son-in-law have the most adorably inoffensive, plump-cheeked baby. Yet there is a pervasive sense that the maintenance of this ideal family structure is contingent upon both the exercise and repression of violence. As a former cop, Big Bob recalls the experience of being shot at, both by the various ethnic minorities he is tasked with policing and, inexplicably, by his own men. There is also a simmering conflict between Bob and his nebbish New York son-in-law, Doug. Yet, such violence is always contained, hidden behind a veneer of middle-class convention.

The fragility of this pretence is exposed when, following an accident in the desert, the Carters find themselves stranded near the Nellis Air Force Base, location of the NTS and four decades' worth of nuclear tests, which would have, in actuality, been still occurring at the time the film was made. Though the Carters never witness an atomic detonation, the violent legacy of nuclear testing manifests in a series of disturbing encounters with a mutant cannibal family who have made their home in the canyons and caves of the wilderness. The cannibal family's origins predate the commencement of atomic testing in Nevada, but that certainly does not mean that they are immune to its effects. An elderly petrol station proprietor they encounter in the opening scenes eventually confesses that the patriarch of the family is his own son, a "devil kid" who grew up to be a "devil man", explaining that in the late 1920s his wife gave birth to a huge grotesque child who tore the family apart and later fled to the desert. There, he made a home with a kidnapped sex worker and produced a whole clan of hideous animalistic children with an inborn propensity for violence and a hunger for flesh. Although it is left unsaid in the film, these children, all of whom are in their twenties or thirties in the late 1970s, would likely have been born during the period of above-ground testing that characterised the region's nuclear programme in the 1950s and early 1960s.

Crucially, though the tests are never referred to directly, clues to the region's history are scattered across the early parts of the film. Both the Carters themselves and the petrol station proprietor reference a military presence in the area. Early shots of a small pink piglet wandering about in the debris behind the gas station recall, albeit loosely, a central component of the Operation Plumbbob tests that were carried out at the NTS in 1957: over one hundred pigs were placed in aluminium containers at the test site, and when one bomb detonated with a greater than expected force, the pigs were exposed to unanticipated levels of radiation (Masco 307). Only two of the 135 test pigs survived for more than a month after the explosion. Images of abandoned homes and businesses, the skeletal structures of rusted cars and rubbish strewn across the highways also invoke the possibility of nuclear apocalypse. Adorned in fragments of bone — O'Keefe's symbol of the desert — the cannibals are death incarnate. Though they are not the only living creatures to creep and crawl through the desert — the canyons teem with snakes, spiders and buzzards — the cannibals emerge from their bone-strewn caves as representatives of a dead or dying world, a landscape that has been transformed through the continued intervention of techno-militaristic interests.

In reality, the long-term environmental impacts of nuclear testing have been difficult to trace, and where scientists have attempted to map the consequences of the tests, some results have been surprising. The NTS remains one of the most radioactive regions of the world. Yet, when I spoke with a staff member at the National Atomic Testing Museum on the Las Vegas Strip, he was eager to highlight that consequences for local flora and fauna were negligible, with local biomes recovering quickly from decades of above- and below-ground detonations. He pointed out that while "we're all carrying some type of body burden from those atmospheric tests", local plant and animal life recovered quickly. Citing experiments conducted by a scientist named Janice Beatley in the 1960s, he explained that while she observed cell changes in animals and plants exposed to radiation sources, when those sources were removed, both flora and fauna returned to normal after a generation. At the same time, vegetables and animals contaminated by fallout during periods of prolonged testing were consumed by local populations. Children, in particular, eagerly drank contaminated milk, unknowingly imbibing high levels of radionuclides.

Regardless of the reality of the nuclear programme and its legacy, *The Hills Have Eyes* imagines a remote rural populace degraded through lengthy, generational exposure to radiation. The members of the cannibal family are not simply wild and animalistic, many of them are caricaturised by physical deformities that suggest some form of environmental contamination or genetic mutation. The family's association with bones — they not only adorn their bodies with skeletal fragments, but also decorate their home with elaborate ornaments forged from rib cages and skulls — links them to both the hidden, uncanny vitality of the desert and to some of the darker facets of atomic science. Joseph Masco, in his lengthy treatise on the nuclear uncanny, draws attention to a bizarre, morbid programme known as Project Sunshine, a series of experiments overseen by the Atomic Energy Commission and based at the University of Chicago. In an attempt to monitor levels of the isotope strontium-90 present in the general populace and determine the wider genetic impact of above-ground testing, scientists sought samples of teeth and bones that could be tested. Because the bones of infants are more susceptible to radiation, the project was particularly eager to work with tissue taken from babies and small children. Consequently, while the ultimate objective of Project Sunshine was to determine how many nuclear tests it would take to undermine the genetic stability of the human race, when the nature of the project was revealed in the latter part of the Fifties, many perceived it as a form of "bodysnatching" whereby government scientists engaged in "a global search for baby bones" (Masco 29).

Craven's cannibals are not only associated with images of bones; in the film's climactic final scenes, they kidnap the Carters' baby granddaughter, planning to kill and cook the infant to ensure their own survival. While this violence appears to situate the cannibals within the larger framework of governmental predation, the film also suggests that the irradiated desert has become so perilous — imbued as it is with a greedy sentience — precisely because of the destruction wrought by atmospheric testing. Because the cannibal family are placed in opposition to the clean, middle-class Carters — a family so all-American that the matriarch has them pray together before setting off to look for help following the accident — they emerge as the sinister, irradiated counterpart to the idealised post-war family. The families are almost identical in structure, comprised as they are of grandparents, children and grandchildren. Yet, where the Carters are clean, respectable and engage only in socially acceptable forms of violence (law enforcement), the cannibals are sexually perverse, sadistic and hungry for flesh. Class, however, may be key to understanding where and how the two families diverge. The cannibals live a life defined by poverty and marginalisation, whereas the Carters are comfortably ensconced within the bourgeoisie. The suggestion here is that the lower socio-economic status of the cannibal clan has rendered them vulnerable to the health and environmental impacts of nuclear testing, while the Carters are shielded from these consequences. Rather than benefiting from scientific advancement as the Carters might, the cannibals become collateral in the pursuit of nuclear primacy and the atomic future.

In 2006, just as the United States was engaged in the post-9/11 "War on Terror", the French director Alexandre Aja directed a remake of *The Hills Have Eyes*. A more brutal, visceral re-imagining of Craven's film, the role of nuclear testing and its abject transformation of desert biomes is rendered much more explicit. In this version, the villainous cannibals are not merely implied to be the victims of radioactive fallout, they are definitively and canonically the descendants of communities ravaged by atomic testing. Although it replicates both the plot and, in places, the dialogue of Craven's original, the remake relocates its cannibals to the New Mexico desert. The cannibals are revealed to be the product of sustained nuclear testing, but New Mexico only witnessed one atmospheric test: Trinity. While most likely a simple oversight, this relocation could also point to the ways in which the entire American desert, the whole Southwest region, has been subsumed into a single, imagined nuclear landscape.

Aja's film is intensely interested in the ways in which atomic testing, and the fears it produced, abutted the utopian fantasies of the post-war period. The opening credits begin with a saccharine country song playing over images of a glamorous mid-century housewife gliding through the chrome arcadia of her brand new kitchen, smiling beatifically as she checks the progress of cakes rising in a high-tech oven. This vision of idealised domesticity quickly switches to a nightmare of destruction as the music hisses and spurts through a staticky interruption, and images of bomb blasts fill the screen. Photographs of children bearing congenital abnormalities follow in a bleak parade of sorrow. Like the 1977 original, this re-imagining of *The Hills Have Eyes* follows the Carter family as they are, once again, stranded in a hostile and seemingly empty desert. Technological advancements are alluded to, with son-in-law Doug noting the lack of cell coverage in the blasted wilderness. Yet, decades removed from the cessation of nuclear testing, the region's atomic history is rendered both enticingly retro and deeply sinister.

Nostalgia and terror become inextricably intertwined in the film's climax, which plays out in a desert "Doom Town", a faux community — seemingly abandoned — that was used during the period of above-ground nuclear testing to determine the impact of atomic blasts on homes, cars and contingency measures like bomb shelters. "Doom Town" — whose apocalyptic name appears to be the inverse of the more pleasingly affluent "Boom Town" — refers to two civil-defence experiments conducted at the NTS in 1953 and 1955. Officially termed "survival towns", the creation of the Doom Towns and the widely publicised images of their eventual destruction were intended to emphasise the importance of "preparedness", and to teach Americans that through hard work — and diligent consumerism — they too could survive a nuclear blast. During two above-ground tests, the Federal Civil Defence Administration (FCDA) carefully recreated ordinary American communities. The first Doom Town was comprised of only two houses, while the second was an entire town, complete with public utilities (Willis, "Exploding" 411–12).

An exercise in propaganda — more than 100 million Americans tuned in to watch the destruction of the second Doom Town live on TV — the Doom Town was also a display of unabashed consumerism. FCDA officials tested everything from venetian blinds to cars in hopes of determining which objects would be best situated to survive an atomic bomb. A company called Atlas Furniture, based in Las Vegas, provided home furnishings for the second experiment (Willis, "Exploding" 415). Ford, Edison Electric and Airstream also contributed products for the test. The construction of the Doom Towns was covered in magazines largely aimed at housewives — *Good Housekeeping*, *Home and Garden*, *American Home* — in rich, lavish detail, as though they were describing the summer homes of movie stars. Humorous "interviews" were conducted with the mannequins who would populate the town, enquiring about their fashion choices and elegant interior décor. Most of the mannequins were dressed in the most up-to-date outfits from the department store J.C. Penney. Later, surviving mannequins that had been returned to their manufacturers embarked on a nationwide tour of shop windows.

The publicity surrounding the Doom Towns not only made celebrities out of their plastic stars and helped to sell products that could now be advertised as "indestructible", they also painted a picture of the kind of Americans who, safe in their modern suburban homes, could be expected to survive an atomic attack. As John Willis explains, the mannequins were, of course, all white, while their positioning in well-appointed, fashionable ranch houses spoke of their class status: they were, to a man (or a mannequin), uniformly middle class ("Doom Town" 399). The appearance and composition of the mannequin families "symbolized for the FCDA a movement that targeted one and all, but in actual imagery excluded black, Hispanic, Asian, and Native American audiences" (400). The 2006 remake of *The Hills Have Eyes* centres on those excluded by the televised spectacle of the Doom Town and its dubious message of survivability. Though the mutant cannibals that torment the Carters are uniformly White, they are portrayed as the descendants of miners, the exploited underclass whose homes were seized by the government to be transformed into a suburban simulacrum for the purposes of determining whether more-valued citizens would survive a nuclear detonation. Initially hiding in deep mines, the miners and their families eventually left their subterranean refuge to populate the remains of a forgotten desert Doom Town.

When Doug tracks his kidnapped daughter to one such ersatz community, he finds the houses, each carefully decorated in mid-century modern style, populated not by the clean White middle-class families imagined by their designers, but by generations of deformed, mutated miners. Framing the monsters at the heart of these films as disfigured victims of radioactive fallout is a complicated, even contradictory strategy. On the one hand, it seems to absolve the cannibals of any responsibility for their crimes — they have been gravely wronged, after all. Conversely, though, the transformation of innocent civilian victims of fallout into grotesque cannibal monsters seems to minimise the more real and certainly less cinematic traumas suffered by the communities that were unfortunate enough to be positioned downwind from both the Trinity test and the NTS.

In any case, through its emphasis on the spectacle of the Doom Town, the 2006 remake of *The Hills Have Eyes* captures the tense interplay of wonder and horror that demarcates the history of Las Vegas and its unusual relationship with the NTS. The way in which the city of Las Vegas seized on the NTS programme of atomic testing, transforming it into a song and dance show, selling cocktails and memorabilia, seems to speak to broader concerns of the American Gothic. Beneath the fantasia of glittering dancers and beauty queens, the sparkle of neon lights flickering quietly against the desert dawn, something more unsettling lingers just beneath the surface. We might take the desert's silence as an indication of its emptiness, seizing upon its muteness and transforming it into something else: a frontier settlement, a hedonistic paradise, an ersatz suburb, a laboratory. Yet, the uncanny vitality of the desert always resists, pushing back against our incursions.

4. CULT OF CELEBRITY: CALIFORNIA GOTHIC

Los Angeles, California

Ever since the Garden of Allah was torn down and supplanted by a respectable savings and loan institution, the furies and ghosts have made their way across Sunset to the Chateau Marmont.
— Eve Babitz, *Slow Days, Fast Company: The World, The Flesh, and LA*

The bus sputtered to a halt in a quiet, mostly empty car park beside a Burger King. It was early morning, and the restaurant was still shuttered. On the other side of the car park, just beyond a small island of gravel decorated with a neat line of palm trees, a huge pink body swelled up out of the flat concrete expanse. The creature's enormous back curved gently, mirroring the distant, sloping peaks of the San Bernadino Mountains. Its incongruously bright colours standing out boldly against the muted brown hues of the Sonoran Desert, this cartoon-like creature was, I would later discover, an apatosaurus. On one side of its body, someone had had painted a brilliant red heart emblazoned with the words "I Love You". A few metres away, an equally immense *Tyrannosaurus rex*, coloured a queasy shade of luminous green, stood with his diminutive arms pulled close to his body. The whole tableau looked as though someone had plucked millennia-old bones from the sand-encrusted depths of the desert earth, reassembled them and wrapped the skeletons in new candy-coloured flesh.

The bus had stopped to pick up additional passengers just next to a popular roadside attraction known as the Cabazon Dinosaurs. The massive creatures were constructed in the 1960s to attract passing tourists to a nearby diner. A few decades later, when the businessman who originally built the dinosaurs passed away, they were taken over by local Christian groups, young-earth creationists, who opened a creation museum inside the huge prehistorical lizards. There was, I felt, a delightful, almost camp hucksterism in transforming a kitsch tourist attraction into a venue for religious proselytising while retaining its essential core of crass commercialism. As the bus pulled back onto the road, we passed a desolate patch of land, nothing but scrub grass and white desert sands ringed by a collapsing fence. A red wooden structure sat alone in the emptiness, accumulating dust and graffiti. Its windows and doors were firmly closed, and a hand-painted sign that was somehow still balanced on its roof read, "Robotic Dinosaur Museum Cave".

As we turned north towards Los Angles, the desert, which crept up tentatively to the roadside, populated itself with the ragged figures of Joshua trees, their limbs stretched imploringly upwards to the sky. Desert succulents, the trees were named by the nineteenth-century Mormon settlers who pushed west through Nevada and California and who, in their profound religious fervour, conflated the plants with the image of a ragged prophet wandering in a howling wilderness. In LA, I spent three nights sleeping in the spare room of friends, who upon hearing that I would be in California insisted I stay with them. Jerome and Faye are grownups, at least a decade older than me. He is a professor at a local college, and she exemplifies the sunny, easy beauty of a native Californian. They drink shakes and smoothies for breakfast most mornings, and Faye does yoga in the afternoons. Their house is a late-twentieth-century split-level structure perched on the edge of one of the many canyons that slice through the hills surrounding Los Angeles. Sitting in their garden, which slopes right down from the hilltops to the canyon floor, you feel as though you have been swallowed by the earth, as if some narrow fissure had opened in the surface of the world and you had somehow slipped through.

Each morning and evening, we would walk their two beautiful, boisterous springer spaniels along the trails that wind along the canyon's sides. They pointed out new houses built along the canyon wall, wedged like a child's building blocks into rocky crevices. They showed me empty lots, ghostly expanses once occupied by homes that were incinerated by the wildfires that sweep down along the hillsides each summer. We passed rough, dusty patches on land stripped bare by the dry, crackling Santa Ana Winds that blow in from the desert, and which according to LA lore carry with them a certain strain of hot, sharp madness. Compelled by windborne psychosis, ordinarily sedate Angelenos become angry, illogical, violent. In a short story titled "Red Wind", Raymond Chandler, perhaps the most esteemed chronicler of LA's dark depths, wrote that when the Santa Anas blow through, "every booze party ends in a fight. Meek little wives feel the edge of the carving knife and study their husbands' necks." We paused to look at dense clusters of cacti and aloe plants that grew around the base of certain canyon homes. Jerome explained that the thick profusion of succulents had protected these houses from wildfires or at least slowed the advancing flames. One evening, while we meandered along a quiet residential road that twisted through the tree-filled groves, the dogs began to bark excitedly and strain at their leads. As we held them back, a single sand-coloured coyote strode across the street, his ears high and alert, tail pointed downwards. He paused momentarily and glanced at us before disappearing into a tangle of trees on the other side of road. At night, when darkness stole in along the hillsides, the yelps and howls of coyotes reverberated along the canyon walls.

***

On a sweltering August afternoon, the first day of my LA sojourn, Faye and I huddled in a little yellow restaurant booth beneath rows of twinkling Christmas lights. Gold-embroidered sombreros hung on one wall alongside colourful murals depicting fiery-feathered parrots. Signed headshots of smiling celebrities multiplied across another wall, even spreading upwards to cover the low, tilted ceiling overhead. Stained glass lanterns illuminated the dim alcoves where groups of immaculately groomed older women clinked margarita glasses, and waitresses swirled past us in brightly coloured peasant blouses and ruffled Mexican skirts. We ordered enchiladas that arrived in front of us like fat, over-stuffed envelopes leaking salsa and cheese, plates heaped high with rice and rich, creamy piles of fried beans. The wide display window in front of the reception was entirely taken over by a hastily constructed set of shelves crowded with toys and trinkets: a pair of porcelain hands holding a heart, ceramic salt and pepper shakers shaped like fish, plastic dinosaurs, shot glasses and off-brand Barbies still in their packaging. I initially though these objects were simply ornaments, but on looking closer, I realised each one had been fixed with a little yellow price tag. Overhead, souvenir T-shirts, neatly hung on plastic hangers, swayed in the gentle breeze that wafted from the nearby air conditioner. On the front of each, the name of the restaurant — El Coyote — was written in careful, looping font.

El Coyote, Los Angeles, California

Outside, El Coyote was painted the kind of brilliant, perfect white that can only be maintained in a city that boasts 275 days of sunshine per year. The red awnings advertised lunch, dinner and cocktails. A red neon sign slumbered, unlit and silent, beneath the deep ocean of afternoon sky. There was little to distinguish El Coyote from the dozens of other single-storey commercial buildings that lined Beverly Boulevard aside from the small, black outline of a glamorous woman with teased hair and heavily mascara'd lashes stencilled just underneath a printed, securely laminated list of opening hours. This single image, a face, beautiful yet inscrutable, was the only indication that on another hot August day more than fifty years ago, an event that would change the course of California history and capture the strange duality of the Golden State had begun with a dinner at El Coyote.

The family-run restaurant has always been popular with celebrities, who, the staff claim, feel comfortable, at home, among the chintzy ornaments and kaleidoscopic lanterns. It's no surprise, then, that on the evening of 8 August 1969, up-and-coming movie star Sharon Tate — the wife of up-and-coming director Roman Polanski — dined at El Coyote with her friends. The next morning, Tate and her companions — heiress Abigail Folger, screenwriter Voytek Frykowski and hairdresser Jay Sebring — were found dead in the Tate-Polanski home, a red-shingled cottage secreted at the end of Cielo Drive in Benedict Canyon. Along with a young visitor named Steven Parent, the friends were victims of a brutal crime that was already, even in the first uncertain hours after its discovery, being whispered about in terms of witchcraft, Satanism, drugs, orgies and occult rituals. The next night, the crime was repeated, as two staid suburbanites — supermarket owner Leno LaBianca and his wife, Rosemary — were murdered in their seemingly secure Los Feliz home. Echoing the Tate murders, both Leno and Rosemary were stabbed, brutally and repeatedly, while the killers left unsettling, occasionally misspelled threats scrawled in blood on walls and furniture. It would take another two months before the Los Angeles Police

Department traced the crimes to a group of peripatetic hippies led by a diminutive former pimp named Charles Manson.

Aside from their very real human tragedy, the Manson murders are often understood in metaphorical terms and picked over for their significance, which seems boundless and endlessly interpretable. For the essayist Joan Didion, the Manson murders signalled the end of the Sixties, marking the bloody denouement of the peace and love decade while also exploding the simmering chaos that lurked beneath its dreamy surface. Didion's recollections of the crimes stagger not so much for their brutality, but rather because of how she presents the murders as unsurprising, expected, even inevitable. The late 1960s, as described in Didion's essay "The White Album", seemed uniquely laden with foreboding and shot through with nascent violence. Didion writes of how, when reports of the murders began to sweep through Hollywood, "The tension broke that day. The paranoia was fulfilled" ("The White Album" 47).

Yet, as well as being a story about the 1960s, the Manson murders are also a quintessential Hollywood story, defined as they are by an uneasy relationship between glitter and filth, glamour and violence. Charles Manson may be remembered as an uncanny guru who bewitched teenage runaways and enchanted the disillusioned children of a complacent post-war middle class, but more than anything else, Manson wanted to be a star. He learned to play guitar in prison and fell in love with the Beatles. He imagined that their music was a secret code only he could understand, a cryptograph that contained the secrets of the universe and clues to his own destiny. Manson courted the attention of celebrities, living for months with Beach Boys drummer Dennis Wilson and attempting to woo music producer and second-generation Hollywood royalty Terry Melcher. Despite his obsessive desire for fame, Manson's ambitions were frustrated, and his dreams of stardom were repeatedly crushed.

That such brilliant, shimmering promise might be deformed into violence and death seems somehow inherently Californian, as if in this blissfully sun-kissed, palm-lined paradise dreams must always be undergirded by some dark seething nightmare. For Bernice Murphy, a scholar of American horror fiction and film, it is precisely this tension between the "California Dream" and the "California Nightmare" that defines the region's Gothic imagination. Murphy explains that if California is "a place of perpetual sunshine with a stunning natural landscape", it is also a precarious territory "beset by natural disasters, pollution, and extreme weather patterns" (9). Similarly, if "California embodies optimistic notions of newness, functioning as a tabula rasa "where anyone can make it", it is also a place poisoned by "corrupt and unaccountable new hierarchies and institutions" (9–10). In this way, while New England Gothic might be understood in terms of the restless disruptions of history's ghosts, and the Southern Gothic might be characterised by the gruesome return of what has been buried, Californian Gothic is structured by an unsettling disjuncture between reality and fantasy, between the golden dream of the West Coast and the nightmarish distortion of that illusion.

In David Lynch's 2001 film *Mulholland Drive*, a naïve young ingenue named Betty frames her arrival in Hollywood as the distillation of a long-held fantasy, explaining that "I just flew in here from Deep River, Ontario, and now I'm in this dream place." Betty's words are not just hyperbole. As the plot unfolds towards its tragic conclusion, it transpires that Betty's dream place is just that, a dream she has created in the wake of a broken heart. Yet the film's central conceit — Hollywood as a dream place — has deep roots in how we think about both Los Angeles in particular and

California more broadly. Hugging the westernmost part of America's Pacific Coastline, much of California is idealised as a warm, placid stretch of land, with the ocean on one side and the harsh environs of either the Mojave Desert or the Sierra Nevada Mountains on the other. It's a little sliver of paradise between huge crashing ocean waves and jagged premonitory cliffs to the west and the hostility of deserts and mountains to the east.

In 1848, in the days before Mexico ceded the territory of Alta California to the United States — another patch of land swallowed by the inexorable march of Manifest Destiny — gold was discovered in the West. Thousands of migrants quit their jobs, sold their homes and headed for the Pacific Coast, dreaming of fortunes buried in the fertile earth of California. Religious exiles also moved west. In another essay on the strange allure of California, Joan Didion notes that Mormons initially attempted to settle this wild new territory, planting the first orange trees in the San Bernadino Valley. While they eventually retreated, the orange groves became a symbol of the fruitful, golden West, and for more than a century afterwards, packs of hard-scrabble Midwesterners moved out from the exposed, unforgiving plains of Iowa and Minnesota in search of a rich climate where one might grow something as fragile and exotic as citrus fruit. These settlers, Didion notes, "brought with them Mid-western ways of building and cooking and praying and [...] tried to graft those ways upon the land" ("Some Dreamers of the Golden Dream" 1). That's the other thing about California: in as much as it is an imaginatively fecund space, rich with its own unique promise, those who drift west invariably try to transform the alien landscape into something more familiar.

A few days later, after leaving Los Angeles behind, I would find myself on a bus winding its way through Santa Barbara County. It was a weekend and the traffic moved sluggishly along Mission Drive. I felt as though I had been caught in a sombre funeral procession. As the bus pushed on through dense traffic, we eventually found ourselves in a strange mountain town that looked as if it had been torn from a book of fairy-tale illustrations. Sheltered by gently curving hills that sloped down to bright yellow and vivid green fields, a sturdy white windmill, with its roof shingled and its four wooden blades painted a cheery red, stood out against the distant mountains. On either side of the road, colourful, half-timbered Scandinavian-style buildings gave the impression of some unreal, chocolate-box world. Faux-wooden signs advertised bakeries and pancake houses. In the windows of shops, colourful Christmas decorations, mostly carved from wood, were already on display. On each building, the stars and stripes fluttered alongside the red-and-white Danish flag. This odd little settlement that had so taken me by surprise was Solvang, a rural town founded in the first decades of the twentieth century by Danish immigrants and which by the 1940s had been transformed into a tourist attraction, a crude simulacrum of a Scandinavian village.

California is awash with strange constructions of this kind, odd pockets of fantasy created in hopes of realising some inborn wish, a whim of the builder's come to life in the golden panoramas of the West Coast. Los Angeles itself appeared to have been conjured up out of some similarly potent desire to render the ephemera of dreams in steel or stone or concrete. When the Santa Fe Railroad reached California in the late nineteenth century, hundreds of thousands of visitors travelled west to the Pacific Coast. In those years, the first concrete pavements were still newly laid, but many of the streets were simply dirt and gravel. Eager estate agents accosted new arrivals, attempting to sell them plots of land at a premium while prospectors snapped up oil-rich land across the city (Stein 5). For a time in the early twentieth century, when oil was not only abundant but close to the surface of the earth, oil derricks proliferated across the city, crowding hillsides like bare winter trees. By the 1920s, Los Angeles was producing around 20 percent of the world's oil supply, and many of the city's first tycoons made their fortune in the black gold that surged beneath the rapidly expanding metropolis.

Around the same time, just as the nearby town of Hollywood was incorporated into Los Angeles, filmmakers began to stream in from the East Coast. Attempting to escape the litigious agents of inventor Thomas Edison, who held patents over much early motion picture technology, film companies established headquarters in Southern California, a cinematic wonderland where the landscape yielded both rugged mountain vistas and a roaring ocean illuminated by year-round sunshine. The first Hollywood film was D.W. Griffith's *In Old California* (1910), an adventure set against the backdrop of Spanish colonialism. Soon after, the stars came west. Lilian Gish, Mary Pickford and Lionel Barrymore all followed the lodestar of cinema to California. New stars were also born. Tom Mix, the quintessential cowboy of the silent years, made his first Western in 1910, solidifying the imaginative connection between Southern California and the mythic Wild West. Even today, our understanding of the American frontier is informed less by the grit and violence of American expansionism than it is by the flickering phantoms of the silver screen.

Hollywood glittered then. It was a "dream place", but it always retained a certain wildness, a frayed edge of frontier danger. Movie stars and moguls built elaborate mansions — palaces, really — by recreating the splendour of the Old World on the edge of a wilderness that had not yet been fully subdued. Mediterranean-style houses were erected in inhospitable cactus patches, and elegant French gardens were hewn from the dusty rocks of the Hollywood hills.

The brand-new homes of brand-new stars gleamed with marble staircases and Moorish tiles. Italian-style piazzas blossomed with jasmine and gardenias. When Jack Warner, one of the most important studio heads of Hollywood's golden age, built his palatial home on Angelo Drive, he first created a weighty, decadent Spanish villa, and later, on the instructions of his second wife, remodelled it as a Southern antebellum mansion. When the house was sold decades later, the new owners discovered that much of the magnificent, "antique" furniture had in fact been produced in the Warner Bros prop department (Stein 45, 48).

***

Part of the Hollywood story has always been grounded in its duplicity, its capacity to enchant and beguile, to summon up ephemeral illusions that dissipate just as soon as they coalesce. The other part of the Hollywood story, one that has become just as axiomatic, is its essential fickleness. Hollywood raises up and deifies a new star simply to let them wilt in the darkness once their initial allure is tarnished. One of the most famous collections of dubious Hollywood scandals, Kenneth Anger's *Hollywood Babylon* abounds with such tales of faded stars who, alone and forgotten, haunt their dark, empty mansions like ghosts.

Anger, who claimed for much of his life to have been a former child star, was a Thelemite, a follower of the infamous British occultist Aleister Crowley. Crowley's religion, Thelema, which he developed during a trip to Egypt in the early part of the twentieth century, emphasised the power of the individual will. Crowley's maxim, "Every man and every woman is a star", opens *Hollywood Babylon* where it is juxtaposed against a hazy, monochrome photograph of glamorous performers poised to take a bow at the end of the kind of absurdly elaborate musical number that defined cinematic productions in the 1940s and 1950s. Crowley's phrase in its original context alludes to the divine energy he imagined each individual to possess. However, its reappropriation in Anger's collection of Hollywood tragedies touches upon both our very human tendency to idealise celebrities, to imbue them with some transcendent quality, and our desire — even potential — to ascend to the celestial heights of fame.

Hollywood Babylon opens with a story that the Anger clearly views as emblematic of the city's merciless caprice. In the book's first pages, Anger describes how D.W. Griffith created an immense replica of the Mesopotamian city of Babylon for his 1916 trans-historical epic *Intolerance*. At Griffith's request, set designers raised up huge white elephants and towering pillars. Thousands of extras, hopeful stars in waiting, lined up day after day to play Babylonian dancers, Assyrian and Median soldiers, slaves and royals. The set was so vast that the filmmaker's camera had to be positioned on a hilltop half a mile away to capture, in spectacular wide-angle shots, the glorious panorama of Babylon. In the opening pages of his gossip-laden tome, Anger describes how, after the commercial failure of *Intolerance*, the elaborate set was simply left to decay in a lot off Sunset Boulevard. He writes of how,

> long after Griffith's great leap into the unknown, his Sun Play of the Ages, *Intolerance*, had failed; long after Belshazzar's court had sprouted weeds and its walls had begun to peel and warp in abandoned movie set disarray; after the Los Angeles Fire Department had condemned it as a fire hazard, still it stood: Griffith's Babylon, something of a reproach and something of a challenge to the burgeoning movie town — something to surpass, something to live down (6).

Although most of the tales collected by Anger in *Hollywood Babylon* have no more substance than whispered rumour or tabloid gossip, there does appear to be a kernel of truth in the story of Babylon's fall. According to podcaster Karina Longworth, the mouldering set stood for a number of years after filming concluded and the movie itself flopped. An article from 1918 claimed that Griffith's Babylon was still "disintegrating in the rain on Sunset Boulevard in Los Angeles, a monument to the greatest play of its type ever produced". Reports suggest that the set was finally torn down around 1919 or 1920, and today the site is occupied by the brightly painted Spanish revival Vista theatre, which opened its doors in 1923. For a time, fibreglass replicas of the *Intolerance* elephants stood alongside reconstructions of the set's faux-Mesopotamian pillars in the centre of the Hollywood and Highland shopping centre. Later in the day, when Faye and I decided to wander along Hollywood Boulevard, following the stars down the walk of fame, dodging performers dressed in cheap superhero costumes and eager Scientologists distributing leaflets, we found even the faux elephants long gone. Apparently, the last traces of Griffith's epic failure — reconstructed fragments of his most ambitious set — had been dismantled in 2021 following concerns about the racist content of his earlier work, *The Birth of a Nation* (1915), the film that revived the waning influence of the Ku Klux Klan.

I was not surprised to see that ghost tours are ubiquitous in Hollywood. Here they function as strange otherworldly counterparts to the innumerable celebrity-spotting bus tours that lumber along Hollywood Boulevard before ascending into the surrounding hills to peer over the iron gates and high walls of celebrity homes. Since the 1930s, a decade when both the studio system and the star machine were at their height, a company called Starline Tours has guided buses full of visitors through the palm-lined streets and dusty hillside roads to ogle the mansions of the rich and famous. The underside of this glittering fantasy can be seen in the many tours that deal specifically in tragedy, scandal and the macabre. In 1987, a former mortician named Greg Smith created a dark reflection of Starline Tours, which he called Graveline Tours, that ferried camera-clutching tourists to infamous locations around the city where stars had breathed their last, dying in some shocking and ignominious ways. The company is now defunct, but dozens of other haunted-history tours still corral tourists along the city's main boulevards and side streets. Guides will gesture towards the iconic Hollywood sign, once a large-scale advertisement for a real-estate development called Hollywoodland, and relay to the assembled crowd the sad story of Peg Entwistle, a British actress who leapt to her death from atop the sign after her role in the 1932 thriller *Thirteen Women* was cut to shreds in the editing room. Tourists will circle the entrance of the towering Roosevelt Hotel, just across the street from the iconic floodlights of Grauman's Chinese Theatre, to hear about how Los Angeles' oldest hotel is haunted by the ghosts of superstars like Marilyn Monroe and Montgomery Clift. Lowering their voices, the guides will promise that if you look carefully, you might just glimpse Marilyn's spectral visage in the mirror that hangs, conveniently, just outside the hotel's gift shop.

Hollywood, I think, has always been haunted by its own death, remaining acutely aware of its own inevitable decay. Even as the stars glittered in the velvet skies and premieres and parties illuminated the warm California night, there was a sense that such beauty, such excitement, could only ever be temporary, a transient flame flickering in the darkness. The early days of Hollywood, at least as they are remembered now, are often imagined to have been as rich and decadent as Griffith's Babylon, an extravagant whirl of beauty and excess that was destined to burn out as quickly as it had come into being. In 1922, when former postmaster general Will Hays became chairman of the Motion Picture Producers and Distributors of America, the major film studios began to introduce morality clauses for their stars, attempting to replace Hollywood's reputation for debauchery with a more staid, middle-class image (Bode 91). After all, even while the medium of film was in its infancy, with the introduction of sound still five years away, scandal had already infiltrated the fledgling industry. By 1922, silent-movie comedian Roscoe "Fatty" Arbuckle had been tried, at least twice, for rape and murder, all-American girl Olive Thomas had died after accidentally ingesting syphilis medication, and director William Desmond Taylor had been murdered in a crime that remains unsolved to this day.

Perhaps it was this early flowering of debauchery, combined with the opulence of the newly born cinematic royalty, but Hollywood has, from the very beginning, expressed an awareness of its own impending decline. Ever since those first scandals broke, the movie people have imagined their beautiful mansions to be haunted, their rich parties populated with ghosts. In her collection of LA stories, writer Eve Babitz captures the ephemerality of early Hollywood in her description of how a glamorous hotel of the silent era was demolished and replaced by a Washington Mutual bank: "Ever since the Garden of Allah was torn down and supplanted by a respectable savings and loan institution, the furies and ghosts have made their way across Sunset to the Chateau Marmont" (139). Those ghosts, displaced from the mythic playground of the silent era, had to go somewhere, flitting across Sunset Boulevard to haunt another Hollywood hotel.

By the 1950s, the power of the Hollywood studio system was beginning to diminish, and the era when the

Paramounts and MGMs of the world exercised absolute control over every aspect of their stars' public personas was growing ever more remote. The first generation of Hollywood royalty was beginning to age, their glamour becoming increasingly frayed and tarnished. The decay that crept in during these years is perhaps most exquisitely portrayed in a series of Hollywood Gothic films produced between the 1950s and the 1970s. Beginning with Billy Wilder's *Sunset Boulevard*, released in 1950, and continuing through to exploitation films like *Hollywood Horror House* (1970), this strange little subgenre transformed the ageing stars of the silent era into restless phantoms haunting the dark hallways of their once luminous mansions. In her study of the California Gothic, Bernice Murphy identifies films of this kind as a central component of the genre, observing how the figure of the faded, often delusional movie star stands as a modern incarnation of the monstrous, corrupt aristocrats who were the first villains of the eighteenth-century Gothic novel. In particular, Murphy singles out Norma Desmond, the washed-up, half-mad silent-movie star played by Gloria Swanson in *Sunset Boulevard*, as the exemplar of the forgotten celebrity as cinematic monster: "Norma Desmond is a 'threat to convention' because she refuses to accept that her time at the top of her industry's social and economic order has ended. [...] she is an extreme representative of Hollywood's 'atrophying aristocracy'" (139).

Sunset Boulevard — often written *Sunset Blvd*, as on a street sign — is a film about Hollywood as a place, about its unique psychogeography and about how an unspoiled paradise can quickly become a decaying, Gothic ruin. The film's title credits begin with a shot of the titular street, the words "Sunset Blvd" stencilled on the side of a kerb. As the foreboding score plays out and the names of the principal players materialise on screen, the camera tracks along the length of Sunset Boulevard, remaining low and close to the tarmac. The name of the film, which is also its primary location, not only locates the film in the heart of Hollywood, named as it is after the road that runs like an artery through the city of Los Angeles, it also captures the profound melancholy that permeates every scene: sunset — the end of the day, the sad golden light that lengthens the shadows as night steals in.

Almost every scene unfolds in a palatial Spanish-style mansion that evokes the beautiful artifice of early Hollywood. The film's protagonist, Joe Gillis — who we meet in the film's opening flashforward floating dead in the house's swimming pool — characterises the mansion as a kind of revenant, a once beautiful body reduced to decomposing flesh and withering, flaking bone. An unsuccessful screenwriter, he first finds the house while fleeing his creditors and personifies it as a tragic old woman, like Miss Havisham in Dickens's *Great Expectations*, sitting alone in the dark in her rotting wedding dress and veil. In a comparison that evokes D.W. Griffith's mouldering Babylon, he refers to the mansion as "a great big white elephant of a place" and observes that it's the kind of overly ornate house that "crazy movie people built in the crazy twenties". The paint is peeling, weeds and rats are reclaiming the swimming pool, and dried, desiccated leaves crunch beneath his feet like crisp, charred flesh.

Joe believes the house is abandoned, occupied only by the ghosts of history, and while it is haunted, its spectres are of another sort entirely. Inside, Joe finds Norma Desmond, an ageing movie queen dressed in black widow's weeds. Along with her faithful servant Max (also her former husband and director), Norma is observing the funeral of a chimpanzee, an exotic pet, emblematic of her equally exotic history, which she buries in a baby coffin in the backyard. The sombre procession uncoils through the overgrown gardens, and the wind howls through the cumbersome pipe organ that occupies the living rooms, playing a melancholic, ghostly tune. *Sunset Boulevard* ends with Norma shooting Joe to death and, shrouded in a tragic delusion, descending the staircase of her crumbling palace to waiting police officers and reporters, all of whom she sees as adoring fans: "All right, Mr DeMille, I'm ready for my close-up."

In 1959, the popular science-fiction anthology *The Twilight Zone* re-imagined *Sunset Boulevard* as an explicitly supernatural story in an episode titled "The Sixteen-Millimeter Shrine". At the heart of the episode is Barbara Jean Trenton, a fading movie star played by Hollywood femme fatale turned pioneering director Ida Lupino. Barbara is an icon of the glamorous, soft-focus Thirties who, by the late 1950s, has become a bitter recluse. The opening monologue describes Barbara Jean as having been "struck down by hit-and-run years" as she spends her days watching her old films in a dark room, illuminated only by flickering celluloid. Like Norma Desmond, she inhabits a weighty Spanish-style mansion, a colossal structure whose emptiness has transformed it into an oppressive mausoleum. In the episode's conclusion, *The Twilight Zone* works its magic and Barbara Jean disappears back into the gaiety, charm and romance of 1930s, becoming a part of the film reels she spent her days watching.

Ten years on, a low-budget exploitation film known in some quarters as *Savage Intruder* and in others as *Hollywood Horror House* combined the archetypal Hollywood Gothic motif of the forgotten movie star with the burgeoning anxieties and incipient chaos of post-Manson LA. The film was written and directed by Donald Wolfe and starred two aging icons of Hollywood's golden age, Miriam Hopkins and Gale Sondergaard. Released in 1970, it was shot in 1969, with some sources inferring that the movie was an immediate and very direct response to the Manson murders. *Hollywood Horror House* weaves together a range of distinct cultural strands, fusing the core motifs of *Sunset Boulevard* with the grotesquery of the more recent film *What Ever Happened to Baby Jane?* Yet, as critic Ian Cooper elucidates, *Hollywood Horror House* exudes unease precisely because of how it "depicts creaky Hollywood glamor menaced by the sinister forces of the counterculture" (58).

The movie opens with images of a glittering premiere at Grauman's Chinese Theatre. Floodlights illuminate the sky; stars sparkle in furs and diamonds. As the credits unfurl, the scene cuts to the Hollywood sign. The camera zooms in, and we are confronted with the grim reality of Hollywood in the late Sixties and early Seventies. Rusted and filthy, the Hollywood sign is crumbling. Parts of its panelling fall off and tumble to the rocks and weeds below. There is no score, and the credits play out with no auditory accompaniment other than the howling wind that stirs the parched scrub grass below. The scene cuts once again, and we are confronted with a dismembered corpse, its limbs scattered around the base of the sign in a way that recalls the tragic death of Peg Entwistle decades earlier. There is a serial killer on the prowl, a disturbed young man named Vic, with all the requisite "mommy issues", who preys solely on middle-aged women. Moving through the darkness of the city, shielded by the guise of a handsome face and a young body, the killer's acts of violence materialise the cruelty of an industry that values only the enchantments of youth.

Ensconcing himself in the home of a forgotten movie queen, Vic haunts the enormous Spanish-style villa in his paisley shirts and long pendants. He consumes various narcotics in the silence of his bedroom, spikes vulnerable girls with acid and has a bright, neon poster of the Sabbatic Goat — a figure often associated with Satanic practice — pinned to his wall. The violent encounter between the deranged, fundamentally inscrutable murderer Vic and the washed-up starlet he first romances and then slaughters gives form to the paranoia that had blossomed in Hollywood following the Tate-LaBianca killings. For a brief period, when the air of the Sixties was still sweet and new, Hollywood opened its doors to itinerant musicians and artists, wandering gurus and aimless runaways. Homes along the secluded canyons and beachfront houses in Malibu throbbed with vibrant music and dynamic cultural exchange. However, after the murders, the divide between stars and ordinary people resumed its insurmountable character, crystallising into a potent strain of paranoia.

***

It was early afternoon when Faye and I pulled into the car park at the Forest Lawn Memorial Park in Glendale. The August heat was already excessive, intolerable, yet I felt a strange, inexplicable guilt about driving everywhere in the chilly comfort of an air-conditioned car. For most of my journey, which was now entering its second month, I had caught trains, hopped on buses and endured the agony of scorching hot streets all across Texas, New Mexico and Nevada. I wondered if I was missing something by sitting in a car as the hills disappeared into dense networks of flat, single-storey buildings before yielding, in an instant, to a thick phalanx of silver skyscrapers and high-rises. Faye, however, assured me that sitting passively in traffic as freeways and pavements streamed by like an unspooled film reel was an essential LA activity. Indeed, Los Angeles had degenerated into an angry snarl of urban freeways and overpasses early in its short history. The 1944 Federal-Aid Highway Act created approximately 1,938 miles of freeway in the state of California, an immense concrete hydra that ploughed through existing communities and ensured that impoverished Black neighbourhoods would be sectioned off from their more affluent White counterparts by treacherous multi-lane roads. Now, Los Angeles was a great congested conveyor belt. Vehicles were carried along slowly, moving often imperceptible distances over clogged roads. Traffic, and how to beat it, was a perennial topic of conversation. Like the weather in Ireland, LA traffic was a persistent yet uncontrollable force of nature, its ubiquity never preventing it from becoming the subject of intense speculation.

We locked the car and walked to the entrance of a massive Tudor Revival house, an imposing structure whose façade was criss-crossed with dark wooden beams. Its severe countenance glowered down at us as we passed through the main door into its cold granite heart. Inside, the staff distributed maps and information booklets. The dense stone walls, thick windows and tiled floors expelled any trace of the outside heat, replacing it with a sepulchral cold. One room sold vibrant, bountiful bouquets of flowers, as well as small porcelain crosses and cherubs, sympathy cards and miniature American flags that could be affixed to gravesides. In other rooms, discretely hidden away in the shadowy bowels of the structure, planning advisors directed grieving relatives and terminal patients to rich velvet couches where they would clutch tissues and study catalogues. Back out in the oppressive sunshine, we squinted at the huge expanse of flat, perfectly maintained grass that stretched across the opposite side of the road. A clear blue pond sparkled in the afternoon light. A fountain located in the centre of the water feature spouted gentle streams of white foam high into the air. The whole scene looked for all the world like a golf course.

Faye has no patience for the summer heat, and so she suggested we drive around the dozens of winding roads that wrapped themselves around Forest Lawn's soft, green hills. We wound our way along circuitous, looping paths, attempting to follow the tourist map that would direct us to the gravesites of Hollywood's greatest stars. The sticky pavements of Hollywood Boulevard may boast the Walk of Fame, but Forest Lawn Memorial Park is likely the city's greatest monument to stardom. Just past the Court of Freedom, where an imposing bronze statue of George Washington stands watch, resting peacefully in the crypts of the Freedom Mausoleum you can find stars of the silent screen Clara Bow and Francis X. Bushman. In the enclosed Garden of Memory, just down the hill, are the graves of Humphrey Bogart and Mary Pickford, while Spencer Tracy and Errol Flynn reside in the Garden of Everlasting Peace. The Great Mausoleum, which is likely the cemetery's centrepiece, looks rather like a medieval castle swallowed a Gothic cathedral. It rises huge and imposing over the green knolls of the memorial park, sheltering marble statues in its arched alcoves, its pointed spire piercing the clouds above. Inside, its cool marble hallways are adorned with replicas of well-known works of art, including Michelangelo's *Pietà* and an elaborate stained-glass iteration of *The Last Supper*. Amongst others, the mausoleum houses the remains of Michael Jackson, Elizabeth Taylor, Jean Harlow, Clark Gable and his wife Carole Lombard, and silent-era vamp Theda Bara.

I couldn't help but notice that the opulence of Forest Lawn is only matched by its disavowal of death. The cemetery is not really a cemetery, but as per its founder's instructions, a "memorial park". Its individual sections bear names like Vesperland, Slumberland, Inspiration Slope and Dawn of Tomorrow. Critics and sceptics have termed it the "Disneyland of Death" due to its outsized and explicit commitment to joy and celebration. Indeed, as if to assert that Forest Lawn might in fact be the happiest place on earth, Walt Disney himself is also buried here.

Forest Lawn was built in 1917 by Hubert Eaton, a man who — as he explained in a philosophical statement now etched on the wall of the Great Mausoleum — believed "in a happy Eternal Life". It was for this reason, Eaton continued, that he dreamed up Forest Lawn as "a great park devoid of misshapen monuments and other customary signs of earthly death, but filled with towering trees, sweeping lawns, splashing fountains, singing birds, beautiful statuary, cheerful flowers, noble memorial architecture with interiors full of light and color, and redolent of the world's best history and romances". In bringing Forest Lawn to life, Eaton created something new and unprecedented in American history, a cemetery severed from the reality of death. As Greg Melville notes, Forest Lawn "doubled as a spectacle of art, Christianity, architecture and patriotism, drawing millions of visitors annually and millions of dollars into [Eaton's] pockets". Moreover, Forest Lawn became a huge success, the burial site of choice for dozens, if not hundreds, of celebrities, and thus commercialised death and mourning in a manner previously unseen in North America.

Years later, British novelist Evelyn Waugh would lampoon Eaton and his philosophies in a 1948 novella called *The Loved One*. In the book, Eaton becomes Wilbur Kenworthy, the Dreamer, whose own insipid creed recalls the saccharine ideals of Wood Lawn's founder: "Young and old, they were happy too. Happy in Beauty, Happy in the certain knowledge that their Loved Ones were very near, in Beauty and Happiness such as the earth cannot give." According to scholar Lisa Colletta, not only does Waugh's slim volume parody the creeping sanitisation of the American funeral industry, a process that had begun with the nineteenth-century image of the exquisite, peaceful corpse, but it also slyly eviscerates Hollywood's obsession with illusion, fantasy and the promise of perpetual, unchanging beauty.

As Faye and I cruised along the roads of Forest Lawn, we noted both the peaceful quality of the landscape and its resemblance to a city park. In accordance with Eaton's instructions, there were no conventional graves, no traces of death's cruel power. Back east, in graveyards from Boston, Massachusetts, to Mobile, Alabama, the spectre of death was very much abroad in the cemeteries I visited. Thick granite headstones crowded the landscape like rows of jagged teeth. Hourglasses and winged cherubs, alongside the occasional airborne death's head, were carved into tombstones, a perennial reminder of mortality. In more-elaborate monuments, the marble bodies of weeping women were draped over cold stone, trails of lichen tears staining their faded cheeks. Here, though, I could not see a trace of sorrow, just verdant hillsides ringed with pine trees, endless stretches of perfectly trimmed green lawns and the occasional family sitting in foldout chairs by the almost invisible marker that indicated the final resting place of their departed loved one.

A few hours later, we parked just off Hollywood Boulevard. Leaving behind the crowds that milled around the star-dust trail on the Walk of Fame, we disappeared into an anonymous side street lined with rows of indistinct commercial and retail units. Just past Sunset Boulevard, the box stores and mirror-fronted modern commercial buildings began to thin out, replaced by the terracotta roofs of early twentieth-century Spanish revival structures on one side, and the high white walls of Gower Studios on the other. Small stage doors and shining plaster stars broke up the huge expanse of wall at regular intervals. After turning onto Santa Monica Boulevard, we came across a placid green landscape incongruously positioned between an auto repair shop and a strip mall. With its small guard post, high stone pillars and monogrammed wrought-iron fences, visitors might mistake the site for a film studio. Actually, this little green oasis in the heart of Hollywood is a cemetery. Marked on its street-facing sign by the eternal coiling loops of the infinity symbol, Hollywood Forever is bounded on one edge by the pulsing traffic of Santa Monica Boulevard and abutted on the other by the Paramount Studios backlot. This is a true Hollywood resting place. If you stand in just the right position in the centre of the cemetery's many winding paths, it's possible to see the Paramount water tower peeking over a back wall. Further in the distance, often shrouded by the mist that hugs the California Coast until well into the afternoon, the Hollywood sign can be seen hovering above the hilltops.

At the vine-covered gift shop that sits solemnly just inside the cemetery gates, Faye and I purchased a map of the grounds — a sort of post-mortem equivalent to the "Maps to Stars' Homes" that are sold all over Hollywood. Less meticulously maintained than Forest Lawn with its resolute disavowal of death, Hollywood Forever is, ironically, more alive because it doesn't seek to deny mortality in the same way. The grounds are eclectic and colourful. Unlike many modern American cemeteries, Hollywood Forever does not limit memorialising to nondescript flat markers embedded in the earth. It doesn't pretend to be a park or garden, though it incorporates elements of both. Headstones of different kinds proliferate throughout the grounds; some are traditional blocks of granite or marble, others are cut to resemble crosses, both Western and Orthodox Christian. In the Buddhist Cremation Garden, brightly tiled funerary stupas — tower-like monuments based on the form of Indian burial mounds — sprout like tropical flowers from the warm earth. Nearby Beth Olam Jewish Cemetery is demarcated by a colourful mosaic featuring a menorah blazing in vibrant shades of red and orange. There is a liveliness to the mausoleums, too. Inside the Abbey of the Psalms, we were enveloped by the cool embrace of pink marble corridors. Everything from the frosted stained glass to the crypts themselves glowed with the kind of gentle pink blush that, a few decades earlier, might have adorned the Beverley Hills mansion of a naïve young starlet. In other parts of the mausoleum, niches were fronted by glass façades containing all kinds of sentimental ephemera: black-and-white photographs of stern ladies in fur hats and serious men in fedoras, pictures of saints, wilted roses, a Star of David, a porcelain statue of the Virgin Mary, even a Fabergé egg.

As we wandered the paths, tall palm trees stood like a guard of honour on each side, their shaggy fronds silhouetted against the sky, a blotch of black ink spreading across the pale blue firmament. Plant and animal life thrived in abundance here. From carefully arranged, eternally geometrical rows of palms and cypresses to erratic elders, oaks and pine trees, Hollywood Forever is a profusion of green. Rubber plants and cacti grow, almost at random, at the edges of grave rows, and sunflowers clamour upwards from the base of headstones. Ducks glide across calm ponds and squirrels scamper along the roadside. Peacocks spread their great fan-like tails and a panoply of green-blue eyes blinks open. A colony of feral cats has even made its home in the bushes and shrubberies, becoming celebrities in their own right.

Hollywood Forever, though less staid than Forest Lawn, houses an equally impressive litany of stars. From the life-sized statue commemorating musician Johnny Ramone to the quiet crypt that holds the remains of Judy Garland, the cemetery is crowded with celebrities. Not too far from Garland's resting place, I was delighted and strangely moved to find a small monument to one of her best-known co-stars, Terry the terrier, the dog who famously played Toto in the 1939 musical spectacular *The Wizard of Oz*. Terry's memorial is, in fact, a cenotaph, a marker commemorating an individual whose remains lie elsewhere. In Terry's case, her original burial plot was paved over during the construction of a freeway — as if it could have been anything else here in Los Angeles — and the monument was built to honour her in 2011. On the day we visited, someone had left a tennis ball as a little gift.

***

That evening, I sat by the window of a bakery in Glendale as streams of people poured through the main doors, rippling and eddying around tables, pulling out chairs, flagging down servers, waving to newly arrived friends. A juice machine whirred behind the counter as it reduced baskets upon baskets of oranges to thick, fleshy pulp. Glass display cases were piled high with pastel-hued macaroons and delicate cupcakes whose iced tops had been whipped to a perfect point.

My evening appointment arrived with the tinkle of a bell as she pushed open a side door and slipped in. Clad in a long black dress, she practically glided across the tiled floor, somehow immune to the oppressive heat and jostling crowds. I waved uncertainly, and the woman approached my table, introducing herself as Myrna. Tall and pale with an air of old-world glamour, Myrna is a tour guide at Hollywood Forever. I wanted to meet her in hopes of understanding the cemetery's powerful allure and the unique, maybe even paradoxical intertwining of death and immortality that draws tens of thousands of visitors each year. The cemetery, Myrna explained, was founded in the last year of the nineteenth century, decades before the film industry was to blossom in Hollywood. Back then, it was simply Hollywood Memorial Park Cemetery, and most of its internments were ordinary people whose lives had ended in the young state of California. In the early years of the twentieth century, unused sections of the cemetery were sold off to studios like Paramount and RKO. In this way, it seems less like the cemetery was constructed in Hollywood and more like Hollywood itself was carved out of the cemetery. Naturally, Hollywood Memorial Park, located so close to many of the city's major studios, became the resting place for many of its first stars.

In the late 1930s, the majority share in the cemetery was bought by Jules Roth, a fast-talking conman who had committed massive fraud and then led authorities on a wild chase across Canada and the Northeastern United States. After serving around five years of a ninety-five-year prison sentence, Roth was released and continued to live a life of disreputable glamour. He bought a yacht and claimed tax deductions by maintaining that the vessel was used solely for the disposal of clients' ashes. He also had a bar installed in his office and boasted an impressive collection of pornographic postcards from around the world. He died in poverty in 1998, his tax scams having finally caught up with him. By the time the cemetery's current owner, Tyler Cassity, acquired the property — having purchased it with his brother Brent in 1998 — the grounds, as well as many of the tombs and monuments, had fallen into disrepair. Decades of neglect had seen many of the graves swallowed up by overgrowth, while crypts and mausoleums were consumed by mould or allowed to crumble into dust. The massive Northridge earthquake of 1994 caused further damage to the monuments, which Roth — heavily in debt — could not afford to repair. Indeed, by the time Roth died, one source claimed that the only revenue being generated by the cemetery came from regular $500 disinterment fees paid by horrified relatives attempting to rescue their loved ones from disintegrating plots.

Myrna went on to tell me about how the cemetery was, fortunately, transformed by Cassity, who not only repaired and renovated the site, but also transformed it into an artistic and cultural hub. "In any case," Myrna said, when Tyler looked at the cemetery "he saw hope, and he saw possibility." While others may have seen decay and a history of scandal, Tyler looked to the future, spending millions of dollars to revive the cemetery, which he renamed Hollywood Forever. "Tyler was a visionary," Myrna continued. "He is very artistic. And I think that's kind of how this cemetery is run. Because under him, starting in about 2001, we started the outdoor movies." Indeed, regular summer screenings are one of Hollywood Forever's major attractions. On warm evenings, when the sky is still tinged with purple dusk, one of the massive blank walls at the far end of the Fairbanks Lawn flickers to life as silver spectres float on the night air. First hundreds and now thousands of visitors camp on lawn chairs and picnic blankets to watch classic films in this historic location. The cemetery also hosts concerts and performances, and in recent years, the annual Día de los Muertos celebration has become one of its most popular events. A local take on a Mexican festival that fuses the Catholic festivals of All Souls and All Saints with pre-Columbian Mesoamerican practices, Día de los Muertos sees Hollywood Forever bloom with blazing orange marigolds and elaborately decorated ofrendas (altars) each October.

I asked Myrna about her work at the cemetery, curious to know what had attracted her to this career and what aspect of the job she finds most enjoyable. "I love Valentino so much. I've been the Lady in Black for twenty years," she responded by way of explanation. I nodded, understanding her enthusiasm immediately. I had seen Valentino's crypt earlier that day. Faye and I had found it, secreted away in a far corner of the Hollywood Cathedral Mausoleum. The unassuming marble vault bore a simple bronze marker that read "Rudolfo Guglielmi Valentino, 1895–1926". Its only decorations were two vases, filled with red flowers, on either side of the name plate. The modest nature of the memorial belies Valentino's superstar status. The star of films such as *The Sheik* (1921), *The Four Horsemen of the Apocalypse* (1921), *Blood and Sand* (1922) and *The Son of the Sheik* (1926), Valentino was the first sex symbol of the silent screen. When he died aged thirty-one, young enough for his beauty to be preserved in popular memory, thousands of fans lined the streets of Los Angeles to watch his funeral cortege as it proceeded from the Church of the Good Shepherd in Beverly Hills to what is now Hollywood Forever. In New York City, where the actor died, riots erupted on the street as fans clamoured to catch a final glimpse of the star.

The first megastar lost in his prime, Valentino is still an object of devotion and of mourning. Beginning sometime in the late 1920s, a mysterious woman in black, her face obscured by a funeral veil, has been known to visit Valentino's crypt on the anniversary of his death, leaving behind a bunch of red roses and solemnly daubing her tear-stained eyes before vanishing once again into the night. Although a 1938 article published in *Time* magazine claimed that the "Lady in Black", as she has since come to be known, was merely a publicity stunt, the tradition continues, with numerous fans and history enthusiasts assuming the role throughout the years. Myrna has played the part for two decades, herself becoming part of the star's mythology.

There's a tragic beauty to early Hollywood which is in many ways bound to its ephemerality, the gossamer frailty of those first flickering motion pictures. In the first few decades of their existence, film studios had little interest in preserving films that were seen to have served their purpose. If a movie had been screened in enough theatres and had turned a sufficient profit, the reels were often destroyed. After all, what use would these old film strips have in the future? Who could possibly want to look back at these old ghosts? As a result of the cavalier attitude adopted by studios during the 1910s and 1920s, many films have been lost to history. Some were intentionally destroyed, while others were simply left to deteriorate in storerooms and warehouses. In the words of film historian Kevin Brownlow, the majority of early American films were carelessly allowed to "rot or burn". In a report conducted for the US Library of Congress, David Pierce found that approximately 75 percent of films produced during the silent period have been lost. For this reason, there is an essential spectrality that clings to early cinema. Not only do the films that survive allow us to glimpse a vanished world, silent and jumpy, but they also speak to an entire mode of cultural production now completely lost.

For Myrna, an important part of her job is calling attention to and memorialising those stars whose names have since been forgotten. She also seeks to rehabilitate performers and artists whose works have been lost to the passing of time or whose lives have been unfairly eclipsed by scandal. One figure Myrna has worked to rehabilitate is Virginia Rappe. Mostly known today for the tragic and somewhat gruesome circumstances surrounding her death, Rappe was an entrepreneur and a fashion designer as well as an actress and model. For a time, all of that was forgotten, and Rappe was reduced to a punchline, portrayed as a loose woman, a victim of the orgiastic excess that characterised early Hollywood. People went so far as to leave rubbish on her grave. In her tours, Myrna tries to bring the real Virginia Rappe to life, introducing her to the public as an artist and businesswoman rather than as a victim or a joke.

Myrna also explained how Rappe's resting place has been cleaned and revitalised thanks to a group, which began on Facebook, called the Silent Film Cemetery Project. Myrna described how the group's members, most of whom are women, adopt the neglected graves of silent-film performers. "They decorate the graves," she explained. "They clean them, they take care of them. People used to leave trash on Virginia's grave. And now they are out there every single week cleaning it."

Myrna and her preservation work, as well as the joyful liveliness of Hollywood Forever, open up new possibilities for thinking about death and haunting. Hollywood's essential spectrality might arise from loss, the atrophy of glamour and stardom, or from the echoes of some terrible crime, but haunting also signifies endurance. A haunting is, after all, the endurance of spirit, or self, beyond death. In this case, and considered within the context of Hollywood history, a haunting might not be understood in terms of menace but as an act of salvaging. The ghosts of Hollywood, if treated with respect and love, can signify the preservation of the past, its endurance into the present.

Ojai, California

It was autumn in Ojai, a small town in the Topatopa Mountains. At least, it felt like autumn. While the air was still warm and the winds that swept along the road crackled with an intense, sinister heat, the ground was blanketed with a thick stratum of crisp, brown l eaves. Beneath my feet, leaves that had been ripped from the branches of the oaks and sycamores by winds stirred up in the high mountain passes crunched loud and satisfying. In the evenings, when the sun dipped behind the mountain top, the light took on a liquid texture as it cast mercurial shades of pink and gold among the hills and trees.

Ojai has an otherworldly air about it. Perhaps that's why I felt as if I had somehow slipped through a crack in time and reached a peaceful, golden autumn in the middle of an oppressively hot Californian summer. Indeed, the entire Ojai Valley has a reputation for spiritual and psychic potency. Some describe it as a vortex, a crucible of preternatural energy that facilitates spiritual connection and transformation. Some residents even believe it was this same psychical force that prevented the town from being consumed by wildfires in 2017.

Though the region has been considered a locus of spiritual energy — a reputation that predates the arrival of European settlers — Ojai was transformed in the late nineteenth century when Yogis, Theosophists and utopian thinkers flooded the valley in what could be viewed as a kind of spiritual gold rush. In subsequent years, these first spiritual settlers were followed by crowds of hippies, healers and health-food enthusiasts. Much like Western New York in the early part of the nineteenth century, the Golden State became, after the 1840s, the end point of America's colonial project and a wellspring of new spiritual possibilities.

Advertised to migrants who headed west — first in wagon trains across the prairies and later by train — as a veritable Garden of Eden, a paradise of lemon groves and fresh ocean breezes, California was conceptualised in utopian terms. Like all frontier regions, it was understood to be fundamentally "unchurched", having no spiritual bedrock other than the eclectic mishmash of faiths imported by settlers. Without an inborn religious tradition, new practices and belief systems could take root and flourish in the fabled Californian soil. And that's just what they did. New religions, esoteric sects and utopian communes sprouted like lemons in the West Coast sunshine.

According to religious studies scholar Philip Jenkins, California's affinity for new religious movements was environmental and cultural as well as practical. As the US frontier pushed further west on its ceaseless march to the Pacific Ocean, newly ceded states like New Mexico, Arizona and California were lauded for their warm, dry weather, which was perceived as healthier than the cold, damp climate of New England and the snowy winters that froze the Midwest. Doctors often recommend these regions to tubercular patients, who they believed would thrive in the arid conditions. Moreover, California law was pretty lax when it came to the establishment of religious entities. The process required little more than the payment of a filing fee and the procurement of a few willing witnesses. Similarly, low property values and abundant land meant that new spiritual communities could easily afford to construct elaborate temples and institutions on huge estates, affording themselves a degree of legitimacy that was then inconceivable in the more heavily populated East. It is for this reason that between 1850 and 1950, the state of California played host to more newly born religious communities than any other part of the US (Murphy 187). In 1913 one writer, presumably taking the city as representative of the entire state, described Los Angeles as filled to the brim with "faddists and mountebanks — Spiritualists, mediums, astrologists, phrenologists, palmists, and all other breeds of esoteric windjammers... whole buildings are devoted to occult and outlandish orders — Mazdaznan clubs, yogi sects, homes of truth, cults of cosmic fluidists, astral planers, Emmanuel movers, Rosicrucian and other boozy transcendentalists" (quoted in Jenkins 90). While many of these groups had their origins on the East Coast — both Transcendentalists and Spiritualists are, as discussed previously, native to New England and New York — it seemed that, for a time, unconventional religious organisations prospered with a peculiar vibrancy in the state of California.

Indeed, during our drives around LA, Faye and I had stopped to take in a number of sites associated with the city's cults and new religious movements. On the corner of Alvarado and Hoover, we paused to view a brick neo-classical church, distinguished by a huge, curved portico and imposing Corinthian columns. Half covered by creeping vines, the building once served as the Los Angeles headquarters of the Peoples Temple, an organisation that had begun as a radically progressive Christian church before eventually succumbing to the egotism and intense paranoia of its leader, Jim Jones. Today, if the Peoples Temple is remembered at all, it is for its apocalyptic implosion in the jungles of Guyana, which resulted in the deaths of over nine hundred people. On the other end of the spectrum, we navigated the perilously narrow road that climbed to the summit of Mount Washington to wander among the gently babbling brooks, koi ponds and tropical gardens of the Self-Realisation Fellowship Meditation Gardens. Established in the 1920s by Paramahansa Yogananda, the guru credited with bringing yoga to America, the gardens are a quiet, rich oasis where adherents and tourists alike can walk, meditate and take in the spectacular views.

The diverse groups that were — and continue to be — nurtured by the sunny climate and salty Pacific breezes of California run the gamut from apocalyptic cults preaching violent jeremiads to peaceful collectives of yogis and pacifists. However, this essential multiplicity hasn't prevented cults from becoming a key component of the California Gothic. Often imagined as abnormal communities presided over by an authoritarian leader who perverts their unquestioned power to manipulate, abuse and even murder, cults are frequently thought of as a dark mirror of the movie-star glamour that has become synonymous with the Golden State. Cult leaders might be understood, then, as satanic incarnations of the handsome matinee idols and sexy pop stars that populate our Hollywood fantasies, while their disciples could be conceived of as devoted fans whose adoration has twisted itself into something grotesque and monstrous. This duality, like the tensions implicit in Hollywood stardom, has lent itself to an enduring literary and cinematic corpus centred on murderous cults. From 1970s Mansonsploitation films, like *The Other Side of Madness* and *The Cult*, to more-recent examples of horror cinema, like *Starry Eyes* (2014) and *The Invitation* (2015), cults have been portrayed as the logical extension of an obsessive celebrity culture.

***

On my last morning in Los Angeles, Jerome and Faye walked me through the huge cathedral halls of Union Station, our footsteps echoing on the gleaming, freshly polished floors. Overhead, the high-vaulted ceilings resounded with echoed shouts and cries. They sent me on my way with a bag full of sandwiches, potato chips and massive slabs of chocolate.

After pulling out of the station, the train ploughed through Los Angeles and its adjacent cities: Glendale, Burbank, Simi Valley — places that had their own separate census designations but which had been long since swallowed up by the outward sprawl of the LA suburbs. After a while, the housing tracts and box stores began to fall away, and somewhere on the western edge of the Simi Valley, the earth creased into hills and mountains. On the side of the freeway that ran parallel to the train tracks, green fields and carefully cultivated ridges of rich soil proliferated. The earth yielded to acres of green shoots that promised rich crops: carrots, onions, cabbage, kale. On neatly arranged patches, strawberry, raspberry and tomato plants wound between thick clods of earth. Trees were ornamented with sunny, yellow lemons. Outside Oxnard, the train pivoted, and suddenly we were alongside the foaming, snarling Pacific Ocean.

I had come to Ojai because of the town's long-standing connection with cults, eccentric spiritualities and unconventional new religions. For much of the twentieth century, philosopher and spiritual leader Jiddu Krishnamurti gave talks and entertained luminaries from around the world in his home in the Ojai Valley. A school based on Krishnamurti's ideals still operates on West Lomita Avenue. Today, the area continues to attract New Age practitioners, devotees of Transcendental Meditation and even the occasional Scientologist. However, Ojai is perhaps best known as the centre of Californian Theosophy. Founded in the latter part of the nineteenth century by Madame Helena Petrovna Blavatsky and Colonel H.S. Olcott, Theosophy is an eclectic spiritual system that many scholars credit with popularising yoga and importing Eastern spiritual concepts like "gurus" and "karma" to the West. Theosophy draws on a range of distinct spiritual strands, including Hinduism, Buddhism, Masonic lore and Spiritualism. However, the core tenets of Theosophy centre around hidden adepts, or Ascended Masters, who exist in different forms throughout the world and are attempting to bring about a rebirth of an ancient religious system. Theosophy also espouses a belief in reincarnation and the spiritual transformation of the soul over successive lifetimes. Another key Theosophical doctrine is the existence of "root races", distinct evolutionary stages of humanity whose ascendance and ultimate decline reflect a broader cosmological schema.

In 1911, Albert P. Warrington, then president of the American Theosophical Society, founded a Theosophical colony in Hollywood. It was named Krotona in honour of the ancient mystical school of Pythagoras. Equipped with a temple, lotus pond, metaphysical library and a Greek theatre, one contemporary novel described this initial iteration of Krotona as "one of the most beautiful spots on the planet and a highly magnetized spiritual center as well" (quoted in Jenkins 91). In the early 1920s, Krotona relocated to Ojai, where it was rebuilt using primarily Spanish architectural styles. According to Warrington, the new Krotona was established in Ojai because, he believed, the entire valley was "impregnated with occult and psychic influences" (quoted in Hoye et al. 114).

Aside from the odd pickup truck or the occasional bus jittering past, the main road that bisected the town was oddly quiet. The shops and houses that bordered the central thoroughfare, Ojai Avenue, were an almost uniform collection of low-slung white buildings with a western motif and bright orange terracotta tiles adorning their roofs. Quirky shops that had been established — hastily, it seemed — in old petrol stations sold hemp clothing and second-hand shoes. The windows of fashionable boutiques were crowded with designer dresses, artisanal foods and a wide array of hand-crafted ornaments. The town's post office featured a tall white bell tower that lengthened into the bright summer sky. On every side, mountains rose above thick, verdant treetops and the clouds hung low in the sky.

I followed a little roadside path that brought me from the busy shops and restaurants of the town centre to a two-lane highway and eventually onto a small country road bordered on both sides by wooden fences and thick mats of yellow-green grass. A narrow lane twisted off to one side and disappeared around a dense grove of trees. According to the wooden sign posted at the top of the lane, this was the Krotona Institute of Theosophy. However, I saw nothing expect for acres and acres of grassland and tress. I resolved to follow the path, which guided me through seemingly infinite meadows. Though Krotona continues to operate as a school of Theosophy and a spiritual centre, I had arrived on a day when the building was closed and the grounds were deserted.

I eventually found myself at a cluster of Spanish-style buildings that constitute the institute's primary structures.

The orange terracotta rooftops blazed in the sun. The School of Theosophy slumbered quietly among the pines; wind chimes jangled on the porch of the shuttered bookshop. I meandered along a few of the countless intersecting paths that coiled through the hills of the institute's grounds. On a stretch of flat land, just at the bottom of a gentle knoll, a rose garden bloomed in vibrant shades of red, yellow, white, pink. Thick and richly scented, the flowers formed an elaborately patterned carpet that seemed, through a trick of perspective, to stretch all the way to the distant, violet mountains. In the centre of the grounds, I came upon the Krotona Institute Library, a low, tiled building that wrapped around a peaceful, shady courtyard. The library boasts over eight thousand books on various occult subjects, spirituality, yoga, healing, philosophy and spirituality. It was closed now, but I wandered around its courtyard picking up brochures on different aspects of Theosophy. Sitting opposite a gently trickling fountain, I watched a hummingbird carefully orbit the streams of water, darting in and then fluttering away in an instant.

I'm not sure whether Theosophy could be described as a cult. It's older now than some stands of Christianity that have made their way into the mainstream. Objectively, a cult is simply a small, unorthodox or novel religious or spiritual system. In recent years, particularly in the aftermath of events like the Manson murders and the tragic dissolution of the Peoples Temple, the word has acquired negative, even frightening associations. According to religious studies scholars Douglas E. Cowan and David G. Bromley, "'cult' has become little more than a convenient, if largely inaccurate and always pejorative, shorthand for a religious group that must be presented as odd or dangerous for the purposes of an emerging news story" (2). The problem with the often-sensational language employed when discussing cultic groups is that it fails to distinguish between the small number of actually dangerous groups and the many organisations that espouse unconventional yet ultimately harmless philosophies. In the system of conceptual binaries that delineates the Californian Gothic, cults, broadly defined, often serve as a convenient antithesis to the dreams of fame and fortune that have long since attached themselves to the region.

In a quiet patch of land at the heart of Krotona, I found a labyrinth formed out of spirals of carefully positioned stones. Later, I read that the labyrinth's concentric circles were intended to replicate the involution and evolution of the universe itself. The Ojai Valley, which spread out around me, was so still, so silent. It was hard to believe that only fifteen miles away great ocean waves were rumbling and breaking against the rugged Pacific Coast. I had read that the Theosophists were drawn to this land precisely because of the looming presence of the Pacific Ocean. In Theosophical thought, the earth has been dominated at various times by great races whose fates have waxed and waned across the aeons. Beginning with the Polarian and the Hyperboreans, continuing through to the Lemurians and the Atlanteans, the earth had now reached the stage when European Aryans were in ascendency. However, that race too would eventually deteriorate and would be replaced by a new, sixth race, which Theosophists expected to arise in the Pacific regions of North America (Jenkins 81–82). California, then, was a site of renewal, holding the promise of a new age.

San Jose, California

The journey north from Ventura to San Jose is a transformative one. Moving up the coast, the landscape shakes off the smooth sandy beaches of Southern California and grows rough, craggy, angry. Most of the way to San Luis Obispo, where we exchanged our train for a connecting bus, the tracks hugged the coast, twisting and turning with the shoreline as it undertook its monstrous transformation. I stared past my own spectral reflection in the glass to watch fecund farmland yield to scrub grasses and thick, spiny sage brush. Patches of resilient yellow flowers sprouted among the dry, papery limbs of skeletal shrubs. The ubiquitous palm trees of Los Angeles were replaced here by strong, resolute pine trees whose bodies had been bent into bizarre contortions by the force of the coastal winds. The ocean appeared ominous as its waves crashed violently against the coast, frothing and seething rabid white foam.

Located inland, just at the bottom curve of the San Francisco Bay, San Jose is a warm, blissful respite from the cutting winds and pervasive chill of the coast. There are still palm trees along its streets, and the plant life has a softness lacking in the hardy grasses and gnarled trees that face onto the Pacific Ocean. If San Jose is known at all by aficionados of horror and the Gothic, it's probably thanks to the Winchester Mystery House, a vast, sprawling Victorian mansion whose construction began in 1886 and continued — ceaselessly, according to most accounts — until 1922. The house was constructed on the orders of Sarah Winchester, whose husband, before his early death from tuberculosis, had been the heir to the Winchester rifle fortune. Most versions of the story assert that Sarah, wracked by grief over the death of her husband, consulted a psychic medium who told her that the misfortunes that plagued her family stemmed from the angry spirits of those killed by Winchester rifles. On the medium's advice, she decided to thwart the spirits by building a huge labyrinthine house filled with staircases that led nowhere, doors that revealed nothing more than brick walls and corridors that culminated in dead ends. Sarah's story, as relayed by guides and tourist brochures, is as compelling as it is chilling. We imagine a tormented, maddened old woman frantically commanding an army of builders to never cease construction on her expansive mansion, to keep building so that she might hide from the spirits she felt eternally at her back. Yet, as Colin Dickey observes, much of Sarah Winchester's story is a fabrication. Her compulsive building and rebuilding, he explains, were not rituals to ward off the spirits of the dead. Instead, he suggests that they may have been an expression of eccentricity, a desire to experiment with architectural form or even an attempt to evade potential houseguests. It could have been any one of these, or a combination of all three, yet Sarah's story is still widely relayed as a tale madness, terror and post-mortem vengeance.

The Winchester House is, of course, one of the many models suggested for Shirley Jackson's Hill House, although in Jackson's version, much of the supernatural mythopoeia is stripped away. Hill House is seemingly devoid of ghosts. It is the house itself that interests Jackson. Unable to determine the source of the revulsion within the walls of Hill House, the characters find themselves preoccupied by its disconcerting architectural qualities, bewitched by this erratic structure that seems to "have formed itself, flying together under the hands of its builders, fitting itself into its own construction of lines and angles" (Jackson 35).

Sarah Winchester's story, as it has been relayed and deformed by countless retellings, seems a quintessentially Californian tale. It is a story of eccentricity, commerce and the repercussions of corporate greed. Most of all, however, it is the story of a move west — after her husband's death, Sarah left Connecticut for the Pacific Coast — and the renewal facilitated by such a journey.

However, on this occasion, I wasn't here for the Mystery House and its forest of turrets or its melancholic statues. Instead, I had come to learn about yet another cultic organisation that had taken root in the warm Californian soil. About two miles from the Winchester House, in an area characterised by neat suburban homes surrounded by carefully trimmed hedges, immaculate lawns and streets sheltered by the boughs of lush green trees, I found myself standing in front of an Egyptian temple. Gargantuan white pillars painted with royal-blue geometrical patterns supported heavy white beams embossed with what appeared to be delicate hieroglyphics. Rows of regal plaster rams, their horns curved back like the ornate headdresses of ancient pharaohs, lined a walkway that led to a high golden door. This odd, anachronistic manifestation was San Jose's illustrious Rosicrucian Egyptian Museum.

Although the museum boasts the largest collection of Egyptian artefacts on the West Coast of the United States, its true power lies in its position at the nexus of American Rosicrucianism. Like Theosophy, the Rosicrucian order was one of the primary conduits through which esoteric philosophies were disseminated in the late nineteenth and

Entrance to the Rosicrucian Egyptian Museum, San Jose, California

early twentieth centuries (Jenkins 82–3). Various strands of Rosicrucianism — a hermetic order whose official history spoke of a secretive cabal of alchemists working to bring enlightenment to the world — have been nurtured in the United States since at least the seventeenth century. The San Jose variety, however, derives from a branch established in 1915 by H. Spencer Lewis, who, in creating an organisation which he called the Ancient and Mystical Order Rosae Crucis (AMORC), drew liberally on the Theosophical teachings and on the structures of other hermetic orders, such as the Golden Dawn. The Rosicrucians, broadly speaking, claim antique origins, dating back to the classical world and the earliest Egyptian dynasties. It is likely this lineage, or imagined lineage, that spurred Lewis to lend his financial support to a series of archaeological expeditions to Tell el-Amarna and other sites across Egypt in the 1920s and 1930s.

Inside, my impression was one of overwhelming darkness. The museum was dimly lit, but display cases glowed, illuminating vast collections of pottery, jewellery, toys and delicate hair ornaments. Human mummies reclined in glass cases while their animal counterparts — cats, birds, baboons — glowered from shelves. Dioramas recreated scenes of everyday life on the Nile Delta, and at the bottom of a dark, winding staircase, I found a replica of a rock-cut tomb. Its corridors were carved from heavy stone and wound in on themselves in disconcerting loops. The walls danced with colourful animal-headed figures that, together, formed a single, inscrutable hieroglyphic story.

On the second floor, I was surprised to find, as if transported there from another era, a detailed recreation of a seventeenth-century alchemist's study. An array of flasks and beakers crowded the surface of a heavy wooden desk; a celestial globe chartered the movements of planets and stars, and what appeared to be a model of a fleshless hand was propped up, as if waving. Moving through the exhibition, I was able to follow, in detail, the seven stages of alchemical transformation. Although the model workshop initially seemed oddly anachronistic — positioned as it was at the summit of a museum dedicated to Ancient Egypt — in the context of Rosicrucian philosophy, it made sense. For members of the order, the wisdom of the alchemists, the power to transform base metal to gold, had its origins in the pyramids of Giza, where secretive schools met to ponder the mysteries of the universe. Moreover, for the AMORC, whose members still run and maintain the museum today, alchemy has become a central metaphor for the kind of spiritual transformation that guides their practice.

Exiting the dark, sepulchral interior of the museum for the Rosicrucian Park at the rear, I was dazzled by the bright swarm of colours that busily arranged themselves into distinct formations. A colourful fountain — its tiles replicating the shape of the rose cross, the group's primary icon — dominated the centre of the park. Flowers burst from every garden and lawn. Replicas of Egyptian temples and obelisks of various sizes stood proudly between the palm fronds and thickets. I sat in the sun and felt the colour wash over me. As with the Theosophy Institute at Krotona, the Rosicrucians didn't seem particularly sinister. Despite the complexity and eccentricity of some of their beliefs, they were simply groups of curious individuals, spiritual seekers searching for new pathways. However, in the anxiety-riddled decades that followed the Manson murders and the collapse of the Sixties' optimism, I could imagine that such groups could, under an appropriately paranoid lens, be contorted into something terrible.

San Francisco, California

It was late afternoon and the diaphanous shroud of fog that usually hovers about the San Francisco Bay until well after midday had finally burned off. Everything shone warm and golden. I sat in a café just a few blocks away from where the small tributaries of Taylor Street, 6th Street and Golden Gate Avenue belched streams of traffic onto the huge intersection of Market Street. I was also just a few streets over from my hotel, a tall, narrow nineteenth-century walk-up whose front-facing exterior wall was caged behind the repetitive zig-zag patterns of a wrought-iron fire escape. Wedged between a halal store and a dive bar with windows so layered in dust that it was impossible to see inside, the hotel was named, incongruously, after an English palace.

The café was crowded, not just with people but with stuff. The tiled countertop somehow managed to accommodate multiple coffee machines, hissing tea kettles, tip jars, plates piled high with pastries, cutlery, napkin dispensers, chocolate bars and a massive glass case filled with cakes and sandwiches. The wall just opposite the counter was crowded too. However, the cluttered shelves and racks sagged with items that might be considered unusual for a café: chains, harnesses, handcuffs, a selection of leather whips in various colours. Rows and rows of dildos were lined up like trophies. Anywhere else, this might have been an unusual juxtaposition — bagels and bondage — but not here. The café, Wicked Grounds, was located in the heart of San Francisco's Leather and LGBTQ Cultural District. The designation is intended to commemorate the history of the city's leather subculture and its role in the advancement of LGBTQ+ rights.

I ordered a cappuccino and joined a man and a woman who were sitting at a table by the window. Her seat seemed to have been carved from — or fused with — a St Andrew's Cross while his looked like a leather dentist's chair. I hit the record button on my phone and tried to recover the dropped threads of the conversation we had just been having: "So you were telling me how you got into Satanism?"

MIRANDA CORCORAN

My interlocutors were Daniel Walker and Simone Lasher, two members of Satanic Bay Area (SBA), an atheistic community organisation based in and around San Francisco. Groups of this kind have become increasingly prominent in recent years, largely in response to the growing influence of Christian fundamentalist groups in the US political sphere, and while they do not believe in a literal Devil, they venerate Satan as a symbol of liberty and intellectual freedom. The Satanic Temple (TST), which is likely the best known contemporary Satanic organisation, began to catch the attention of the media and the public more broadly around 2012, as it launched a series of campaigns to highlight infringements against the separation of church and state as it is defined in the US constitution. Many of TST's tactics are intentionally confrontational, often veering closer to performance art than conventional political protest. Most notably, the group commissioned a statue of the goat-headed deity Baphomet to stand on the grounds of the Oklahoma State Capitol, a challenge to the conservative Republicans who had just installed a monument to the Ten Commandments in the same building.

The use of Satanic iconography by groups such as TST is intended to be challenging and defiant, to force us to reconsider the role of religion in public life and to satirise the way in which US political life had become imbricated with reactionary modes of Christianity. Adopting Satan as the figurehead of an antinomian struggle against repressive social and political strictures is not, however, a new strategy. In the nineteenth century, Romantic writers — such as Lord Byron, Percy Bysshe Shelley and William Blake — as well radical political thinkers like Mikhail Bakunin, Stanisław Przybyszewski and Pierre-Joseph Proudhon reconfigured Lucifer as the embodied spirit of rebellion, enlightenment and sexual and civic freedom.

TST and like-minded organisations treat Satan in much the same way, using the cultural cache and the frisson of danger associated with the Dark Lord as a means to restage debates about religion and secularism in contemporary American life.

SBA, although it shares many of TST's core principals, is an independent entity. Shaking out his long, dark hair, Daniel explained that the group owes its origins to Halloween night, 2015, when he and a friend decided to host a Black Mass, for fun and simply because it was something they'd always wanted to do. The organisation grew from there, and while they are not devoted to activism in the same way that TST might be, SBA often hosts community events — concerts, variety shows, burlesque performances, picnics — and donates the proceeds to various local charities. They give generously to organisations that support marginalised groups, particularly LGBTQ+ youth, sex workers and victims of sexual violence. Every summer, SBA gathers in a local park for what they call Pazuzu's Blessing, an expression of community joy where attendees celebrate their accomplishments and congratulate each other on their achievements. The festivities centre around a small stone statue of Pazuzu, the demon from 1973's *The Exorcist*, who, Daniel stressed, was historically both the Mesopotamian king of wind demons and a protector of infants and their mothers. Daniel continued: "I would say that, actually, relative to a lot of other Satanist groups, we do relatively little activism. We do benefit shows and we do direct action, but I feel like the bulk of what we do are things that are more community based... like creating space where people who do not necessarily feel comfortable in any kind of conventional religious setting can hopefully be open and welcome and accepted."

I couldn't help but feel drawn to Simone and Daniel's open, welcoming brand of Satanism, which also occasionally includes fieldtrips to petting zoos where they have the opportunity to play with baby goats. In my academic life, I do study Satanism, at least as it manifests in film and literature, and so I was well aware of the existence of activist groups like the TST and other manifestations of both theistic and atheistic Satanism before I sat down with Simone and Daniel. However, I appreciated the joy they took in their Satanic practice, the fun they had in subverting and playing around with both religious and cultural norms. As a child, growing up in Ireland during the 1990s, when the country was still overwhelmingly, suffocatingly Catholic, I lived in terror of the Devil. One of my earliest memories of primary school dates from junior infants — I would have been about five at the time — when an elderly nun named Sister Rose would supervise during our lunch break. In her late eighties, Sister Rose always wore a heavy, black veil pulled tight around her deeply creased face. As we sat in a circle, fifteen or more tiny children tucking into soft, doughy sandwiches, she would tell us about the Devil and the fires of hell. In those years, I would dream about the Devil almost every night, envisioning him waiting for me in a darkened kitchen, at the foot of the stairs. Indistinct, but forceful, he sometimes wore a bushy black beard. He always came with his arms outstretched, ready to drag me down to the fiery furnaces that blazed in the bowels of the earth. Perhaps, like Daniel and Simone, I too was ready to have some fun with the Prince of Darkness.

***

SBA is not the only group of diabolists operating in San Francisco. There have been and continue to be many Satanic or broadly Luciferian organisations at work in this vertiginous city of steep slopes and disconcerting peaks. We are in California, after all, and for much of its history

San Francisco has pulsed with a dark, diabolic energy. While there have been many individuals and sects that have displayed characteristics of what we now call Satanism, religious studies scholars tend to agree that Satanism as a cohesive, highly visible and properly documented religious entity only came into being in the late Sixties and early Seventies, and moreover they concur that it was born here, in one of the grand Victorian homes of old San Francisco.

The by now mythic origin story of modern Satanism tends to run like this: on the night of 30 April 1966, the fabled Walpurgisnacht, when witches and demons are believed to roam the countryside, one Anton Szandor LaVey (born Howard Levey) shaved his head, donned a cloak and breathed into being the Church of Satan. Declaring 1966 to be Year One, Anno Satanas, the first year of the age of Satan, LaVey pronounced the establishment of a new, carnivalesque mode of Satanism that would swiftly grab the attention of novelists, filmmakers and journalists around the world. The rituals performed by the church were characterised by an explicitly theatrical bent and many were inspired either by earlier horror movies, like *The Black Cat* (1934) and *The Seventh Victim* (1943), or by literary accounts of Satanism such as J.K. Huysmans' *Là-Bas* (1891). LaVey's brand of Satanism is generally understood as atheistic, and in his *Satanic Bible* (1969) he refers to the elaborate rituals he presided over as "psychodramas", a sort of psychological decompression chamber that would allow participants to break free from any pre-existing religious or social conditioning. Rituals often featured a nude woman lying prone in the form of an altar, a strange echo or distortion of the nascent sexual revolution. LaVey himself often dressed in garments reminiscent of a Catholic priest, perhaps hoping to evoke the image of a fallen man of God, or in a cape adorned with plastic devil horns. In a ritual filmed for the documentary

Satanis: The Devil's Mass (1970), a man dressed as the pope has his buttocks flogged while lying atop a naked woman. Although claiming to adhere to a rationalist, materialist philosophy, LaVey did also frame his rituals as potent acts that could impact the wider world. For him, "magic" could be divided into two categories: lesser magic, which was little more than psychological manipulation, and greater magic, which unleashed powerful emotions that could manipulate the physical world in accordance with one's own will.

LaVey is a controversial figure, largely because both his philosophies and his carefully cultivated public persona appear lacking in consistency. In a 1964 article bearing the intriguing headline "He's a Ghost Inspector at Night", the *San Francisco Chronicle* describes LaVey as an "organist, hypnotist and psychic investigator". He also claimed at various times to have been a carnie, or carnival roustabout, a lion tamer, a psychic investigator and the lover of Marilyn Monroe. However, it is difficult to track down definitive evidence supporting any of these claims. More disturbingly, despite claiming both Roma and Jewish heritage, LaVey flirted with Far Right and neo-Nazi groups later in his career (though, as scholar Joseph Laycock observes, it's likely that LaVey's engagement with their philosophies was ambivalent, and in all probability the High Priest of the Church of Satan simply found "the idea of totalitarianism romantic and admired the Nazis' aesthetics"). In any case, LaVey's most intense flirtation was always with the press. A consummate showman, he understood how to attract attention and court media interest. When LaVey officiated at a Satanic wedding in 1967, one reporter described the spectacle as "the largest gathering of the press since the opening of the Golden Gate Bridge".

The Church of Satan was born in a small wooden house at 6114 California Street. A classic San Francisco Victorian building, LaVey had the house painted a deep, obsidian black. In photographs, it seems to trap light, its individual features becoming indistinguishable in the overwhelming gloom. The organisation grew out of a series of weekly lectures where friends, acquaintances and the morbidly curious would gather to hear LaVey hold court on a range of disturbing subjects, from the occult to medieval torture and cannibalism. When the gatherings evolved into the Church of Satan, apparently at the urging of a friend who encouraged LaVey to start his own church, the High Priest began to recruit through adverts and a range of novel activities guaranteed to draw a crowd. In addition to lectures, LaVey hosted weekly Friday night rituals and specialty events, such as a women-only "witches workshop". For a time, LaVey was also responsible for the "Topless Witches Revue", a nightclub performance whose dancers included Susan Atkins, a pale dark-haired girl who would later become notorious as one of Charles Manson's most devoted acolytes.

From early in its existence, the Church of Satan shimmered with a strange, lustrous glamour. Not long after the new religion's foundation, LaVey developed a relationship — perhaps personal, perhaps professional — with Jayne Mansfield, a beautiful blonde movie star whose risqué performances often pushed the boundaries of what was permissible in a still conservative Hollywood. Carefully staged photos from the period show LaVey and Mansfield attending parties together, with the Satanic High Priest holding the door for Jayne as she steps out of a Cadillac in a glistening, sequined dress. In another series of photos, LaVey, robed in a silken cape and devil horns, visits Mansfield at her opulent pink mansion on Sunset Boulevard. In one photograph, LaVey and Mansfield pose by the heart-shaped pool built by the actress's former husband, bodybuilder Mickey Hargitay. In another, Mansfield clutches a plastic skull while LaVey looms over her, sword in hand. In one of the most entertaining images, captured during what was clearly a publicity stunt, LaVey, all black goatee and sinister cape, tenderly cradles one of Mansfield's tiny Chihuahuas in his arms.

LaVey's play with celebrity culture and theatricality was an essential component of the early Church of Satan. In both his public persona and his religious rituals, LaVey borrowed heavily from pulp magazines, weird fiction and popular Hollywood cinema. However, his influence and that of his Church would also creep into the very genres from which he drew inspiration. In a convoluted instance of life imitating art and art then imitating life once again, a number of popular novels and films cast LaVey-style Satanists as their villains. Ira Levin, a writer of popular thrillers, began plotting his most famous novel, *Rosemary's Baby*, in 1965, and later claimed that he included the Devil, in whom he did not believe, for convenience more than anything else. He wanted to write a suspenseful horror novel in which the main character was wracked with anxiety knowing that she was incubating a monstrous foetus. Because alien impregnation had already been taken — in John Wyndham's *The Midwich Cuckoos* — Levin conceded that he was "stuck with Satan". The novel was published in 1967, and its vision of a Satanic cult populated by ordinary middle-class Americans closely resembles LaVey's church, a collection of ostensibly respectable businessmen, doctors, academics and police officers. Moreover, just as LaVey announced the birth of his Satanic congregation by declaring 1966 to be Anno Satanas, the first year in the age of Satan, so too does Levin's Satanic priest, Roman Castevet, declare that "God is dead and Satan lives! The year is one, the first year of our Lord!"

When the film adaptation of *Rosemary's Baby* was released in 1968, LaVey praised the film as the "the best ad for Satanism ever screened". He also claimed to have acted as a consultant on the film and to have played the role of the Devil in the infamous scene where a semi-conscious Rosemary is raped by the Devil. These assertions have since been disproven; however, the devil's hoofed footprints and LaVey's fingerprints can still be discerned in other popular films of the period. He acted as a technical advisor for both *The Car* (1977) and *The Devil's Rain* (1975). In the latter film, LaVey himself can be seen in the background of one scene. Clad in black, with a shining gold helmet atop his head, LaVey plays a member of a Satanic order presided over by a monstrous, goat-headed high priest. Even beyond the films he had a direct hand in, LaVey and his church undoubtedly contributed to the broad public fascination with the diabolical in the 1960s and 1970s as well as to the poisonous Satanic Panic that swept through much of the anglophone world in the 1980s and 1990s. As Kier-La Janisse writes in her study of the phenomenon, by the early Eighties, after two decades of celebrity Satanism and devilish pop culture, most Americans were primed to believe that Satanists could — and might! — be living next door to them (Janisse 15). La Vey and his San Francisco Satanists had made Satanism as American as apple pie. No longer associated with an obscure pseudo-medieval past or strange works of European literature, Satanism flourished in US popular culture. Not only was the Devil abroad in 1960s California, but he was living the American dream, flanked by beautiful woman and hobnobbing with movie stars.

Earlier that day, before sitting down to drink coffee in a kink café with a friendly group of Satanists, I set out to find the site where LaVey's house had once stood. Taking a city bus that rattled up and down the rugged peaks of San Francisco, I made my way to the Richmond District, not far from where the great steel expanse of the Golden Gate Bridge swept out of the clouds and into the tree-filled parks of the Presidio. California Street, where the

Black House had stood, was a long, wide road lined with pastel-hued Victorian homes. Each pavement was strung with telephone wires that stretched all the way downhill to the bright blue waters of the bay. The birthplace of the Church of Satan was long gone, having been demolished in 2001 and replaced with a non-descript condo. Yet there was something about the street — it's eclectic architecture and its faded Victorian gilding — that spoke of the strange Gothic glamour of its past.

Turning off California Street, I followed 23rd Street down a gentle slope to Golden Gate Park. All along my route, colourful Victorian houses shone under the midday sun like gleaming fragments of coral. In the summer of 1967, while Anton LaVey was developing the Church of Satan just a few blocks away, Golden Gate Park teemed with young people seeking to break away from the bourgeois conventions that bounded their suburban childhoods. These kids, who flooded San Francisco in huge numbers during what would be called the Summer of Love, weren't about to join LaVey's Satanic order, which was at heart anti-drug and respectful of law and order. Instead, they cleaved to new gurus and leaders offering alternatives to the suffocating post-war consensus from which they were trying to free themselves. Sprawled across the rich green pastures of the thousand-acre park, a festival called the Human Be-In played host to music, art, speeches, chanting sessions and performances. Established to counter a new law banning LSD, a drug which many treated as a potent spiritual accelerant, the festival drew somewhere in the region of thirty thousand people. It was here that former Harvard professor and LSD proselytiser Timothy Leary encouraged America's youth to "turn on, tune in, and drop out".

Leaving the park behind, I crossed a street interlaced with overhead tram wires and made my way up hill, along Haight Street. The intersection of Haight and Ashbury

Streets is still infamous as the epicentre of the hippie movement and Sixties counterculturalism. These days, although succumbing to the creeping gentrification that plagues most major cities, the Haight still retains at least some of its original countercultural allure. Street art still explodes bright, psychedelic colours across the walls of homes and businesses. Everywhere, crowds of young people stream in and out of restaurants, record shops and vintage clothing stores. The area's characteristic Victorian houses, all painted different colours and constructed in a wide array of shapes and sizes, give the impression of a haphazard collection of children's toys, an art project gone awry.

In the late nineteenth century, Haight-Ashbury had been a comfortable, solidly middle-class neighbourhood. However, as James Riley observes, the economic fallout of the Great Depression, as well as an unrealised municipal proposal to build a freeway through the area, reduced it to a "ghost town" (14). By the 1960s, Haight-Ashbury was practically abandoned, its once grand Victorian homes falling into disrepair. As such, the rents were low, and this attracted many rootless young people who were enchanted by the romance of Old San Francisco, which they perceived as the last gasp of frontier freedom. Not only did they set up homes in the crumbling ruins of a century past, but many adopted the fashions of the era. Young people wandered the streets of San Francisco dressed in self-consciously Victorian outfits, with stiff-collared shirts and velvet riding coats. They grew their hair long under Western-style hats and posed like prospectors ready to strike gold. The new residents of Haight-Asbury also created a dynamic new culture in the city blocks they settled, establishing shops, restaurants and a vibrant arts scene. Some residents, such as the radical Diggers, envisioned a society existing freely outside of capitalism. Taking unwanted food from supermarkets, they cooked and dispensed free meals — typically stew — to other residents. They also distributed free clothing and organised medical care, transport and other community initiatives.

The young people who were drawn, as if under a spell, to Haight-Ashbury in the mid- to late Sixties were, for the most part, searching for a new way of life, something more profound, more meaningful than the staid consumerism that demarcated the middle-class, overwhelmingly White suburbs many of them had fled. Yet the utopian impulse that birthed the Haight community was also haunted by something much darker. Gurus, preachers and aspiring messiahs wandered the streets seeking followers and new converts. While some had good intentions, or were simply greedy, others were monsters wrapped in the guise of gentle hippies. Charles Manson — whose trail of destruction would eventually lead him three hundred miles south to Hollywood and then out to the scorching desert dunes — lived in a house just off Haight, on Cole Street. He showed up in San Francisco in 1967, having spent more than half of his life in prison, and seized the opportunity to exploit the new sexual and social freedoms that had blossomed during his incarceration. It was in San Francisco that he found his first disciple, university librarian Mary Brunner, and from there he quickly built a devoted circle of acolytes.

Emerging as a dark reflection of hippie idealism, Manson employed a potent admixture of LSD, psychological manipulation, and vague mysticism to reprogramme his followers. Dr David Smith, who founded the Haight Ashbury Free Clinic and treated a number of "Charlie's girls", later recalled how Manson treated the girls "like objects", wearing down their defences to transform them "into self-acknowledged 'computers,' empty vessels that would accept almost anything he poured in" (quoted in O'Neill). When I turned onto Cole Street and followed a gentle incline to Manson's former home, I found a couple in their twenties taking photographs. They were, they told me, on vacation, with one partner explaining that he was a "huge true crime nerd". Gesturing towards his boyfriend, he laughed, "But Cam here thinks I'm a total weirdo." By now, the house was utterly innocuous, its pale yellow paint and clean bay windows blending in easily with its neighbours. Like LaVey's notorious Black House, it had simply melted into obscurity.

It wasn't just Manson that threatened the utopia of Haight-Ashbury. The arrival of so many young people from all over the country in the summer of 1967 threatened to destabilise the neighbourhood's fragile ecosystem. These kids had seen pictures of the newly awakened San Francisco in newspapers and magazines, and heard radio reports about hippies and happenings. In bedrooms all across the silent plains of the Midwest and in small, suffocating East Coast towns, they dreamed about following the trail of freedom all the way out to California. However, with somewhere in the region of one hundred thousand young people arriving in the Haight during that pivotal summer, the scant resources cobbled together by volunteers and activist groups were stretched to their limit. Kids fell into the abyss of bad trips or caught sexually transmitted diseases that, untreated, spread across the community. Some overdosed, while others sickened from filth or malnutrition.

In an essay written that summer, Joan Didion borrowed the apocalyptic language of W.B. Yeats's poem "The Second Coming" to describe the chaos of San Francisco in 1967. "The center was not holding," she wrote, describing a nation where dissatisfied kids and frustrated parents vanished into the great American night before reappearing, reconstituted as blissful flower children, in Golden Gate Park. In those years, at the end of the Sixties, San Francisco was a bubbling cauldron of tension, a powder keg of barely suppressed violence, the dirt and the chaos, the disease and the predatory faux messiahs shaping themselves into a sinister, apocalyptic distortion of an innocent utopian dream.

In my conversation with SBA members Daniel and Simone, I asked them why they thought Satanism had first grown up, in its modern religious incarnation, in San Francisco. LaVey's brand of Satanism, with its nude female altars, Social Darwinist philosophies and occasionally fascistic aesthetics, differs immensely from the left-leaning, radically accepting ideals of both the Satanic Temple and SBA. However, I wondered if either of my interlocutors saw something unique in San Francisco, something that might lend itself to growth of such radically unconventional institutions.

Simone, who described herself as a proud "third-generation, California Bay Area-ian", suggested that it was perhaps San Francisco's position at the furthest reaches of the frontier that invoked this spirit of rebellion. "Since the gold rush," she said, California has "always offered this promise of a new start... being able to have a better life. And, you know, that really did centralise in San Francisco, and also in Los Angeles in a different way." Although Daniel resists the narrative that the Church of Satan codified Satanism as we understand it today, pointing towards smaller organisations that existed at various times between the eighteenth and early twentieth centuries, he observed that San Francisco was perhaps the ideal ecosystem in which such ideologies could thrive. Daniel pursued that train of thought: "There is a quote that I can't remember who it was... a travel writer from the nineteenth century, where he said San Francisco furnishes the best bad things in America, but he talked about all the great bars he'd been to and how drunk he'd been and how the sex workers here were the prettiest he'd ever seen, and so, like, that kind of caught on."

I nodded. Daniel's observation aligned with what I'd been hearing throughout my travels, that California, positioned at the edge of the frontier, lawless and ostensibly unchurched, was a uniquely fertile ground for new ideas, new beliefs and new ways of living. However, Daniel contended that some of this mythology might be just that, a story, a carefully woven narrative intended to simplify a complex range of social, historical and political upheavals. "There is a degree to which the history of San Francisco is kind of deceptive," he explained, "because up to about the Reagan years, San Francisco, like other American cities at the time, was generally quite conservative. But those are not the things people will remember. There were not that many Beats; there were not that many flower children... if you go back to the Gold Rush, there were not that many outlaws and vigilantes." California, it seems, seeks a simple story, a romantic tale of freedom and individuality to bind together the messy strands of history. Such neat stories, however, are often tenuous, cracking apart easily to reveal a mass of chaos and disorder.

***

I followed telephone lines and tram wires downhill from Haight Street, past wooden houses painted with delicate, gold-tinged details, each one as lustrous and ornate as a Fabergé egg. After crossing through green parks and climbing endless, contiguous hills, I eventually stopped outside a tall, imperious Victorian house. Dark and brooding, yet also richly decorated with gold cornices and Gothic wrought-iron spires, the house is known by locals as the Russian Embassy in honour of the refugee Russian royalists who took up residence there in the 1920s. In his LSD-laced counterculture classic *The Electric Kool-Aid Acid Test*, Tom Wolfe called it a "decayed giant". However, the building is officially known as the Westerfeld House, after the German confectioner who built it in the late nineteenth century. The house is a towering monolith, flanked by palms on one side and twisted eucalyptus trees on the other. Haunted-house enthusiasts have claimed that not only did inventor Guglielmo Marconi send radio singles from the building's high tower room, but escape artist Harry Houdini also used the Westerfeld's uppermost reaches to project psychic messages to his wife on the other side of the Bay.

In the 1960s, Kenneth Anger, the occultist gossipmonger and filmmaker who eulogised Griffith's rotting Mesopotamian film set as a metaphor for Hollywood caprice, lived here with Bobby Beausoleil, another wild youngster who would hitch his wagon to Charles Manson's dark star. In 1968, Anger created a short film entitled *Invocation of my Demon Brother*, starring the beautiful Beausoleil as Lucifer and Anger's friend Anton LaVey as "His Satanic Majesty". The music for the film was composed by Mick Jagger, and the film features clips of his performances with the Rolling Stones, making *Invocation* a unique, filmic microcosm of San Francisco counterculture at the tail end of the 1960s. Rumour has it the while filming, LaVey performed Satanic rituals in the tower room, although diabolical insignia scratched into the floorboards have long since been covered over with carpet.

A highly charged melange of occult symbolism, *Invocation of my Demon Brother* was, according to James Riley, "a fragment made in fury... the last blast of Haight consciousness" (220). Anger, it appears, knew that the age of peaceful hippie consciousness was on the verge of disintegration, that the Summer of Love was about to burn out in the flames of violence and paranoia. The film itself is deeply, intriguingly sinister. A synthesiser drones menacingly over images of a ritual broken down into fragments: glimpses of movement and the flash of a knife. Intercut with this spectacle are scenes, likely culled from news footage, of US troops unloading from helicopters. Musicians play in a shadowy room and a group of longhaired young people smoke pot from a tiny skull. The music speeds up, colours melt and merge as the robes of a frantic magician (Anger himself) explode in a fiery dance. Faces overlap, laughing disconcertingly as they are superimposed over ritualistic imagery. Bodies melt into an indistinct kaleidoscope of colour. LaVey appears in his horned headdress and waves his hands over a skull. His image fades into and is consumed by a gang of leather-clad bikers. A cat is cremated in a Satanic funeral ceremony, and the promise of the 1960s explodes in saturated plumes of smoke.

The film dramatises the birth of a new age, an emerging spiritual aeon. However, it also sounds the death knell of the 1960s. Anger believed that film itself could function as a magic spell, an incantation that could evoke primal forces and perhaps even demons. If that is the case, then perhaps he conjured something potent in the dim hallways and darkened rooms of the Russian Embassy. Writing about the texture of Anger's film, James Riley observes that the filmmaker's use of parallel film strips enabled him to "imbue *Invocation* with the visual density of a sigil: an inscribed, typically multi-layered symbol saturated with magical potency" (221). Indeed, watching the film, Anger seems to have caught something, some wayward spirit or devil, between the erratically juxtaposed images that flit across the screen in erratic explosions of colour.

Just outside of the Russian Embassy, a small park called Alamo Square rises to a high green knoll, dotted with thick, densely knotted Monterey cypresses. From there, if you cast your eye towards the bay, one of the city's most famous and frequently photographed views begins to materialise. Directly in the foreground, just below the park, a diagonal row of Victorian houses, known as the "Painted Ladies", extends itself in increments up the hillside. Just behind them, growing from the tops of trees, a phalanx of modern skyscrapers pushes up towards the sky. Finally, in the background, you can just about make out a distant assemblage of hills sweeping down to the barges and container ships that glide on the blue waters beneath.

There's something potent in this image. It reveals itself like a collage of different landscapes, different historical eras, somehow brought together in a single mystical point. Like Anger's celluloid sigil, the overlapping landscapes and architectures evoke something powerful, wondrous yet uneasy. Perhaps it is this unique intersection of built environment and natural topography that stirs up occult forces in San Francisco and indeed across California. There's something almost preternatural in the way settlers, fleeing the bustling cities of the East Coast and vast plains of the Midwest, attempted to eke out a familiar world in this alien landscape. Planting oranges in the Southern Californian valleys and building elaborate bourgeois homes along the rugged peaks of San Francisco, it's almost as if these new arrivals were engaged in some occult act of transformation, attempting to remake a strange new land according to their own dreams. No wonder, then, that California quickly became a dream world, a site of renewal and metamorphosis, where a brand-new Beverly Hills mansion could become a colonial Spanish villa, a pale, trembling creature from the Midwest could become a star, and a seedy conman could become a guru.

EPILOGUE

American Gothic

The crickets were listening. The night was listening to her. For a change, all of the far summer-night meadows and close summer-night trees were suspending motion [...] And perhaps a thousand miles away, across locomotive-lonely country, in an empty way station, a single traveler reading a dim newspaper under a solitary naked bulb, might raise up his head, listen, and think, What's that?
— Ray Bradbury, *Dandelion Wine*

In the first half of Jack Kerouac's novel *On the Road*, the protagonist, Sal Paradise, is obsessed with reaching Denver. It's all he thinks about. All his plans and conversations centre around how he's going to reach this mile-high city on the western edge of the Great Plains. When Sal sets off on his journey into the Far West, he imagines "Denver looming ahead of me like the Promised Land, way out there beneath the stars, across the prairie of Iowa and the plains of Nebraska" (12). For Sal, Denver is a boundary line, an invisible marker, separating the East of his past from the West of his future.

I made the journey backwards, travelling from San Francisco to Denver (thirty-five hours by train), riding the bus from Denver to Omaha, Nebraska, and then, eventually, taking another bus through the Iowa prairies to the little town of Ottumwa. Where Sal's journey was one of liberation, sloughing off the traditions and strictures of the East Coast in favour of the free, boundless West, I was moving back towards the Atlantic Seaboard, where my journey had commenced three months prior.

Travelling from northern California across the state line to Nevada, the hills assumed a radiant, golden cast. As the train climbed high into the Sierra Nevada Mountains, we glimpsed the shining aquamarine waters of Donner Lake through a canopy of pine trees. It was here, in the winter of 1846 and the early months of 1847, that a group of pioneers, following the call of Manifest Destiny into the West, were forced to resort to cannibalism in order to survive. Further east, the train moved sluggishly through deep orange pastures where horses grazed on peaceful, rolling hills. The bridges and railway lines that cut across the landscape were so dwarfed by gargantuan pines and the (at times unbearable) vastness of the terrain that they looked like tiny, fragile matchsticks. By the time we reached the deserts of Utah, the sky began to grow dark, a huge dust cloud obscuring the setting sun. A large pile of bones — animal, presumably — sat alone beside the railroad tracks. The headlights of distant cars and trucks occasionally rose out of the darkness of nearby highways before disappearing once again into the night. I fell asleep and woke up not sure where I was. A sign blinked red in the distance, illuminating the words "Rio Grande".

The culmination of this particular journey was Ottumwa, Iowa, a little town on the banks of the Des Moines River, in the southeast corner of the state. As I climbed out of the bus, I was joined by a crowd of passengers disembarking for a smoke break. Most clustered in the shade of a bus shelter to light cigarettes, except for one elderly Amish man who immediately began to puff on an ancient wooden pipe.

Aside from one section of Main Street, the town was largely deserted. Wide streets were lined with stony-

Heading east, through Nevada to Utah

faced brick commercial buildings, all identically flat and industrial in aspect. Roads and footpaths were riven with cracks that sprouted surprisingly lush patches of grass and weeds. Heading for my accommodation, another rented room, I stopped to rest momentarily outside a trailer park. Wedged into the hollow of an ancient elm tree that shaded one of the mobile homes, a parched white cow skull grinned at me out of the darkness. Further along the same street, beside an abandoned auto-repair shop whose deteriorating signage hung empty and wordless from the front gate, I came to a single-storey motor inn that wrapped itself around a massive concrete parking lot. Outside the main office, whose screen door creaked loosely on its hinges, a group of elderly men sat on plastic furniture and played cards. A younger man, probably in his early twenties, who had been lounging on a nearby lawn chair, jumped up and jogged over to me. His fingernails were painted a bright

Cattle skull in Ottumwa, Iowa

electric blue, and he told me that his name was Michael. He had been in the military, and a recruiter had dropped him off at the motel a few weeks ago. I asked if he was from the area and why the recruiter had left him here. He simply shrugged and said that he was trying to decide whether to rejoin the army. For now, he seemed to be marooned in a small town with little to no public transport and absolutely nothing to do. He was profoundly sad and very bored.

***

The Midwest, the region of the US that stretches from the flat prairies of Iowa and Kansas to the Great Lakes on the Canadian border, has long been understood in terms of homogeny, a lack of variation in both its populace and landscape. It's a region often caught in the sticky, molasses grip of nostalgia, representing for many an idealised past. For others, however, it represents backwardness, and is seen as being inhabited by people who are believed to cling too tightly to the past.

Once, the region we now call the Midwest was the frontier, encompassing the western edge of Euro-American settlement on the continent. When the frontier finally extended all the way to the Pacific Coast in the final decades of the nineteenth century — when there was, at last, no more West left to "win" — historians and public intellectuals began to reflect on the central plains with increasing nostalgia. Frederick Jackson Turner, a turn-of-the-century historian who spent much of his career theorising the effects of the frontier on the American psyche, reacted to the settlement of the Far West by projecting a nostalgic vision of frontier life onto the Midwest. Positioned halfway between the traditions of the established East and the promise of the developing West, the Midwest was, for Turner, a kind of eternal frontier. As

Adam Ochonicky explains, although western expansion was no longer possible, with Euro-American settlements now stretching all the way to the Pacific, the Midwest's location in the centre of the United States allowed it to retain those qualities Turner viewed as emblematic of the frontier: bravery, pragmatism, individuality, an independent spirit (3). In this way, the Midwest becomes, at least in the popular imagination, a place outside of time, a place where those values we idealise as fundamentally American might continue to thrive.

On the day I arrived in Ottumwa, a stall had been set up in one of the town's many empty car parks selling Trump merchandise. Among the Trump 2024 T-shirts and "Let's Go Brandon" placards, there were numerous hats and banners bearing the ubiquitous MAGA, or "Make America Great Again", slogan. Much like Turner's nostalgic view of the Midwest as a place where progress continues up to a point before turning in on itself, "Make America Great Again" was a slogan and a concept predicated on the notion of moving forwards by retreating into the past. Trump doesn't promise to "make America great", but rather to make it great "*AGAIN*". The restoration of the nation's glory depends upon a return to an imagined past where things were better, richer, safer. The implication, of course, is that this better America was an America prior to women's liberation, desegregation and civil and LGBTQ+ rights. This is nostalgia that shades into stagnation, even decay. While such nostalgic conceptions of a lost America are certainly not confined to the Midwest and its inhabitants, it is precisely this region — eternally caught in a pioneer push West — that many Americans imagine when they try to conjure that eternally elusive historical greatness.

About fifteen miles south of Ottumwa, there's an even smaller town, a town so small that its city hall appears to be a shuttered storefront and the bank, judging by the decades-old coke machine gathering dust by its barred front door, has been closed for longer than I've been alive. Aside from a single general store that seems to do a brisk trade in petrol and junk food, the place is a ghost town. People do live here — it's a town of clapboard houses, sunflowers and grain silos — but it seems devoid of any commercial and cultural life. This is Eldon, a town that is most famous for a small, inscrutable painting of a man and a woman standing stock still and sour-faced outside of a little white country house. The painting in question is Grant Wood's *American Gothic*, an image that has been parodied and reproduced so often that it's often difficult to recall the original painting without imagining some embellishments or satirical transformations. The actual work, however, is an oil painting which portrays in muted, washed-out tones a stern farmer, holding a pitchfork, alongside a severe, old-fashioned woman whom Wood intended to be the man's daughter. Many people, however, interpret her as his wife. In the background, the vaulted roof of a white house creates a symmetrical point, neatly dividing the pair.

The grim couple were modelled on Wood's sister and his dentist, both of whom had to transform themselves into dour farmers for the artist. However, the house itself is very real and required little in the way of transformation. Wood, an Iowa native, discovered the odd little house with its incongruous church window while driving through Eldon in 1929. He was struck by the building's appearance and what he called its "severe Gothic lines" (quoted in in Baigell 116). Based on this, he endeavoured "to find two people who by their severely straight-laced characters would fit into such a home" (quoted in Baigell 116). The completed painting was displayed in the Chicago Art Institute, where it continues to generate a wide array of diverging interpretations. In the 1930s, many who saw the painting viewed it through the lens of Wood's Regionalist approach to art — a desire to

The small town of Eldon, Iowa

shift cultural production away the Europeanised influences of major urban centres and towards "more authentic" rural communities — and as such, interpreted the image as a portrait of "real" Americans. Others interpreted the painting as condescending or satirical, an attempt to mock the perceived conservatism, religious fundamentalism and self-imposed ignorance of the rural Midwest.

From Elm Street, where shuttered windows stared blankly at empty pavements, I turned onto a residential street, all silent clapboard houses, huge protective trees and flags flapping on neat lawns. Another turn brought me to Finney Avenue, a narrow country lane bordered on all sides by farmland and backyard vegetable patches. The Dibble House, better known as the American Gothic House, stood almost entirely alone at the edge of a curved driveway. It was startlingly small, a little cottage with a severe arch and an oddly ecclesiastical Gothic window looming above the porch.

Not far from the house itself, a small museum houses exhibitions on the building's history and the complex afterlife of Wood's painting. The staff I met inside were friendly and enthusiastic about both the painting and the town of Eldon more broadly. However, they were also careful to stress that *American Gothic* has absolutely nothing to do with Goth music or fashion. Indeed, when I mentioned that I often use the painting in my classes on Edgar Allan Poe to illustrate the tension between surface and reality, I was told they in no way want to portray the house or museum as connected to anything sinister. Their stance makes sense, of course. The organisation relies on donations and broad public appeal to survive, and they don't want to jeopardise that by aligning themselves with anything outside the norm. Similarly, it is true that when Wood painted the image, his conjunction of the words "American" and "Gothic" would have been both novel and jarring. Critics hadn't yet begun to think of early American literature — Poe, Hawthorne and Melville — in terms of the Gothic, and so the term was almost uniformly applied to medieval European art (Soltysik

The Dibble House, also known as the American Gothic House

239). As it relates to the Dibble House, the word "Gothic" refers to the Carpenter Gothic style of the architecture and that intriguing little window.

While I respect the museum's desire to distance themselves from the tenebrous realms of horror and the Gothic, I also feel that the painting does embody a very specific style of Midwestern unease. Wood himself posed and costumed his models to reflect the kinds of people that might live in that house, basing their appearance on old photographs from family albums (Corn 256). This doesn't necessarily mean that he was attempting to condemn or satirise the imagined "backwardness" of the Midwest, but the image nevertheless evinces the kind of duality that characterises a great deal of Midwestern literature. The painting is tinged with nostalgia. The muted colours and awkward poses evoke the nebulous, monochrome sadness of a lost family photograph. The white wooden cottage, its porch decorated with lovingly tended plants, and the red barn in the background suggest a simpler, pre-industrial world. At the same time, there's a forlorn look on the farmer's face, a lost quality, while the woman, with her severe hairdo and sideways glance, seems to express a quiet rage.

There is, I think, an essential ambivalence to the painting. It is at once nostalgic and unsettling, a duality which defines a large number of texts that we might group together under the banner of Midwestern Gothic. Unlike the Gothic modes of New England, California and the South, the Midwestern Gothic, if it exists at all, has been sadly under-theorised. However, for me, this genre is defined by an intermingling of nostalgia and unease, a yearning for a romanticised past that is always undermined by a lingering fear of violence, death and the obliteration of the individual by the immense, endless flatness of the plains. The Midwestern Gothic finds expression in films like Terrence Malick's 1973 *Badlands*, in which a nostalgic vision of 1950s South Dakota is shot through with intense, meaningless violence. Similarly, Michael Lesy's *Wisconsin Death Trip*, a nonfiction photography book from the same year, evokes an analogous tension between the romance of the past and uncanny horror. Comprised of hundreds of nineteenth-century photographs, typically of ordinary people and scenarios, the images are accompanied by news items describing murders, suicides, fires and mysterious disappearances. According to the historian Warren Susman, who wrote the preface to Lesy's book, *Wisconsin Death Trip* serves as a potent counter-narrative to both "the Frontier Myth" and "the vision of a happier agrarian America".

Other incarnations of the Midwestern Gothic emerge in the short fiction of the Ohio writer Sherwood Anderson. In "Death in the Woods" (1933), Anderson tells the story of a small rural community and its sad secrets from the perspective of an adult man recalling his Midwest boyhood. The narrator remembers the lonely death of a poor old woman in a snow-covered wood. The nostalgic tone of his reflections is tempered by an awareness of both the abuses that often occur — silently, secretly — in small communities and of the eerie quality of the landscape. Describing the spot where the old woman's body was found, Anderson observes how, "in a woods, in the late afternoon, when the trees are all bare and there is white snow on the ground, when all is silent, something creepy steals over the mind and body". An equally potent tension between nostalgia and terror emerges throughout the extensive literary corpus of Illinois native Ray Bradbury. Many of his tales turn a tender eye towards the Midwest of his childhood. However, idyllic small-town life is invariably underpinned by something more insidious: children are carried away by the forces of darkness and wicked carnivals set up shop in unsuspecting country towns. In one of his most well-known novels, *Dandelion Wine* (1957), Bradbury portrays a small country town, a place of porch lights and lemonade, menaced by a serial killer called the Lonely One. In one particularly striking passage, he imagines the unseen killer's presence casting a pall over the normally peaceful community and freezing its residents with a deep, icy terror. As one woman makes her way through the darkened streets, she imagines the criminal as an omnipresent force, tracking her movements and infecting her with dread:

The crickets were *listening*. The night was listening to *her*. For a change, all of the far summer-night meadows and close summer-night trees were suspending motion [...] And perhaps a thousand miles away, across locomotive-lonely country, in an empty way station, a single traveler reading a dim newspaper under a solitary naked bulb, might raise up his head, listen, and think, What's that?

Although Grant Wood's *American Gothic* does not contain the kind of grotesque imagery or pervasive dread found in the works of Ray Bradbury or Sherwood Anderson, there is an ambivalence in his painting that connects it to these more overtly Gothic tales. There is a sense in the illegible faces of its characters, the ambiguity of the church-like window, that something is simmering beneath the surface.

I caught a taxi from Eldon back to Ottumwa. There didn't seem to be any buses running, at least not according to any reliable service. As the car drove the wide, straight roads that bisected inexpressibly vast cornfields, I felt as if I, myself, had begun to come apart, to vanish into the far-flung horizon, a tiny dot feeling the enormity of the earth around me. Iowa, like many of the surrounding Midwestern states, is possessed of a disconcerting flatness, an unsettling topographical homogeneity. While this can be attributed to the natural evenness of the prairie landscape, Iowa was also rendered homogenous by settlers who, advancing west across the continent in the nineteenth century, attempted to transform the region into a simulacrum of European — or at the very least East Coast — farmland. While Indigenous inhabitants made careful use of natural resources, taking what they needed from native plant and animal communities without eliminating them, Euro-American settlers who arrived from the 1830s onwards cut down woods, drained wetlands and destroyed native prairie grasses (Mutel). Today, to travel in the Midwest is to cover thousands of miles of flat land, past endless corn fields, and find nothing to distract the eye aside from the silver glint of a grain silo.

The Midwestern Gothic is far from simple. Though it often engages with themes of nostalgia, particularly as it shades into conservatism and stagnation, as well as notions of conformity and the disconcerting vastness of the landscape, its aim isn't necessarily to critique the region and its inhabitants. Often, the Midwestern Gothic, with its emphasis on the sinister underpinnings of supposedly idyllic small towns and the inexplicable eruption of violence in the heart of bucolic farmland, forces us to reconsider our relationship to the past. In an American context, the Midwestern Gothic asks us to question our nostalgic affinity for the frontier and our belief in the existence of some pure, authentic American self.

***

What is America to me now? A fly buzzing behind a screen door? A porch light flickering on a warm prairie night? A cow skull wedged into the hollow of an ancient tree somewhere in the infinite Iowa plains? For three months, I travelled thousands of miles hoping to understand the immense haunted house that is America, yet I was still unable to perceive the spirits that walk its corridors and rattle its attics. One night, on a bus that passed silently through a sea of cornfields, I woke from my sleep to see a white sheet covering a body on the floor. It moved slightly, breathing deeply. After a few moments, I realised that someone was trying to sleep in the aisle and had covered themselves with a sheet to block out the dim LED lights that occasionally flickered overhead.

I spent my last American night in New York City, having finally returned to the East Coast, where my journey commenced. As I prepared to leave, I was alert to the enduring presence of my own scepticism. It sat within me, still soft and ductile, but nevertheless present. I had seen no ghosts, felt no supernatural stirrings either within my own soul or in the world beyond. Certainly, I had been warmed by the ardent, blazing faith of believers. Spiritualists like Tracy in Hydesville and the mediums in Lily Dale had made me feel so welcome, enfolding me within a joyful, comforting warmth that had endeared me profoundly to their faith and their communities. Similarly, I had felt Voodoo as a potent force in New Orleans. Like Spiritualism, it is a religion that burns with a powerful fervour. I caught glimpses of its power in the saints that stared at me from the walls of churches and the windows of stores, in the vèvès scrawled on alters that glowed, like beacons in the night, in the dim recesses of botánicas. Yet, like the ghosts that had failed to materialise in my childhood home, these spirits also eluded me.

I opened this book with the words of Joseph Glanvill, the seventeenth-century thinker who attempted to apply rational scientific principles to the realm of the spirits. He hoped that one day scientists could utilise empirical, repeatable experiments and carefully observed evidence to decode the mysteries of the supernatural, and in doing so, understand its inscrutable machinations. For him the "LAND of SPIRITS", was a "kinde of AMERICA", a place of unknown dimensions and uninterpretable inhabitants. However, after travelling the length and breadth of the nation, I was beginning to feel that Glanvill's maxim could also be reversed. America itself is akin to the spiritual realm: inchoate, unfathomable, fundamentally strange. It's impossible, I think, to sum up what America is, even in a book. There is no single American character or culture. Each region is utterly distinct. The vast red deserts of New Mexico not only resemble the surface of Mars, they might as well *be* Mars, or any other planet, when compared to the green hills of Vermont. Moreover, the population is diverse, both across regions and within regions, while the political landscape — always contentious — has become increasingly fractured.

Approaches to and uses of the supernatural, or the Gothic more broadly, are equally fragmented. We might speak of the American Gothic, but the Gothic imagination is anything but monolithic. In California, the Gothic is a prism through which to interrogate the state's association with bright, golden promise and utopian dreams. Here, horror takes the form of spectral, maddened starlets and slithery, treacherous gurus. Conversely, in the deserts of Nevada and New Mexico, horror expands to fill the eternity of their vast landscapes. The buzzing, vital life that scurries beneath sand dunes or coils in the shadow of ragged cacti grows gargantuan, becoming a terrible magnification of the desert's uncanny liveliness. The aridity of desert space finds expression in images of parched, desiccated bones. Deep in the swamplands of the South, the region's haunted history merges with its oppressive climate to produce nightmarish images of undeath, reanimated corpses and restless burials. Ghosts proliferate in the Northeast, haunting the white-steepled towns and dense forests of New York and New England. Some are garrulous, extroverted beings who return to commune with the living, passing on messages of hope, while others are silent, indecipherable wisps. Yet each of these distinct regions contains multitudes, and the function of the supernatural varies immensely even within the narrow confines of a single community. Ghosts can speak of the repressed horrors of the past or the promise of the future, sometimes even embodying both simultaneously. In the South, tales of the unburied dead might gesture towards resurgent historical guilt intermingled with an anxiety about the swampy, flood-prone landscape. However, as in the folktales collected by Zora Neale Hurston, such stories might also be a source of joy, community bonding and even resistance. Even as far west as California, the Gothic is possessed of a strange duality. While murderous cults and the ubiquitous aesthetic of faded glamour speak to the underside of the Hollywood dream, joy and hope also form part of the multifaceted, ever-shifting Gothic imaginary. Here, celebrity graves become not just a means of connecting with a favourite star, but also a way to preserve history and educate a new generation about the icons of the past.

There is, as I have previously stated, something almost contradictory about the notion of a Gothic road trip. Such journeys, especially in America, where people seem to possess an ardent faith in the healing power of open highways, are usually imagined through the prism of golden sunlight and the freedom of boundless landscapes racing to meet the horizon. Yet American culture has continuously imagined the ways in which such liberatory journeys might sour: stumbling upon a strange, isolated community with monstrous intentions; meeting a killer on the road; losing oneself forever in that great American night. Moreover, the mobility inherent to such journeys reflects the endlessly transformative nature of the American Gothic. It is a mode that never allows itself to rest, and which is forever morphing to fit the contours of distinct histories, landscapes and cultures.

The academic consensus on the American Gothic is that it is a literary, cinematic and artistic mode that undermines the optimistic myth of American exceptionalism, the belief that the US is, by virtue of its democratic character and utopian foundations, unique among the nations of the world and therefore has a special duty to shine the torch of liberty across the globe. The Gothic, scholars argue, reveals the dark, mouldering foundations upon which that narrative has been built. In its restless spectres and violent, uncanny returns, the Gothic illuminates the brutality embedded in American history, excavating a bloody legacy of genocide, slavery, religious zealotry and avaricious imperialism. Yet, in my travels, the Gothic unveiled a panoply of different aspects. It did, of course, give voice to the many historical abuses that run counter to more idealistic accounts of the nation's history. However, it also performed a wide range of other tasks. In Upstate New York, the home of Spiritualism, ghosts articulated hopes for a new and better world shaped by emerging technologies as well as racial and gender equality. In the South, uncanny corporeal returns form the core of horror stories meant to terrify, but they also appeared in humorous or subversive tales. The Gothic therefore becomes a means of resisting abusive power structures or giving form to secret desires. It is a way of conceptualising the unimaginable — nuclear disaster or the insidious invisibility of radiation — or interrogating the power of a fantasy, like the Hollywood dream, for instance. America, like the Gothic tales that haunt its unconscious, is complex, multifaceted and fragmented. It is a ghost, ephemeral, powerful and impossible to capture. It is haunted, if not by ghosts, then by a plethora of dreams, terrors and desires. Like the hard, stony faces of Grant Wood's *American Gothic*, the nation itself refuses interpretation, opening itself up to endless, often contradictory, readings. As much as I might try to pin it down, to unstick my tongue and articulate the haunting power of America, its ghosts simply stare back at me, silent and eternally mysterious.

WORKS CITED

Introduction

Botting, Fred. *Gothic. The New Critical Idiom*. 2nd ed., Routledge, 2014.

Cohen, Jeffrey Jerome. "Monster Culture: Seven Theses". *The Monster Theory Reader*, edited by Jeffrey Andrew Weinstock, University of Minnesota Press, 2020, pp. 37–56.

Debord, Guy. "Introduction to a Critique of Urban Geography". *Les Lèvres Nues* #6 (September 1955), translated by Ken Knabb, *Situationist International Online*, https://www.cddc.vt.edu/sionline/presitu/geography.html. Accessed 7 February 2024.

Fiedler, Leslie A. *Love and Death in the American Novel*. Criterion Books, 1960.

Glanvill, Joseph. *A blow at modern Sadducism in some philosophical considerations about witchcraft. To which is added, the relation of the fam'd disturbance by the drummer, in the house of Mr John Mompesson, with some reflections on drollery and atheisme. / By a member of the Royal Society*. Printed by E.C. for James Collins, at the Kings Head in Westminster-Hall, 1668. *Early English Books*, https://quod.lib.umich.edu/e/eebo/A70179.0001.001?view=toc. Accessed 2 February 2024.

Morrison, Toni. *Playing in the Dark: Whiteness and the American Literary Imagination*. Vintage, 1993.

Owens, Susan. *The Ghost: A Cultural History*. Tate, 2017.

Pitts, Jr, Leonard. "Abominations From America's Past Haunt Us". *Chicago Tribune*, 20 October 1998, https://www.chicagotribune.com/1998/10/20/abominations-from-americas-past-haunt-us/. Accessed 11 Feb. 2024.

Chapter 1

Abramovich, Chad. "The Vanished Town of Glastenbury and the Bennington Triangle". *Obscure Vermont*, 7 April 2015, https://urbanpostmortem.wordpress.com/2015/04/07/the-vanished-town-of-glastenbury-and-the-bennington-triangle/. Accessed 19 August 2023.

Anolik, Lili. "The Secret Oral History of Bennington: The 1980s' Most Decadent College". *Esquire*, 28 May 2019, https://www.esquire.com/entertainment/a27434009/bennington-college-oral-history-bret-easton-ellis/. Accessed 10 August 2023.

Bachelard, Gaston. *The Poetics of Space Paperback*. Translated by Maria Jolas, Beacon Press, 1994.

Bailey, Dale. *American Nightmares: The Haunted House Formula in American Popular Fiction*. Bowling Green University Popular Press, 1999.

Behringer, Wolfgang. *Witches and Witch-Hunts*. Polity Press, 2004.

Bergland, Renée. *The National Uncanny: Indian Ghosts and American Subjects*. University Press of New England, 2000.

Blauweiss, Stephen, and Karen Berelowitz. "The Lenape, Mohicans and Iroquois were native to New York State". *Hudson Valley 1*, 13 October 2021, https://hudsonvalleyone.com/2021/10/08/the-lenape-mohicans-and-iroquois-were-native-to-new-york-state/. Accessed 2 August 2023.

Birdle, Deborah. "The Geography of Horror: Lovecraft's (Re) construction of New England". *Journal of the Short Story in English: Les Cahiers de la nouvelle*, vol. 71, 2018, pp. 1–16.

Boyer, Paul, and Stephen Nissenbaum. *Salem Possessed: The Social Origins of Witchcraft*. Harvard University Press, 1974.

Breslaw, Elaine G. *Tituba, Reluctant Witch of Salem: Devilish Indians and Puritan Fantasies,* New York University Press, 1997.

Braude, Ann. *Radical Spirits: Spiritualism and Women's Rights in Nineteenth-Century America*. 2nd ed., Indiana University Press, 2001.

Brodhead, Richard. *Hawthorne, Melville, and the Novel*. University of Chicago Press, 1977.

Buckland, Raymond. *The Spirit Book*. Visible Ink, 2013.

Cross, Whitney R. *The Burned-Over District; The Social and Intellectual History of Enthusiastic Religion in Western New York, 1800–1850*. Cornell University Press, 1950.

Curtis, Barry. *Dark Places: The Haunted House in Film*. Reaktion Books, 2008.

Davis, Colin. "Hauntology, Spectres and Phantoms". *French Studies*, vol. 59, no. 3, 2005, pp. 373–9.

Elizabeth, S. *The Art of the Occult: A Visual Sourcebook for the Modern Mystic*. Francis Lincoln, 2020.

Fetsko Petrie, Kathye. "In Search of Shirley Jackson's House". *Lithub*, 28 September 2016, https://lithub.com/in-search-of-shirley-jacksons-house/. Accessed 20 August 2023.

Fisher, Mark. "What Is Hauntology?" *Film Quarterly*, vol. 66, no. 1, 2012, pp. 16–24.

Franklin, Ruth. *Shirley Jackson: A Rather Haunted Life*. Liverlight, 2016.

Freud, Sigmund. "The Uncanny". Translated by Alix Strachey, https://web.mit.edu/allanmc/www/freud1.pdf. Accessed 14 August 2023.

Godwin, Joscelyn. *Upstate Cauldron: Eccentric Spiritual Movements in Early New York State*. CUNY Press, 2015.

Gordon, Avery. *Ghostly Matters: Haunting and the Sociological Imagination*. Minnesota University Press, 2008.

Hawthorne, Nathaniel. *The House of the Seven Gables*. Project Gutenberg, 2021, https://gutenberg.org/cache/epub/77/pg77-images.html.

---. *The Scarlet Letter*. Project Gutenberg, 2008, https://www.gutenberg.org/files/25344/25344-h/25344-h.htm.

Hill, Frances. *Hunting for Witches: A Visitor's Guide to the Salem Witch Trials*. 2nd ed., Commonwealth Editions, 2019.

Hughes, Robert. "Sleepy Hollow: Fearful Pleasures and the Nightmare of History". *Arizona Quarterly: A Journal of American Literature, Culture, and Theory*, vol. 61, no. 3, 2005, pp. 1–26.

"Inside Spirit Cabinets with the mediums of the Spiritualist Era". *American Hauntings*, https://www.americanhauntingsink.com/cabinets. Accessed 8 Aug. 2023.

Irving, Washington. "The Legend of Sleepy Hollow". *Project Gutenberg*, 2008, https://www.gutenberg.org/cache/epub/41/pg41-images.html

---. "Rip Van Winkle". *The Sketch Book of Geoffrey Crayon, Gent.* Penguin, 1988, pp. 29–41.

Jackson, Jr, Herbert G. "Spiritualist Landmark Becomes One Man's 'Calling.'" *New York Times*, 29 March 1970, https://www.nytimes.com/1970/03/29/archives/spiritualist-landmark-becomes-one-mans-calling.html. Accessed 2 August 2023.

Jackson, Shirley. *Hangsaman*. Penguin, 2013.

---. *The Haunting of Hill House*. Penguin, 2006.

---. *Life Among the Savages*. Penguin, 2019.

---. "The Lovely House [A Visit]". *Come Along with Me*. Penguin, 2013, pp. 93–116.

Kleiman, Jordan. "Love Canal: A Brief History". Geneseo Honors College, https://www.geneseo.edu/history/love_canal_history. Accessed 6 Aug. 2023.

Lewis, E.E. *A Report of the mysterious noises heard in the house of Mr John D. Fox, in Hydesville, Arcadia, Wayne County, N.Y. : authenticated by the certificates, and confirmed by the statements of the citizens of that place and vicinity.* Self-published, 1848.

"Love Canal Chronologies". SUNY Buffalo, https://library2.buffalo.edu/archives/lovecanal/about/chronologies.html/. Accessed 7 August 2023.

Lovecraft, H.P. "The Dreams in the Witch House", *Project Gutenberg Australia*, 2015, https://gutenberg.net.au/ebooks15/1500441h.html.

---. "The Unnameable". *Lovecraft Archive*, 20 August 2009, https://www.hplovecraft.com/writings/texts/fiction/u.aspx. Accessed 7 August 2023.

Luna-Firebaugh, Eileen M. "The Border Crossed Us: Border Crossing Issues of the Indigenous Peoples of the Americas". *Wicazo Sa Review*, vol. 17, no. 1, 2002, pp. 159–81.

Mather, Cotton. *The Wonders of the Invisible World*. Project Gutenberg, 2009, https://www.gutenberg.org/cache/epub/28513/pg28513-images.html.

Miller, Arthur. *The Crucible: A Play in Four Acts*. Penguin, 2015.

Moore, William D. "'To hold communion with nature and the spirit-world': New England's spiritualist camp meetings, 1865–1910". *Perspectives in Vernacular Architecture*, vol. 7, 1997, pp. 230–48.

Natale, Simone. *Supernatural Entertainments: Victorian Spiritualism and the Rise of Modern Media Culture*. Pennsylvania State University Press, 2016.

Norton, Mary Beth. *In the Devil's Snare: The Salem Witchcraft Crisis of 1692*. Knopf Doubleday, 2003.

Pearsall, Ronald. *The Table-Rappers*. St Martin's Press, 1972.

Poole, Scott W. *Satan in America: The Devil We Know*. Rowman & Littlefield, 2010.

Richardson, Judith. "Possessing High Tor Mountain". *Medium*, 31 October 2019, Harvard University Press, https://hup.medium.com/possessing-high-tor-mountain-d474e14da5f4. Accessed 2 August 2023.

---. *Possessions: The History and Uses of Haunting in the Hudson Valley*. Harvard University Press, 2005.

Ringel, Faye. "I am Providence: H.P. Lovecraft". *A Companion to American Gothic*, edited by Charles L. Crow, Blackwell, 2014, pp. 267–78.

Schiff, Stacy. *The Witches: Salem, 1692: A History*. Weidenfeld & Nicholson, 2015.

Schill, Brian. *Stalking Darkness*. 2nd ed., International Parapsychology Research Foundation, 2008.

Tesfastion, Master. "Twin Border Cities of Niagara Falls Face Economic Challenges". *Two Borders,* Walter Cronkite School of Journalism and Mass Communication at Arizona State University, 24 September 2013, https://cronkite.asu.edu/projects/buffett/canada/bordercities.html. Accessed 17 August 2023.

The Spirit Rooms of Lily Dale. Matt's Next Level Media and Paula D'Amico Productions, 2021.

Troy, Kathryn. *The Specter of the Indian: Race, Gender, and Ghosts in American Seances, 1848–1890*. State University of New York Press, 2017.

van der Veen, Arancha. "Lives Behind the Legends: Mae West — Spiritual Vixen". *CMH Blog*, 27 June 2021, https://www.classicmoviehub.com/blog/lives-behind-the-legends-mae-west-spiritual-vixen/. Accessed 6 August 2023.

Vidler, Anthony. *The Architectural Uncanny: Essays in the Modern Unhomely*. MIT Press, 1992.

Weir, Robert E. "Bewitched and Bewildered: Salem Witches, Empty Factories, and Tourist Dollars". *Historical Journal of Massachusetts*, vol. 40, no, 1/2, 2012, pp. 178–211.

Weisberg, Barbara. *Talking to the Dead: Kate and Maggie Fox and the Rise of Spiritualism*. Bravo Ltd., 2004.

Winsser, Johan. "Mary Dyer and the 'Monster' Story". *Quaker History*, vol. 79, no. 1, 1990, pp. 20–34.

Chapter 2

Anderson, Jeffrey E., *Hoodoo, Voodoo, and Conjure: A Handbook*. Greenwood Press, 2008.

Atwill, Nicole. "Slavery in the French Colonies: Le Code Noir (the Black Code) of 1685". *Library of Congress Blogs*, 13 January 2011, https://blogs.loc.gov/law/2011/01/slavery-in-the-french-colonies/. Accessed 20 September 2023.

Blayde, Ariadne. *Ash Tuesday*. April Gloaming Publishing, 2022.

Boyd, Valerie. *Wrapped in Rainbows: The Life of Zora Neale Hurston*. Scribner, 2004.

Bradford, Adam C. *Communities of Death: Whitman, Poe and the American Culture of Mourning*. University of Missouri Press, 2014.

Cave, Damian. "In a Town Apart, the Pride and Trials of Black Life". *New York Times*, 29 September 2008, https://www.nytimes.com/2008/09/29/us/29florida.html. Accessed 12 September 2023.

Chireau, Yvonne P. *Black Magic: Religion and the African American Conjuring Tradition*. University of California Press, 2003.

Dickson, Dickson, Jr. "The 'John and Old Master' Stories and the World of Slavery: A Study in Folktales and History". *Phylon*, vol. 35, no. 4, 1974, pp. 418–29.

Dixon, Terrence. "Black History Month: Honoring Untold RVA 11:11 Portal". *12onyourside.com*, 28 February 2020, https://www.12onyourside.com/2020/02/28/black-history-month-honoring-untold-rva-portal/. Accessed 17 September 2023.

Due, Tananarive. *Ghost Summer: Stories*. Prime, 2015.

The Eastside Environmental Council, https://theeec.org/. Accessed 19 September 2023.

"Eatonville, the Town that Freedom Built, Still Stands as a Beacon of Hope and Progress". *Orange County Government Florida*, 28 February 2023, https://newsroom.ocfl.net/2023/02/eatonville-the-town-that-freedom-built-still-stands-as-a-beacon-of-hope-and-progress/. Accessed 16 September 2023.

Edelson, S. Max. "Clearing Swamps, Harvesting Forests: Trees and the Making of a Plantation Landscape in the Colonial South Carolina Lowcountry". *Agricultural History*, vol. 81, no. 3., 2007, pp. 381–406.

Faulkner, William. *As I Lay Dying*. Vintage, 2004.

French, Scott. "Historic Eatonville Timeline". *Association to Preserve*

Eatonville, https://preserveeatonville.org/about-eatonville/.
Accessed 21 September 2023.

Frisby, Helen. *Traditions of Death and Burial*. Shire, 2019.

Gan, Vicky. "America's Failure to Preserve Historic Slave Markets".
Bloomberg, 13 February 2015, https://www.bloomberg.com/news/
articles/2015-02-13/america-s-failure-to-preserve-historic-slave-
markets?embedded-checkout=true. Accessed 4 September 2023.

Gates, Jr, Henry Louis, and Maria Tatar, editors. *The Annotated
African American Folktales*. Liveright, 2017.

Giblett, Rodney James. *Postmodern Wetlands: Culture, History,
Ecology*. Edinburgh University Press, 1996.

Goddu, Teresa A., *Gothic America: Narrative, History and Nation*.
Columbia University Press, 1997.

Grant, Richard. "Deep in the Swamps, Archaeologists Are Finding
How Fugitive Slaves Kept Their Freedom". *Smithsonian*, September
2016, https://www.smithsonianmag.com/history/deep-swamps-
archaeologists-fugitive-slaves-kept-freedom-180960122/. Accessed
26 September 2023.

Harris, Charlaine. *Dead Until Dark*. Ace Books, 2001.

"History of the Codes of Louisiana: Black Code". *Law
Library of Louisiana*, https://lasc.libguides.com/c.
php?g=254608&p=1697971. Accessed 23 September 2023.

Hurston, Zora Neale. *Dust Tracks on a Road*. Harper, 2010.

---. *Mules and Men*. Harper, 1990.

---. *Their Eyes Were Watching God*. Harper Collins, 2006.

Katić, Elvira K. "Exploring Contortions of the Authentic: Voodoo in New Orleans". *Southern Semiotic Review*, vol. 13, no. 2, 2020, pp. 6–30.

Newman, Christopher L. "'Savages and Sable Subjects': White Fear, Racism, and the Demonization of New Orleans Voodoo in the Nineteenth Century". *Madison Historical Review*, vol. 20, 2023, pp. 1–31.

McInnis, Maurice D. "Mapping the Slave Trade in Richmond and New Orleans". *Buildings & Landscapes: Journal of the Vernacular Architecture Forum*, vol. 20, no. 2, 2013, pp. 102–25.

Morrow Long, Carolyn. "High John the Conqueror Root". *An Encyclopedia of African American History*, edited by Leslie M. Alexander and Walter C. Rucker, ABC-Clio, 2010, pp. 207–8.

---. *Spiritual Merchants: Religion, Magic, and Commerce*. University of Tennessee Press, 2001.

---. *A New Orleans Voudou Priestess: The Legend and Reality of Marie Laveau*. University Press of Florida, 2006.

O'Connor, Flannery. "The Grotesque in Southern Fiction". *Mystery and Manners*, edited by Sally Fitzgerald and Robert Fitzgerald. Faber & Faber, 2014.

Pike, Judith, E. "Poe and the Revenge of the Exquisite Corpse". *Studies in American Fiction*, vol. 26, no. 2, 1998, pp. 171–92.

Poe, Edgar Allan. "The Black Cat". *The Complete Tales and Poems of Edgar Allan Poe*. Penguin, 1982, pp. 223–30.

---. "Dream-Land" *The Complete Tales and Poems of Edgar Allan Poe*. Penguin, 1982, pp. 967–8.

---. "The Fall of the House of Usher". *The Complete Tales and Poems of Edgar Allan Poe*. Penguin, 1982, pp. 231–45.

---. "Instinct vs Reason: A Black Cat". *The Edgar Allan Poe Society of Baltimore*, https://www.eapoe.org/works/essays/ivrbcata.htm. Accessed 15 September 2023.

---. "The Lake". *The Complete Tales and Poems of Edgar Allan Poe*. Penguin, 1982, pp. 1015.

---. "The Premature Burial". *The Complete Tales and Poems of Edgar Allan Poe*. Penguin, 1982, pp. 258–68.

Ocker, J.W. *Poe–Land — The Hallowed Haunts of Edgar Allan Poe*. Countryman Press, 2017.

Owens, Susan. *The Ghost: A Cultural History*. Tate, 2017.

Ray, Victor. *On Critical Race Theory: Why It Matters & Why You Should Care*. Random House, 2022.

Rothstein, Richard. *The Colour of Law: A Forgotten History of How Our Government Segregated America*. Norton, 2018.

Rice, Anne. *Interview with the Vampire*. Ballantine, 1977.

Ruggles, Jeffrey. "The Burial Ground: An early African-American site in Richmond. Notes on its history and location". December 2009, https://www.scribd.com/document/42051809/Burial-Ground-Ruggles-12-09. Accessed 23 September 2023.

Sago, Renata. "Ella Augusta Johnson Dinkins, Champion Of Zora

Neale Hurston's Hometown, Dies At 102". *NPR*, 14. December 2020, https://www.npr.org/2020/12/14/945164861/ella-augusta-johnson-dinkins-champion-of-zora-neale-hurstons-hometown-dies-at-10. Accessed 17 September 2023.

Schneider, Gregory S. "Where's Kitty Cary? The answer unlocked Black history Richmond tried to hide". *The Washington Post*, 28 October 2022, https://www.washingtonpost.com/dc-md-va/2022/10/27/richmond-shockoe-african-burying-ground/. Accessed 14 September 2023.

Stromberg, Joseph. "The real reason American public transportation is such a disaster". *Vox*, 10 August 2015, https://www.vox.com/2015/8/10/9118199/public-transportation-subway-buses. Accessed 17 September 2023.

Stevenson, Christopher M. "Burial Ground for Negroes, Richmond, Virginia: Validation and Assessment". *The Virginia Department of Historic Resources*, 25 June 2008, https://www.dhr.virginia.gov/pdf_files/SlaveCemeteryReport.pdf. Accessed 14 September 2023.

"Vampires in the Deep South". *Terrebone Parish Library*, https://mytpl.org/project/vampires-in-the-deep-south-the-casket-girls-and-comte-de-st-germain/. Accessed 30 September 2023.

Vincent, Joshua, and Lydia Lindsey. "Jazz is African Diasporic Music: Reconfiguring the Uniquely American Definition of Jazz". *Africology: The Journal of Pan African Studies*, vol. 10, no. 5, 2017, pp. 156–89.

Ward, Martha. *Voodoo Queen: The Spirited Lives of Marie Laveau*. University of Mississippi Press, 2004.

"What is Haint Blue?" *Lowcountry Gullah*, 15 July 2021, https://

lowcountrygullah.com/what-is-haint-blue/. Accessed 17 September 2023.

Wilson, Anthony. *Shadow and Shelter: The Swamp in Southern Culture*, University of Mississippi Press, 2006.

Young, Jason. "Of Moses, Mules, and Men: Zora Neale Hurston and the Politics of Folk Art". *Obsidian*, vol. 9, no. 1, 2008, pp. 9–19.

Zitter, Emmy Stark. "Language, Race, and Authority in the Stories of Edgar Allan Poe". *Studies in Popular Culture*, vol. 21, no. 2, 1998, pp. 53–69.

Chapter 3

Abbott, Carl. "Building the Atomic Cities: Richland, Los Alamos, and the American Planning Language". *The Atomic West*, edited by Bruce Hevly and John M. Findlay, University of Washington Press, 1998, pp. 90–115.

"Amarillo, Texas". *Encyclopedia of the Great Plains*, 2011, http://plainshumanities.unl.edu/encyclopedia/doc/egp.ct.004. Accessed 14 November 2023.

Amigos Bravos and Concerned Citizens for Nuclear Safety. *Historic and Current Discharges from Los Alamos National Laboratory: Analysis and Recommendations*, September 2006, https://nukewatch.org/wp-content/uploads/2019/08/amigos_bravos.pdf. Accessed 5 November 2023.

Anaïs, Seantel, and Kevin Walby. "Secrecy, publicity, and the bomb: Nuclear publics and objects of the Nevada Test Site, 1951–1992". *Cultural Studies*, vol. 30, no. 6, pp. 949–68.

"Atomic Tourism in Nevada". *PBS American Experience*, https://

www.pbs.org/wgbh/americanexperience/features/atomic-tourism-nevada/. Accessed 13 November 2023.

"Beauty Passing Through Us: Natural History and Art as Intervention". *Extraction*, 2021, https://www.extractionart.org/nhi. Accessed 20 November 2023.

Bradbury, Ray. "There Will Come Soft Rains". *The Martian Chronicles*, Harper, 2008.

Brown, Jennifer. *Cannibalism in Literature and Film*. Palgrave, 2013.

Carroll, Noel. "Fantastic Biologies and the Structures of Horrific Imagery". *The Monster Theory Reader*, edited by Jeffrey Andrew Weinstock, University of Minnesota Press, 2020, pp. 136–47.

Del Pilar Blanco, Maria. *Ghost-Watching American Modernity: Haunting, Landscape, and the Hemispheric Imagination*. Fordham University Press, 2012.

Dunbar-Ortiz, Roxanne. *An Indigenous Peoples' History of the United States*. Beacon, 2015.

Giaimo, Cara. "The Long, Weird Half-Life of Trinitite". *Atlas Obscura*, 30 June 2017, https://www.atlasobscura.com/articles/trinitite-trinity-test-mineral-cultural-jewelry. Accessed 7 November 2023.

Goffe, Nadira. "Oppenheimer's Glaring Omission". *Slate*, 26 July 2023, https://slate.com/culture/2023/07/oppenheimer-christopher-nolan-manhattan-project-nuclear-testing-los-alamos-trinity-victims.html. Accessed 17 November 2023.

Hendershot, Cyndy. "Mythical and Modern: Representations of Los Alamos". *Journal of the Southwest*, vol. 41, no. 4, 1999, pp. 477–85.

Hacker, Barton C. "'Hotter Than a $2 Pistol': Fallout, Sheep, and the Atomic Energy Commission, 1953–1986". *The Atomic West*, edited by Bruce Hevly and John M. Findlay, University of Washington Press, 1998, pp. 157–75.

Hevly, Bruce and John M. Findlay. "The Atomic West: Region and Nation, 1942–1992". *The Atomic West*, edited by Bruce Hevly and John M. Findlay, University of Washington Press, 1998, pp. 3–18.

The Hills Have Eyes. Directed by Wes Craven, Vanguard, 1977.

The Hills Have Eyes. Directed by Alexandre Aja, Fox Searchlight, 2006.

"Hispanic Homesteaders and the Los Alamos National Laboratory". *National Parks Service*, https://www.nps.gov/articles/000/hispanic-homesteaders-and-the-los-alamos-national-laboratory.htm. Accessed 22 November 2023.

Hunner, Jon. "Family Secrets: The Growth of Community at Los Alamos". *New Mexico Historical Review*, vol. 72, no. 1, 1997, pp. 39–46.

Jasper, David. *The Sacred Desert: Religion, Literature, Art, and Culture*. Blackwell, 2006.

Jentsch, Ernst. "On the psychology of the uncanny (1906)". *Angelaki: Journal of the Theoretical Humanities*, vol. 2, no. 1, 1997, pp. 7–16.

Kaiser, David. "In the Shadow of Los Alamos". *American Scientist*, vol. 95, no. 1, https://www.americanscientist.org/article/in-the-shadow-of-los-alamos. Accessed 15 November 2023.

Kirk, Andrew, and Kristian Purcell. *Doom Towns: The People and*

Landscapes of Atomic Testing, A Graphic History. Oxford University Press, 2016.

Kirsch, Scott. "Watching the Bombs Go Off: Photography, Nuclear Landscapes and Spectator Democracy". *Antipode*, vol. 29, no. 3, 1997, pp. 227–55.

Kordas, Ann Marie. *The Politics of Childhood in Cold War America*. Routledge, 2016.

Kristeva, Julia. *The Powers of Horror: An Essay on Abjection*. Translated by Leon S. Roudiez, Columbia University Press, 1982.

Laurence, William. L. *Dawn Over Zero*. Museum Press Ltd., 1947.

"Los Alamos: Beginning of an Era 1943–1945". *Atomic Archive*, https://www.atomicarchive.com/resources/documents/los-alamos/los_alamos_part_2.html. Accessed 7 November 2023.

Masco, Joseph. *The Nuclear Borderlands: The Manhattan Project in Post–Cold War New Mexico*. Princeton University Press, 2006.

Matlock, Staci. "Los Alamos Will Never Be Clean". *Santa Fe New Mexican*, 13 July 2015, https://www.santafenewmexican.com/news/local_news/los-alamos-will-never-be-clean/article_a3cc7ce1-8af0-5113-8f38-5d4aa673fd7a.html. Accessed 4 November 2023.

Morley, David. "A Short History of the Sublime". *The MIT Press Reader*, https://thereader.mitpress.mit.edu/a-short-history-of-the-sublime/. Accessed 16 November 2023.

Nakamura, Masako. "'Miss Atomic Bomb' Contests in Nagasaki and Nevada: The Politics of Beauty, Memory, and the Cold War". *U.S.-Japan Women's Journal*, no. 37, 2009, pp. 117–43.

"Nevada Test Site". *Atomic Heritage Foundation*, https://ahf.nuclearmuseum.org/ahf/location/nevada-test-site/#:~:text=The%20Nevada%20Test%20Site%20(NTS,here%20between%201951%20and%201992. Accessed 7 November 2023.

"The Old Mormon Fort: Birthplace of Las Vegas, Nevada". *National Park Service*, https://www.nps.gov/articles/the-old-mormon-fort-birthplace-of-las-vegas-nevada-teaching-with-historic-places.htm. Accessed 30 November 2023.

ORAU Museum of Radiation and Radioactivity, https://orau.org/health-physics-museum/index.html. Accessed 27 November 2023.

Ortiz, Simon J. *Woven Stone*. University of Arizona Press, 1992.

Pounders, Lisa A. "Her 'Symbols of the Desert': An Emerging Alchemical Impression in the Bone Paintings of Georgia O'Keeffe". *Journal of Jungian Scholarly Studies*, vol. 14, no. 1, 2019, pp. 16–29.

Provost, Claire. "Atomic City, USA: how once-secret Los Alamos became a millionaire's enclave". *Guardian*, 1 November 2016, https://www.theguardian.com/cities/2016/nov/01/atomic-city-los-alamos-secret-town-nuclear-millionaires. Accessed 12 November 2023.

Rhodes, Richard. "A Chunk of Trinitite Reminds Us of the Sheer, Devastating Power of the Atomic Bomb". *Smithsonian*, September 2019, https://www.smithsonianmag.com/smithsonian-institution/chunk-trinitite-reminds-sheer-devastating-power-atomic-bomb-180972848/#:~:text=Once%20the%20site%20was%20opened,was%20collected%20before%20the%20ban. Accessed 4 November 2023.

Rice, James C. *Downwind of the Atomic State: Atmospheric Testing and the Rise of the Risk Society*. New York University Press, 2023.

Sandweiss, Martha A. "John Gast, American Progress, 1872". *Picturing United States History — CUNY*, https://picturinghistory. gc.cuny.edu/john-gast-american-progress-1872/. Accessed 24 November 2023.

Schneider, Steven Jay. "The Hills Have Eyes". *Senses of Cinema*, March 2002, https://www.sensesofcinema.com/2002/cteq/hills/. Accessed 17 November 2023.

Slaughter, Amy. "Performing the Manhattan Project in Los Alamos". *History of Science*, 2023, pp. 1–21.

Tarantula. Directed by Jack Arnold, Universal, 1955.

The Texas Chain Saw Massacre. Directed by Tobe Hooper, Vortex, 1974.

Them! Directed by Gordon Douglas, Warner Bros, 1954.

"Trinity: The first nuclear bomb test". *Bulletin of the Atomic Scientists*, https://thebulletin.org/virtual-tour/trinity-the-first-nuclear-bomb-test/. Accessed 23 November 2023.

Tsutsui, William M. "Looking Straight at 'Them!' Understanding the Big Bug Movies of the 1950s". *Environmental History*, vol. 12, no. 2, 2007, pp. 237–53.

United States, Department of Energy. *Acid/Pueblo Canyon Fact Sheet, New Mexico, Site,* https://www.energy.gov/lm/acidpueblo-canyon-new-mexico-site. Accessed 2 November 2023.

Wheller, Joshua. "In the Shadow of Oppenheimer". *Science History Institute Museum and Library*, 16 July 2023, https:// www.sciencehistory.org/stories/magazine/in-the-shadow-of-oppenheimer/. Accessed 6 November 2023.

Willis, John. "Doom Town, Nevada Test Site, and the Popular Imagination of Atomic Disaster". *Journal of American Studies*, vol. 57, no. 3, pp. 393–415.

---. "Exploding the 1950s Consumer Dream". *Pacific Historical Review*, vol. 88, no. 3, 2019, pp. 410–38.

Wood, Robin. "An Introduction to the American Horror Film". *Robin Wood on the Horror Film: Collected Essays and Reviews*, edited by Barry Keith Grant, Wayne State University Press, 2018, pp. 73–110.

Chapter 4

Anger, Kenneth. *Hollywood Babylon*. Dell Books, 1975.

Babitz, Eve. *Slow Days, Fast Company: The World, the Flesh and L.A.* New York Review Books, 2016.

Beckley, Cody. *Ojai: the Crucible of Southern California's Cultic Milieu*. California State University Northridge, 2016.

Blaine, Adrienne. "San Jose's Egyptian Museum Vibes off its Secret Society Roots". *KQED*, 30 June 2015, https://www.kqed.org/arts/10669130/san-joses-egyptian-museum-still-magically-mesmerising. Accessed 15 January 2024.

Bode, Lisa. "Fade out/fade in: dead 1920s and 1930s Hollywood stars and the mechanisms of posthumous stardom." *Celebrity Studies*, vol. 5, no. 1–2, 2014, pp. 90–92.

"Cabazon Dinosaurs". *Atlas Obscura*, https://www.atlasobscura.com/places/cabazon-dinosaurs. Accessed 5 January 2024.

Chandler, Raymond. "Red Wind". *The Collected Stories of Raymond Chandler*. Everyman, 2002.

Colletta, Lisa. *British Novelists in Hollywood, 1935–1965: Travellers, Exiles, and Expats*. Palgrave, 2013.

Cooper, Ian. *The Manson Family on Film and Television*. MacFarland, 2018.

Cowan, Douglas E. and David G. Bromley. *Cults and New Religions: A Brief History*. Wiley Blackwell, 2015.

Dickey, Colin. *Ghostland: An American History in Haunted Places*. Viking, 2016.

Didion, Joan. "Slouching Towards Bethlehem". *Slouching Towards Bethlehem*. Farrar, Straus and Giroux, 2008. E-Book.

--- "Some Dreamers of the Golden Dream". *Slouching Towards Bethlehem*. Farrar, Straus and Giroux, 2008. E-Book.

---. "The White Album". *The White Album*. Farrar, Straus and Giroux, 2009, pp. 11–48.

Dyrendel, Asbjørn, et al. *The Invention of Satanism*. Oxford University Press, 2016.

Fleischer, Matthew. "Opinion: Want to tear down insidious monuments to racism and segregation? Bulldoze L.A. freeways". *LA Times*, 20 June 2020, https://www.latimes.com/opinion/story/2020-06-24/bulldoze-la-freeways-racism-monument. Accessed 7 January 2024.

"Grave Business". *Forbes*, 1 November 2002, https://www.forbes.

com/2002/11/01/cx_bs_1101homea.html?sh=13d971db2a01. Accessed 18 January 2024.

Hartlaub, Peter. "A satanic priest raised a lion in an S.F. neighborhood. Then things got really wild". *San Francisco Chronicle*, 26 October 2023, https://www.sfchronicle.com/oursf/article/ church-satan-lavey-lion-18444967.php. Accessed 19 January 2024.

Hedenborg White, Manon, and Fredrik Gregorius. "The Satanic Temple: Secularist Activism and Occulture in the American Political Landscape". *International Journal for the Study of New Religions*, vol. 10, no 1, p. 89–110.

Hollywood Horror House (AKA *Savage Intruder*). Directed by Donald Wolfe, Congdon Productions, 1970.

Hoye, Richard, Tom Moore and Craig Walker. *Ojai*. Arcadia, 2010.

Jackson, Shirley. *The Haunting of Hill House*. Penguin, 2006.

Janisse, Kier-La. "Introduction: Could It Be... Satan?" *Satanic Panic: Pop-Cultural Paranoia in the 1980s*, edited by Kier-La Janisse and Paul Corupe, FAB Press, 2018, pp. 1–25.

Jenkins, Philip. *Mystics and Messiahs: Cults and New Religions in American History*. Oxford University Press, 2000.

Johnston, Jill, and Bhavna Shamasunder. "LA's long, troubled history with urban oil drilling is nearing an end after years of health concerns". *The Conversation*, 27 January 2023, https:// theconversation.com/las-long-troubled-history-with-urban-oil- drilling-is-nearing-an-end-after-years-of-health-concerns-198650. Accessed 15 January 2024.

Kamin, Debra. "Ojai, California: A Valley of Wellness". *New York*

Times, 17 October 2020, https://www.nytimes.com/2020/03/03/
realestate/ojai-calif-a-valley-of-wellness-but-no-chain-stores-
in-ventura county.html#:~:text=Ojai's%20quiet%20nature%20
has%20long,medicine%20shops%20and%20vegan%20eateries.
Accessed 19 January 2024.

Laycock, Joseph. *Satanism: Elements in New Religious Movements*.
Cambridge University Press, 2023.

Leorne, Ana. "This Alamo Square Victorian holds 100 years of SF
counterculture history". *SF Gate*, 19 October 2020, https://www.
sfgate.com/characters/article/This-Alamo-Square-Victorian-holds-
100-years-of-SF-15651657.php. Accessed 18 January 2024.

Levin, Ira. *Rosemary's Baby*. Random House, 1967.

---. "Stuck with Satan". *Criterion*, 5 November 2012, https://www.
criterion.com/current/posts/2541--stuck-with-satan-ira-levin-on-
the-origins-of-rosemary-s-baby. Accessed 4 January 2024.

Levitt, Linda. "Death on Display: Reifying Stardom through
Hollywood's Dark Tourism". *The Velvet Light Trap*, no. 65, 2010, pp.
62–70.

Longworth, Karina, host. "DW Griffith, the Gish Sisters and
the Origin of *Hollywood Babylon*, 2 July 2018, https://www.
youmustrememberthispodcast.com/episodes/2018/6/26/dw-
griffith-the-gish-sisters-and-the-origin-of-hollywood-babylon-
fake-news-fact-checking-hollywood-babylon-episode-1. Accessed
25 October 2023.

Melville, Greg. "Inside the Disneyland of Graveyards". *Smithsonian*,
29 September 2022, https://www.smithsonianmag.com/history/
inside-the-disneyland-of-graveyards-180980510/. Accessed 18
January 2024.

Mulholland Drive. Directed by David Lynch, Universal, 2001.

Murphy, Bernice M. *The California Gothic in Fiction and Film*, Edinburgh University Press, 2022.

O'Neill, Tom, with Dan Pipenbring. *Chaos: Charles Manson, the CIA, and the Secret History of the Sixties*. Little, Brown and Company, 2019.

Parks, Shosi. "A secret alchemist society — at the heart of a Bay Area museum — wants to unlock the mysteries of humankind". *Roadtrippers*, 14 May 2019, https://roadtrippers.com/magazine/rosicrucian-egyptian-museum-alchemy/. Accessed 19 January 2024.

Pierce, David. "The Survival of American Silent Feature Films: 1912–1929". Council on Library and Information Resources and the Library of Congress Washington, D.C., 2013.

Riley, James. *The Bad Trip: Dark Omens, New Worlds and the End of the Sixties*. Icon, 2019.

"Self-Realization Fellowship Meditation Gardens". *Atlas Obscura*, https://www.atlasobscura.com/places/self-realization-fellowship-headquarters-gardens-mount-washington. Accessed 20 January 2024.

Silverman, Jacob. "Burial Plots". *Tablet*, 22 September 2011, https://www.tabletmag.com/sections/arts-letters/articles/burial-plots. Accessed 17 September 2024.

"The Sixteen-Millimeter Shrine". *The Twilight Zone*, season 1, episode 4, CBS Productions, 1959.

Sklarz, Ellen. "Krishnamurti and the Ojai Valley". *Ojai History*, 27

May 2011, https://ojaihistory.com/krishnamurti-and-the-ojai-valley/. Accessed 18 January 2024.

Stein, Jean. *West of Eden: An American Place*, Vintage, 2016.

Strube, Julian. "Theosophy, Race, and the Study of Esotericism". *Journal of the American Academy of Religion*, vol. 89, no. 4, 2021, pp. 1180–9.

Ulin, David L. "The Santa Ana winds and the literature of Los Angeles". *LA Times*, 14 May 2014, https://www.latimes.com/books/jacketcopy/la-et-jc-the-santa-ana-and-the-literature-of-los-angeles-20140514-story.html. Accessed 17 January 2024.

Van Luijk, Ruben. *Children of Lucifer: The Origins of Modern Religious Satanism*. Oxford University Press, 2016.

Waugh, Evelyn. *The Loved One: An Anglo-American Tragedy*. Back Bay Books, 2012.

Weller, Sheila. "Suddenly That Summer". *Vanity Fair*, July 2012, https://www.vanityfair.com/culture/2012/07/lsd-drugs-summer-of-love-sixties. Accessed 3 January 2024.

Willis, Alfred. "A Survey of the Surviving Buildings of the Krotona Colony in Hollywood". *Architronic*, vol. 8, no. 1, pp. 1–18.

"Woman in Black". *Time Magazine*, 5 September 1938, https://web.archive.org/web/20081113142932/http://www.time.com/time/magazine/article/0,9171,760116,00.html. Accessed 17 January 2024.

Epilogue

Anderson, Sherwood. "Death in the Woods". *Death in the Woods and Other Stories*, Project Gutenberg of Australia, 1933, https://gutenberg.net.au/ebooks04/0400491h.html.

Badlands. Directed by Terrence Malick, Warner Bros., 1973.

Baigell, Matthew. "Grant Wood Revisited". *Art Journal*, vol. 26, no. 2, 1966–1967, pp. 116–22.

Bradbury, Ray. *Dandelion Wine*. Bantam, 1978

Corn, Wanda M. "The Birth of a National Icon: Grant Wood's 'American Gothic". *Art Institute of Chicago Museum Studies*, vol. 10, pp. 252–75.

Kerouac, Jack. *On the Road*. Penguin, 2000.

Mutel, Cornelia. *The Emerald Horizon: The History of Nature in Iowa*. University of Iowa Press, 2007.

Nichols, William D. "Shifting Rurality American Gothic, Iowa Nice, Biotech and Political Expectations in Rural America". *Landscapes: the Journal of the International Centre for Landscape and Language*, vol. 8, no. 1, 2018, pp. 1–25.

Ochonicky, Adam R. *The American Midwest in Film and Literature: Nostalgia, Violence, and Regionalism*. Indiana University Press, 2020.

Soltysik, Agnieszka M. "The uses of the American Gothic: The politics of a critical term in post-war American literary criticism". *Comparative American Studies: An International Journal*, vol. 3, no. 2, 2005, 237–48.

Susman, Warren. "Preface". *Wisconsin Death Trip*, by Michael Lesy, 3rd ed., University of New Mexico Press, 2000.

Repeater Books

is dedicated to the creation of a new reality. The landscape of twenty-first-century arts and letters is faded and inert, riven by fashionable cynicism, egotistical self-reference and a nostalgia for the recent past. Repeater intends to add its voice to those movements that wish to enter history and assert control over its currents, gathering together scattered and isolated voices with those who have already called for an escape from Capitalist Realism. Our desire is to publish in every sphere and genre, combining vigorous dissent and a pragmatic willingness to succeed where messianic abstraction and quiescent co-option have stalled: abstention is not an option: we are alive and we don't agree.